Truth at Last

Why Black Folks were Punished and Placed in America for 400 Years

The 'True' Bible Story Revealed

by
brother ahjamal

1663 Liberty Drive, Suite 200
Bloomington, Indiana 47403
(800) 839-8640
www.AuthorHouse.com

This book is designed to provide information in regard to the subject matter covered. It is not the purpose of this book to reprint all the information that is otherwise available to the author and/or publisher, but to compliment, amplify and supplement other texts.

Every effort has been made to make this book as complete and as accurate as possible. However, there may be mistakes both typographical and in content. Therefore, this text should be used only as a general guide and not as the ultimate or only source of information.

The purpose of this book is to inform and entertain. The author and publisher is neither liable nor responsible to any person or entity with respect to any loss or damage caused or alleged to be caused directly or indirectly by the information contained in this book.

© 2005 brother ahjamal. All Rights Reserved.
© 1973, 1994 By Ahjamal Jacob Weathers
First edition 1973
First revision 1992

No part of this book may be reproduced, stored in a retrieval system, or transmitted by any means without the written permission of the author.

First published by AuthorHouse 06/16/05

ISBN: 1-4208-5241-8 (sc)

Library of Congress Control Number: 2005903759

Printed in the United States of America
Bloomington, Indiana

This book is printed on acid-free paper.

The Book That Explains Why 'Black Folks' Were Punished and Placed In America For 400 Years, And How All Mankind Were Created..

DEDICATION

This Revelation is dedicated to the "Lost Sheep of the House of Israel, the True African Hebrew Israelites, the so-called "Black man", who GOD placed in America in the year 1619, (5380) to serve a 400 year captivity for breaking God's Ten Commandments while living in Africa.

(Genesis 15:13-14) And he said unto Abram, Know of a surety that thy seed shall be a stranger in a land that is not theirs, and shall serve them; and they shall afflict them four hundred years;

14 And also that nation, whom they shall serve, will I judge: and afterward shall they come out with great substance.

(Genesis 15:13-14).

INTRODUCTION

“And ye shall know the TRUTH, and the TRUTH shall make you free”.

The purpose of this book is to provide true information that will explain why “Black Folks” were punished and placed in America for 400 years. If your mind is open and ready to receive the knowledge of TRUTH, this book will be of great benefit to you. However, if you read this book with a closed mind, the information will be shocking and very disturbing to you. Nevertheless, it is the TRUTH, and those that worship GOD, must worship in Spirit and in TRUTH. What is TRUTH? TRUTH is an expression of ‘reality’. TRUTH is perceived by two faculties; ‘intuition’ and ‘intellect’. The intellect is trained in logic, reason and scientific study. The intuition is based on the great source of ‘inner feeling’. All thoughts must be weighed by these two faculties before it can be accepted as TRUTH. TRUTH stands alone, and TRUTH will always verify itself. A strong mind must be established upon TRUTH. Why? Because TRUTH never fails. When we view the world today, we can clearly see that the cause of most sorrow, grief and disappointment, is because of the lack of TRUTH. Without TRUTH, there can be no peace. Look around you at the amount of misery in the world. Everyone is searching for ‘grief-relief’. Alcohol, prescription pills of all kinds, and street drugs of all kinds, have been used to solve the problems of sorrow and hopelessness, but only TRUTH can free your troubled mind. Only TRUTH can give you the peace of mind that will lead you to the ‘higher life’. Did you know that ‘peace of mind’ is the most ‘coveted’ possession of all mankind? Did you know that there is no peace outside the Commandments of God? For it is written in the Scripture of TRUTH; ‘great peace have they, that love Thy law (Commandments), and nothing shall offend them’. (Psalms 119: 165) Therefore, the first step is to free your mind of the mental garbage and all of your false beliefs. Your mind and beliefs must be established upon absolute, unfailing, TRUTH. There is only one TRUTH that you can rely on. ‘GOD’S TRUTH’.

Only God’s TRUTH can free you from the misery that is locked inside of your head. We are not talking about ‘religion’ either. We are talking about the TRUTH that separates the ‘IS’, from the ‘IS NOT’. We are talking about the TRUTH as in Joshua 24:14;

"Now therefore fear the Lord, and serve Him in sincerity and in TRUTH".

Many are professing the Truth, but God can't find any.

(Jere. 5:1)

1 Run ye to and fro through the streets of Jerusalem, and see now, and know, and seek in the broad places thereof, if ye can find a man, if there be any that executeth judgment, that seeketh the TRUTH; and I will pardon it.

(Jeremiah 5:1).

God is punishing the world and will continue until TRUTH is established.

(Jere. 5:3).

3 O LORD, are not thine eyes upon the TRUTH? thou hast stricken them, but they have not grieved; thou hast consumed them, but they have refused to receive correction: they have made their faces harder than a rock; they have refused to return.

(Jeremiah 5:3).

TRUTH has perished from the earth.

(Jere. 7:28).

28 But thou shalt say unto them, This is a nation that obeyeth not the voice of the LORD their God, nor receiveth correction: TRUTH is perished, and is cut off from their mouth.

(Jeremiah 7:28).

God said everyone is deceiving each other because there is no TRUTH.

(Jere. 9:2-6)

2 Oh that I had in the wilderness a lodging place of wayfaring men; that I might leave my people, and go from them! for they be all adulterers, an assembly of treacherous men.

3 And they bend their tongues like their bow for lies: but they are not valiant for the TRUTH upon the earth; for they proceed from evil to evil, and they know not me, saith the LORD.

4 Take ye heed every one of his neighbour, and trust ye not in any brother: for every brother will utterly supplant, and every neighbour will walk with slanders.

5 And they will deceive every one his neighbour, and will not speak the TRUTH: they have taught their tongue to speak lies, and weary themselves to commit iniquity.

6 Thine habitation is in the midst of deceit; through deceit they refuse to know me, saith the LORD.

(Jeremiah 9:2-6).

Lies, Lies, Lies. It should be a crime when you consider the amount of lies that have been told over the years to generations of black and white folk. Most black folks were born of parents who were taught that their race had no history and that they were inferior. Many black children grew up, lived their limited lives, and died of old age being ashamed of being black. WHY? You will find out when you read this book, because the TRUTH is poured out onto every page. "TRUTH AT LAST" is about TRUTH. GOD'S TRUTH.

NOTE: This is not a 'novel', but more a 'study guide' that will explain the deep, dark sayings in the Old Testament. This book is not intended to please the 'intellect'. It is written so that even a child can understand it, so please pardon it's crudeness and please forgive all grammatical imperfections.

"VITAL"

As you read and study this book, it is critical that you refer only to the specific Bible chapters and specific Bible verses that are indicated. This is necessary because most of the books of the Bible do not follow in the order of their time of writing, or of the events which they record. Referring to the specific Bible chapters and verses will provide you with a good understanding of God's TRUTH, and give you a clear understanding of why African people were punished and placed in America for 400 years, and what God is preparing to do in the very near future.

This Revelation is presented in chronological date sequence, matching the B.C.E. with the actual TRUE year (4222/0001). The following Key, or Legend will help you understand the references and descriptions of the people and places referred to in this Revelation.

We're not trying to create a new language, and we are certainly not trying to cause any more division between the 'races', for surely there exist enough issues regarding that matter, but it is imperative to point out that it isn't an issue of 'color', it is an issue of 'truth'. Therefore we will use 'Old Folks' and 'New Folks', instead of Black Folks' and 'White Folks'.

OLD FOLKS: (SO-CALLED 'BLACK FOLKS)

THE FIRST PEOPLE; ALL AFRICAN PEOPLE; THE CHILDREN OF ISRAEL; AFRICAN HEBREW ISRAELITES; ISRAEL; JUDAH . The term 'Old Folks' is quite fitting because 'black folks' have existed for almost 6000 years. They are very 'Old".

GENTILE OLD FOLKS:

THE AFRICANS OR OLD FOLKS THAT CHOSE NOT TO WORSHIP AND SERVE THE SAME GOD AS THE CHILDREN OF ISRAEL WHILE IN AFRICA.

NEW FOLKS: (SO-CALLED 'WHITE FOLKS')

CAUCASIAN PEOPLE; ; ALL NON-AFRICAN PEOPLE. (According to the Old Testament, "New Folks' were created 3760 years after 'Old Folks)

ANACHRONISM: A chronological misplacing of persons, names, events, locations, objects, or customs in regard to each other.

The Old Testament is full of 'Anachronisms', which is the primary reason why people cannot understand what God is saying to the Prophets in the Old Testament. This Revelation will uncover and reveal the true descriptions of all anachronisms. Anachronisms had to be used in the Old Testament to address names, people and locations that did not exist during the time of the Old Testament. Anachronisms also had to be used to address the coming of 'new folks' (white folks) because New Folks (White Folks) did not exist during the time of the Old Testament.

This is a portion of the 'Revelation' that the writer received in 1973 (5734).

As you read and study this revelation, you will learn that in the beginning when GOD created man, He created the 'Black Man', and 'Black Folks' (Old Folks), were the only people on earth in Africa for the first 3760 years.

You will also discover that God created 'White Folks' also, but not for the same **reason**, not at the same **time**, and not out of the same **'matter' and 'substance'** that was used to create the African people. This is why there is a distinct difference between the two peoples, and this is why we have an 'Old Testament', and a 'New Testament' in the Bible. The 'Old Testament' is the pure, true history of all African people. It explains how African people started out in the Garden of Eden, and ended up in America for 400 years. The 'New Testament' was created by the European 'new folks' for political expediency, and to justify their newly created existence.

'Truth at Last' will prove without a doubt, that African people have existed for over 5700 years; they have been here for a long, long time, and could be called 'Old Folks' instead of 'Black Folks', because it is a matter of TRUTH, not 'color'.. This book will also prove that 'new folks (white folks) have not existed as long as African people, and could be called 'New Folks' ..Even though 'new folks' have existed for over one thousand years, they are still quite 'NEW' to most logical and natural things. **When color is used to describe or define a people, "white" becomes "superior", "black" becomes "inferior".** Therefore, African people degrade their intelligence by accepting and referring to themselves as "black". If African people looked at the definition of 'black', as defined in 'Webster's Dictionary', they would quickly discard 'black' as their race. 'Black' is defined as **negative, dirty, soiled, thoroughly sinister or evil, wicked, very sad, and gloomy.**

If the Children of Israel would have obeyed God, and kept the Ten Commandments while in Africa, there would have been no need for a 'New Testament', or 'New Folks'. but 'Old Folks' were disobedient to God's laws, so it was necessary for God to create "New Folks", (white folks).

The Old Testament contains the True history of the African people, and the TRUTH to why God had to create the \"New Folks" (white folks) thousands of years later, to punish and place 'Old Folks' (black folks) in America for 400 years. The New Testament contains the work that God prepared Jesus to do, so that the 'new folks' (white folks) would know what God did before they were created. God knew that when He created 'new folks', (white folks) that they would not believe the things reported in the 'Holy Scriptures' (Old Testament). That's why GOD made Jesus do so many things that appeared to be 'miraculous'. God worked His power so strong on Jesus, that the 'new folks' thought Jesus was God, and the European Councils sanctioned the fallacy. Even in these present days, many folks are being misled into believing that Jesus is their Saviour, and are waiting for Jesus to come back. We will get to the TRUTH about Jesus when we complete the Old Testament, but right now get your King James version of the Bible and follow this Revelation from God, and the Spirit of TRUTH will be revealed before your very eyes. Of all the many different types of Bibles and books, the writer chose the "Kings James Version" dated 1612 as his base of reference . Why? ,because no other book of any kind has affected, inspired and influenced the entire life of English -speaking people.

Before we start, we must understand that this 'unknowable something' that we call GOD, is not a person, has no sex or gender, is more '**WHAT**' then '**WHO**', and the best we have to describe it, is the term **'SPIRIT'**. But since we have used the term "GOD" throughout the ages, we will without any religious connection use the term "GOD" during this Revelation.

The 'Spirit-God' revealed, that there should be no conflict between Creation and Evolution, because everything evolved from what was created. God was very pleased with the creation when the Universal elements and the Heaven and the Earth were finished, for GOD saw that it was all good. All of the Universal elements that GOD made prior to man, obeyed the natural law in which they were created. The Spirit always existed, the Spirit created everything that was, is, and will be, and everything evolved from what the Spirit created. We now begin the chronology of life according to the Bible.

1st Day Genesis 1: 3-5 Water, Daylight, Night.

And God said, Let there be light: and there was light. And God saw the light, that it was good: and God divided the light from the darkness. And God called the light Day, and the darkness he called Night. And the evening and the morning were the first day. (Gen 1:3-5).

2nd Day Genesis 1: 6-8 Firmament, Heaven

And God said, Let there be a firmament in the midst of the waters, and let it divide the waters from the waters. And God made the firmament, and divided the waters which were under the firmament from the waters which were above the firmament: and it was so. And God called the firmament Heaven. And the evening and the morning were the second day. (gen 1:6-8).

3rd Day Genesis 1: 9-13 Firmament, Earth, Seas, Herb, Trees Grass, Seed and Fruit Trees

And God said, Let the waters under the heaven be gathered together unto one place, and let the dry land appear: and it was so. And God called the dry land Earth; and the gathering together of the waters called he Seas: and God saw that it was good. And God said, Let the earth bring forth grass, the herb yielding seed, and the fruit tree yielding fruit after his kind, whose seed is in itself, upon the earth: and it was so. And the earth brought forth grass, and herb yielding seed after his kind, and the tree yielding fruit, whose seed was in itself, after his kind: and God saw that it was good. And the evening and the morning were the third day. (gen 1:9-13).

4th Day Genesis 1: 14-19 Lights, Sun, Moon, Stars

And God said, Let there be lights in the firmament of the heaven to divide the day from the night; and let them be for signs, and for seasons, and for days, and years: And let them be for lights in the firmament of the heaven to give light upon the earth: and it was so. And God made two great lights; the greater light to rule the day, and the lesser light to rule the night: he made the stars also. And God set them in the firmament of the heaven to give light upon the earth, And to rule over the day and over the night, and to divide the light from the darkness: and God saw that it was good. And the evening and the morning were the fourth day. (gen 1:14-19).

5th Day Genesis 1: 20-23 Fish, Fowl from water.

And God said, Let the waters bring forth abundantly the moving creature that hath life, and fowl that may fly above the earth in the open firmament of heaven. And God created great whales, and every living creature that moveth, which the waters brought forth abundantly, after their kind, and every winged fowl after his kind: and God saw that it was good. And God blessed them, saying, Be fruitful, and multiply, and fill the waters in the seas, and let fowl multiply in the earth. And the evening and the morning were the fifth day. (gen 1:20-23).

6th Day Genesis 1: 24-31 Beast, Creeping things from the earth, Man and Woman.

And God said, Let the earth bring forth the living creature after his kind, cattle, and creeping thing, and beast of the earth after his kind: and it was so. And God made the beast of the earth after his kind, and cattle after their kind, and every thing that creepeth upon the earth after his kind: and God saw that it was good. And God said, Let us make man in our image, after our likeness: and let them have dominion over the fish of the sea, and over the fowl of the air, and over the cattle, and over all the earth, and over every creeping thing that creepeth upon the earth. So God created man in his own image, in the image of God created he him; male and female created he them. And God blessed them, and God said unto them, Be fruitful, and multiply, and replenish the earth, and subdue it: and have dominion over the fish of the sea, and over the fowl of the air, and over every living thing that moveth upon the earth. And God said, Behold, I have given you every herb bearing seed, which is upon the face of all the earth, and every tree, in the which is the fruit of a tree yielding seed; to you it shall be for meat. And to every beast of the earth, and to every fowl of the air, and to every thing that creepeth upon the earth, wherein there is life, I have given every green herb for meat: and it was so. And God saw every thing that he had made, and, behold, it was very good. And the evening and the morning were the sixth day. (gen 1:24-31).

<u>7th Day Genesis 2: 1-3 Sabbath Day Rest.</u>

Thus the heavens and the earth were finished, and all the host of them. And on the seventh day God ended his work which he had made; and he rested on the seventh day from all his work which he had made. And God blessed the seventh day, and sanctified it: because that in it he had rested from all his work which God created and made. (gen 2:1-3).

4222/0001

The geographic situation of the Bible cannot be overlooked. You will note that all of the events cited from Genesis to Revelation took place on the continents of Africa and Asia, land inhabited by African people thousands of years before 'new folks' (white folks) were created, and even today...Therefore, the creation took place in AFRICA.

In Gen. 1:26, Let US make man in our image..

The **<u>us</u>,** is referring to all of the **109** elements of the universe. God's plan was to create the African man out of the universal elements that existed, and have man function according to 'natural law', or in other words, since man was created from the elements, man was expected to live his life in obedience to the 'WILL' of God, as the elements did. (GOD'S WILL IS **"LAW"**)

4222/0001

Gen. 2:7 shows how the African man was created. "Out of the dust of the ground".

7 And the LORD God formed man of the dust of the ground, and breathed into his nostrils the breath of life; and man became a living soul.

(Genesis 2:7).

All forms of life can only come from three areas; (1). The **heavens** above. (2). The **earth** beneath. (3). The **waters** thereof. These are the only three areas that contain **"ATOMS"**, which are the unitary particles of which <u>all matter and life</u> are formed. Atoms contain all 109 elements of the universe. This is why the color of the African people's skin represents the many shades of soil (dust/dirt) in the earth. Also, how could 'old folks' (Black folks) have possibly endured the horrors that took place in this earth, unless they were made from something 'everlasting', and by God? Genesis Chapter 5 shews the life span of the African people in the beginning. Many people do not believe that they lived for almost a thousand years. We must remember that when God made the African man, GOD intended for man to live forever because the African man was created from an everlasting substance. God provided man with everything that enabled him to live forever. At that time man's 'life-style' was much different, and man's total intake was 'natural', from the earth. That's why the African people in the beginning lived so long; natural food went into a natural body. Today our life span is very short, because of our 'life-styles' and we allow too many man-made destructive chemicals to enter the natural system. Let's take a look at African longevity from Genesis chapter 5.

4222/0001	Adam created.
4092/0130	Adam begat Seth at 130 years old.
3987/0235	Seth begat Enos at 105 years old.
3897/0325	Enos begat Cainan at 90 years old.
3827/0395	Cainan begat Mahalaleel at 70 years old.
3762/0462	Mahalaleel begat Jared at 65 years old.
3600/0622	Jared begat Enoch at 162 years old.
3535/0687	Enoch begat Methuselah at 65 years old.
3348/0874	Methuselah begat Lamech at 187 years old.
3292/0930	Adam died at 930 years old.
3235/0987	Enoch died at 365 years old.
3180/1042	Seth died at 912 years old.
3166/1056	Lamech begat Noah at 182 years old.
3082/1140	Enos died at 905 years old.
2987/1235	Cainan died at 910 years old.
2932/1290	Mahalaleel died at 805 years old.
2800/1422	Jared died at 962 years old.
2666/1556	Noah begat Shem, Ham, Japheth.
2571/1651	Lamech died at 777 years old.
2566/1656	Methuselah died at 969 years old.

2566/1656

Gen. 6:3 So the African people in the beginning lived a long time, enjoying all the wonderful things that God had created. But as they multiplied on the face of the earth of Africa, God saw that It's spirit would not always strive with man, so God reduced man's life span to 120 years.

3 And the LORD said, My spirit shall not always strive with man, for that he also is flesh: yet his days shall be an hundred and twenty years.

(Genesis 6:3).

2566/1656

Gen. 6:5-6; Man became so wicked before God that God was sorry that HE made man. It grieved God so much, that HE decided to destroy the African people from the face of Africa.

5 And GOD saw that the wickedness of man was great in the earth, and that every imagination of the thoughts of his heart was only evil continually.

6 And it repented the LORD that he had made man on the earth, and it grieved him at his heart.

(Genesis 6:5-6).

2566/1656

Gen. 6:7 All flesh in Africa destroyed by the flood.

7 And the LORD said, I will destroy man whom I have created from the face of the earth; both man, and beast, and the creeping thing, and the fowls of the air; for it repenteth me that I have made them.

(Genesis 6:7).

2566/1656

Gen. 6: 8-9 But there was one African man who found grace in the eyes of God. 'Noah'. Noah and his family were saved from the great flood that destroyed the first people of Africa, 1656 years after God created the heavens and the earth.

8 But Noah found grace in the eyes of the LORD.

9 These are the generations of Noah: Noah was a just man and perfect in his generations, and Noah walked with God.

(Genesis 6:8-9).

2566/1656

Gen. 7:6 Noah was 600 years old at the time of the flood.

2566/1656

Gen. 7:23.. So God destroyed all the African people (except Noah and his family), and every living substance which was upon the face of Africa, with the flood. Remembering that God made everything for His pleasure, we should be able to understand why God destroyed the first batch of African people. They were not good, and God wanted everything that He created to be good. God was hurt and very disappointed, so He destroyed the first African people that He created. But God did not give up because He was determined that man would live his life according to the natural law that governs the universe (The Golden Rule).

2347/1875

Gen. Chapter 9. Not only did God save Noah and his family because of his righteousness, God also saved Noah so that his seed could be used to replenish Africa with more people. (We still have a long way to go before the Bible addresses the creation of 'new folks' (White folks). Versus 18 & 19. Noah's sons replenished the nations in Africa, which was the whole earth at that time.

2247/1975

Gen. 11:1 Shews that when God made man out of the dust of the earth, He only made one kind, (the African) which needed only one language, and one speech.

1 And the whole earth was of one language, and of one speech.

(Genesis 11:1).

If GOD had made new folks (white folks) at that time, GOD would have made it known unto us, because God is specific , and more languages would have been necessary. Also, if the new folks (white folks) existed during the time of the Old Testament, why is there no report or record of 'Racial unrest', Segregation, Apartheid, etc.,? 'Racism' did not exist during the Old Testament because new folks (white folks) did not exist during the time of the Old Testament.

2247/1975

11:3-4 God gave the African people everything, for He had no other people to give it to. He gave them so much, that they thought they were God.

3 And they said one to another, Go to, let us make brick, and burn them throughly. And they had brick for stone, and slime had they for morter.

4 And they said, Go to, let us build us a city and a tower, whose top may reach unto heaven; and let us make us a name, lest we be scattered abroad upon the face of the whole earth.

(Genesis 11:3-4).

2247/1975

Gen. 11:6 God shewing us that African people were the only people that He made in the beginning.

6 And the LORD said, Behold, the people is one, and they have all one language; and this they begin to do: and now nothing will be restrained from them, which they have imagined to do.

(Genesis 11:6).

2247/1975

Gen. 11:7 God shewing us why each African nation speaks a different language.

7 Go to, let us go down, and there confound their language, that they may not understand one another's speech.

(Genesis 11:7).

2247/1975

Gen. 11:8-9 No matter where you go in the world, you will always find 'old folks' (Black folks) We will explain why as this Revelation unfolds.

8 So the LORD scattered them abroad from thence upon the face of all the earth: and they left off to build the city.

9 Therefore is the name of it called Babel; because the LORD did there confound the language of all the earth: and from thence did the LORD scatter them abroad upon the face of all the earth. (Africa)

(Genesis 11:8-9).

2216/2006

Noah died at 950 years old. Gen. 9:29

Now it was time for God to go forward with the next part of His plan. God had to destroy the first batch of 'old folks' in Africa because they did not live according to 'natural law', and now we have another batch of the same kind of African people. The African people before the flood did not understand 'Universal Law' and the general rule of nature, and unfortunately did not reach the stage of development where they were perfect channels for expressing the Spirit of God. God knew that this new batch of African people would experience the same level of destruction unless something different was established.

The question became, 'what could be done so that these people would live in harmony with the 'law of life'? What could be done to make these people understand that everything in the universe is governed by absolute, unfailing LAW, and that this natural law governs and judges all human behavior? God knew that in order for this people to understand natural law, someone would have to be chosen to train the people.and teach them "LAW".. Abram was selected for this task.

1996/2226

Gen. 11:26 Abram born unto Terah.

26 And Terah lived seventy years, and begat Abram, Nahor, and Haran.

(Genesis 11:26).

1921/2301

Gen. 12:1-9 Abram chosen by God to be the father of God's chosen people. (African Hebrews) God told Abram to be obedient and do everything that he was commanded to do, and he would be blessed and become the father of a great nation of people. Abram believed and obeyed God. No matter what God asked him to do, Abram did it without question. God was pleased with Abram, and blessed him greatly. When the people saw that Abram would sacrifice anything in obedience to the will of God, and saw how greatly God blessed him, they wanted to share in this peculiar treasure.

1 Now the LORD had said unto Abram, Get thee out of thy country, and from thy kindred, and from thy father's house, unto a land that I will shew thee:

2 And I will make of thee a great nation, and I will bless thee, and make thy name great; and thou shalt be a blessing:

3 And I will bless them that bless thee, and curse him that curseth thee: and in thee shall all families of the earth be blessed.

4 So Abram departed, as the LORD had spoken unto him; and Lot went with him: and Abram was seventy and five years old when he departed out of Haran.

5 And Abram took Sarai his wife, and Lot his brother's son, and all their substance that they had gathered, and the souls that they had gotten in Haran; and they went forth to go into the land of Canaan; and into the land of Canaan they came.

6 And Abram passed through the land unto the place of Sichem, unto the plain of Moreh. And the Canaanite was then in the land.

7 And the LORD appeared unto Abram, and said, Unto thy seed will I give this land: and there builded he an altar unto the LORD, who appeared unto him.

8 And he removed from thence unto a mountain on the east of Bethel, and pitched his tent, having Bethel on the west, and Hai on the east: and there he builded an altar unto the LORD, and called upon the name of the LORD.

9 And Abram journeyed, going on still toward the south.

(Genesis 12:1-9).

"VITAL"

At this point we must point out something that's very important. Out of all of the African people on earth in Africa at this time, God reached down and grabbed a handful of them and said, "I know now that all men won't do as I command, so I want you to represent Me down there". "And ye shall be unto me, a Kingdom of Priests, and a Holy Nation". Abram's job was to teach Universal Law and lead this people in such a way that they would become a source of blessing for all mankind. All of the people that believed and followed Abram were, 'The Children of Abram'. Abram and his children were set apart from the rest of the African people in Africa by God, so that they could be trained in the wisdom of natural law, which is the true worship to God. This is where God selected, "His chosen people". At this point God is dealing with two types of African people; 'The Children of Abram', and the 'Gentile African people'. Gentile, was the name given to the African people who chose not to serve the God of Abram. The name "BETH-EL" is highlighted in this writing to explain it's origin, and to shew that in 'TRUTH', it was stolen from Africa by 'new folks', and is presently used to name many of their churches and synagogues. When God chose Abram to be the father of the African Hebrews, He also established the first "House of God". As Abram journeyed to the place chosen by God, He would always build an altar unto the Lord and name it "BETH-EL". (Please read Gen. 12:6-8)

6 And Abram passed through the land unto the place of Sichem, unto the plain of Moreh. And the Canaanite was then in the land.

7 And the LORD appeared unto Abram, and said, Unto thy seed will I give this land: and there builded he an altar unto the LORD, who appeared unto him.

8 And he removed from thence unto a mountain on the east of Bethel, and pitched his tent, having Bethel on the west, and Hai on the east: and there he builded an altar unto the LORD, and called upon the name of the LORD.

(Genesis 12:6-8).

Naming the place of worship "BETH-EL" became a tradition of the African Hebrew Israelites. "BETH-EL", the House of God, is mentioned sixty-six time from Genesis Chapter 12 thru Amos 13. Notice how this African Hebrew tradition continued with Jacob. (Gen. 28:10-22).

10 And Jacob went out from Beersheba, and went toward Haran.

11 And he lighted upon a certain place, and tarried there all night, because the sun was set; and he took of the stones of that place, and put them for his pillows, and lay down in that place to sleep.

12 And he dreamed, and behold a ladder set up on the earth, and the top of it reached to heaven: and behold the angels of God ascending and descending on it.

13 And, behold, the LORD stood above it, and said, I am the LORD God of Abraham thy father, and the God of Isaac: the land whereon thou liest, to thee will I give it, and to thy seed;

14 And thy seed shall be as the dust of the earth, and thou shalt spread abroad to the west, and to the east, and to the north, and to the south: and in thee and in thy seed shall all the families of the earth be blessed.

15 And, behold, I am with thee, and will keep thee in all places whither thou goest, and will bring thee again into this land; for I will not leave thee, until I have done that which I have spoken to thee of.

16 And Jacob awaked out of his sleep, and he said, Surely the LORD is in this place; and I knew it not.

17 And he was afraid, and said, How dreadful is this place! this is none other but the house of God, and this is the gate of heaven.

18 And Jacob rose up early in the morning, and took the stone that he had put for his pillows, and set it up for a pillar, and poured oil upon the top of it.

19 And he called the name of that place Bethel: but the name of that city was called Luz at the first.

20 And Jacob vowed a vow, saying, If God will be with me, and will keep me in this way that I go, and will give me bread to eat, and raiment to put on,

21 So that I come again to my father's house in peace; then shall the LORD be my God:

22 And this stone, which I have set for a pillar, shall be God's house: and of all that thou shalt give me I will surely give the tenth unto thee.

(Genesis 28:10-22).

1913/2309

After observing the behavior of the African people for the first 2309 years, it was quite apparent to GOD that they would violate universal law, and ultimately experience retribution, punishment and destruction from Africa.

1913/2309

God tells Abram that the African Hebrew Israelites would be placed in America for 400 years. Many people are under the misconception that the 400 years mentioned in Genesis 15:13-14, pertain to the 430 years that the African Hebrew Israelites sojourned in the land of Egypt. Gen. 15:13-14 specifically states that the African Hebrew Israelites would be afflicted in a land that is not theirs. America is not the African Americans land. We must understand "affliction". Afflict means, to strike down, to cause pain and suffering, to distress and to overthrow with calamity. (This is what 'old folks' (black folks) experienced since being placed in America for almost 400 years, according to Gen. 15:13-14. The African Hebrew Israelites sojourned in the land of Egypt for 430 years where they were subjected to hard labour for 266 years; they lived in 'peace' in Egypt for the other 164 years. (Sojourn means; to stay as a temporary resident.)

40 Now the sojourning of the children of Israel, who dwelt in Egypt, was four hundred and thirty years.

41 And it came to pass at the end of the four hundred and thirty years, even the selfsame day it came to pass, that all the hosts of the LORD went out from the land of Egypt.

(Exodus 12:40-41).

The African Israelites lived free from bondage in Egypt for 164 years. They served in bondage/captivity in Egypt for 266 years, not 400 years as recorded in Gen. 15:13-14.

13 And he said unto Abram, Know of a surety that thy seed shall be a stranger in a land that is not theirs, and shall serve them; and they shall afflict them four hundred years;

14 And also that nation, whom they shall serve, will I judge: and afterward shall they come out with great substance.

(Genesis 15:13-14).

1913/2309

Gen. 16:1-6 Sarai, Abram's wife was baren, and could not have children, so she gave her handmaid , Hagar , to Abram to be his wife. When Hagar got pregnant by Abram, Sarai got jealous, mad, and kicked her out, and Hagar fled from them.

1 Now Sarai Abram's wife bare him no children: and she had an handmaid, an Egyptian, whose name was Hagar.

2 And Sarai said unto Abram, Behold now, the LORD hath restrained me from bearing: I pray thee, go in unto my maid; it may be that I may obtain children by her. And Abram hearkened to the voice of Sarai.

3 And Sarai Abram's wife took Hagar her maid the Egyptian, after Abram had dwelt ten years in the land of Canaan, and gave her to her husband Abram to be his wife.

4 And he went in unto Hagar, and she conceived: and when she saw that she had conceived, her mistress was despised in her eyes.

5 And Sarai said unto Abram, My wrong be upon thee: I have given my maid into thy bosom; and when she saw that she had conceived, I was despised in her eyes: the LORD judge between me and thee.

6 But Abram said unto Sarai, Behold, thy maid is in thy hand; do to her as it pleaseth thee. And when Sarai dealt hardly with her, she fled from her face.

(Genesis 16:1-6)

Gen. 16:7-16. When the angel of the Lord caught up with Hagar, she told the angel what happen. The angel told her to return to Abram's house, and told her that her seed would be multiplied. She was also told that her son Ishmael would be a wild man. He would be after every man, and every man would be against him

7 And the angel of the LORD found her by a fountain of water in the wilderness, by the fountain in the way to Shur.

8 And he said, Hagar, Sarai's maid, whence camest thou? and whither wilt thou go? And she said, I flee from the face of my mistress Sarai.

9 And the angel of the LORD said unto her, Return to thy mistress, and submit thyself under her hands.

10 And the angel of the LORD said unto her, I will multiply thy seed exceedingly, that it shall not be numbered for multitude.

11 And the angel of the LORD said unto her, Behold, thou art with child, and shalt bear a son, and shalt call his name Ishmael; because the LORD hath heard thy affliction.

12 And he will be a wild man; his hand will be against every man, and every man's hand against him; and he shall dwell in the presence of all his brethren.

13 And she called the name of the LORD that spake unto her, Thou God seest me: for she said, Have I also here looked after him that seeth me?

14 Wherefore the well was called Beerlahairoi; behold, it is between Kadesh and Bered.

15 And Hagar bare Abram a son: and Abram called his son's name, which Hagar bare, Ishmael.

16 And Abram was fourscore and six years old, when Hagar bare Ishmael to Abram.

(Genesis 16:7-16).

1910/2312

Gen. 17:1-8 . When Abram was 99 years old, GOD changed his name to Abraham, and told him that 'nations' and 'kings' shall come from his loins.

1 And when Abram was ninety years old and nine, the LORD appeared to Abram, and said unto him, I am the Almighty God; walk before me, and be thou perfect.

2 And I will make my covenant between me and thee, and will multiply thee exceedingly.

3 And Abram fell on his face: and God talked with him, saying,

4 As for me, behold, my covenant is with thee, and thou shalt be a father of many nations.

5 Neither shall thy name any more be called Abram, but thy name shall be Abraham; for a father of many nations have I made thee.

6 And I will make thee exceeding fruitful, and I will make nations of thee, and kings shall come out of thee.

7 And I will establish my covenant between me and thee and thy seed after thee in their generations for an everlasting covenant, to be a God unto thee, and to thy seed after thee.

8 And I will give unto thee, and to thy seed after thee, the land wherein thou art a stranger, all the land of Canaan, for an everlasting possession; and I will be their God.

(Genesis 17:1-8).

1910/2312

Gen. 17:15 God changed Sarai's name to Sarah.

15 And God said unto Abraham, As for Sarai thy wife, thou shalt not call her name Sarai, but Sarah shall her name be.

(Genesis 17:15).

1898/2324

Gen. Chapters 18 and 19. Sodom and Gomorrah destroyed because of homosexuality and wickedness.

1896/2326

Gen. 21:5 When Abraham was 100 years old, his son Isaac was born unto him and Sarah. Sarah became the mother of the nation of African Hebrew Israelites. Abraham became the father of the African Hebrew Israelites and the father of the African Islam/ Muslims. Based on this, it would be utterly ridiculous for people of African descent to worship other than as Hebrew or Muslim.

1872/2350

Gen. 22:1-19 Abraham was put on trial and his faith was tested by being asked to sacrifice his son Isaac. Abraham passed the test because he believed God, he knew what God wanted of him, he was determined to obey God's command and Abraham was willing to pay the price for his spiritual convictions, regardless of the cost.

1 And it came to pass after these things, that God did tempt Abraham, and said unto him, Abraham: and he said, Behold, here I am.

2 And he said, Take now thy son, thine only son Isaac, whom thou lovest, and get thee into the land of Moriah; and offer him there for a burnt offering upon one of the mountains which I will tell thee of.

3 And Abraham rose up early in the morning, and saddled his ass, and took two of his young men with him, and Isaac his son, and clave the wood for the burnt offering, and rose up, and went unto the place of which God had told him.

4 Then on the third day Abraham lifted up his eyes, and saw the place afar off.

5 And Abraham said unto his young men, Abide ye here with the ass; and I and the lad will go yonder and worship, and come again to you.

6 And Abraham took the wood of the burnt offering, and laid it upon Isaac his son; and he took the fire in his hand, and a knife; and they went both of them together.

7 And Isaac spake unto Abraham his father, and said, My father: and he said, Here am I, my son. And he said, Behold the fire and the wood: but where is the lamb for a burnt offering?

8 And Abraham said, My son, God will provide himself a lamb for a burnt offering: so they went both of them together.

9 And they came to the place which God had told him of; and Abraham built an altar there, and laid the wood in order, and bound Isaac his son, and laid him on the altar upon the wood.

10 And Abraham stretched forth his hand, and took the knife to slay his son.

11 And the angel of the LORD called unto him out of heaven, and said, Abraham, Abraham: and he said, Here am I.

12 And he said, Lay not thine hand upon the lad, neither do thou any thing unto him: for now I know that thou fearest God, seeing thou hast not withheld thy son, thine only son from me.

13 And Abraham lifted up his eyes, and looked, and behold behind him a ram caught in a thicket by his horns: and Abraham went and took the ram, and offered him up for a burnt offering in the stead of his son.

14 And Abraham called the name of that place Jehovahjireh: as it is said to this day, In the mount of the LORD it shall be seen.

15 And the angel of the LORD called unto Abraham out of heaven the second time,

16 And said, By myself have I sworn, saith the LORD, for because thou hast done this thing, and hast not withheld thy son, thine only son:

17 That in blessing I will bless thee, and in multiplying I will multiply thy seed as the stars of the heaven, and as the sand which is upon the sea shore; and thy seed shall possess the gate of his enemies;

18 And in thy seed shall all the nations of the earth be blessed; because thou hast obeyed my voice.

19 So Abraham returned unto his young men, and they rose up and went together to Beersheba; and Abraham dwelt at Beersheba.

(Genesis 22:1-19).

1860/2362

Gen. 23:1,2 Sarah, the mother of the original African Hebrews, died at the age of 127.

1 And Sarah was an hundred and seven and twenty years old: these were the years of the life of Sarah.

2 And Sarah died in Kirjatharba; the same is Hebron in the land of Canaan: and Abraham came to mourn for Sarah, and to weep for her.

(Genesis 23:1-2).

1837/2385

Gen. 25:26 Jacob was borned unto Isaac and Rebekah when Isaac was 60 years old.

1821/2401

Gen. 25:7,8 Abraham dies at 175 years old. Abraham was the first African Prophet of God.

7 And these are the days of the years of Abraham's life which he lived, an hundred threescore and fifteen years.

8 Then Abraham gave up the ghost, and died in a good old age, an old man, and full of years; and was gathered to his people.

(Genesis 25:7-8).

1800/2422

Gen. 25:11 God chose Isaac to lead the African Hebrews. (The Children of Isaac)

11 And it came to pass after the death of Abraham, that God blessed his son Isaac; and Isaac dwelt by the well Lahairoi.

(Genesis 25:11).

Gen. 25:12-18 The nations and generations of the African Muslims are identified.

12 Now these are the generations of Ishmael, Abraham's son, whom Hagar the Egyptian, Sarah's handmaid, bare unto Abraham:

13 And these are the names of the sons of Ishmael, by their names, according to their generations: the firstborn of Ishmael, Nebajoth; and Kedar, and Adbeel, and Mibsam,

14 And Mishma, and Dumah, and Massa,

15 Hadar, and Tema, Jetur, Naphish, and Kedemah:

16 These are the sons of Ishmael, and these are their names, by their towns, and by their castles; twelve princes according to their nations.

17 And these are the years of the life of Ishmael, an hundred and thirty and seven years: and he gave up the ghost and died; and was gathered unto his people.

18 And they dwelt from Havilah unto Shur, that is before Egypt, as thou goest toward Assyria: and he died in the presence of all his brethren.

(Genesis 25:12-18).

1773/2449

Gen. 25:17 Ishmael, who established the African Muslim nations of Islam, died at the age of 137.

1752/2470

Gen. 30. The 12 sons of Jacob. When God changed Jacob's name to 'Israel', his sons developed into the 'Twelve Tribes of Israel', or, the Children of Israel', the original African Hebrew Israelites, many of the African Americans today.

1729/2493

Gen. 39:1 Joseph was sold by his brothers and placed in Potiphar's house in Egypt. Joseph was the first of the Children of Israel who began the 430 year sojourn in the land of Egypt.

1716/2506

Gen. 35:10-15 God changed Jacob's name to ISRAEL. This is where the name "THE CHILDREN OF ISRAEL" came from. They were 'old folks' (black folks) then, and they are 'old folks' now, and, the whole world will soon know it. God chose Israel (Jacob) to lead the African Hebrews. So the "Children of Israel" were the nation of 'black folks' (old folks) that God chose and set apart from the rest of the 'gentile old folks' in Africa. For the rest of this revelation, you will find that the 'Old Testament', is a historical report of the relationship between GOD, and HIS chosen people. (The Children of Israel) who are 'old folks', the so-called black people of the world.

1716/2506

Gen. 35:28-29 Isaac dies at the age of 180.

1715/2507

Gen. 41:37-46 Joseph was made Governor over Egypt at the age of 30.

1706/2516

Gen.46:1-27 God told Jacob to take the Children of Israel into Egypt where they would become a great nation of people.

1689/2533

Gen. 47:28 Jacob lived in the land of Egypt 17 years and died at the age of 147.

28 And Jacob lived in the land of Egypt seventeen years: so the whole age of Jacob was an hundred forty and seven years.

(Genesis 47:28).

1689/2533

Gen.Chapter 49 Before he died, Jacob blessed his sons and told them of the things that would befall the African Children of Israel in the last days.

1 And Jacob called unto his sons, and said, Gather yourselves together, that I may tell you that which shall befall you in the last days.

2 Gather yourselves together, and hear, ye sons of Jacob; and hearken unto Israel your father.

3 Reuben, thou art my firstborn, my might, and the beginning of my strength, the excellency of dignity, and the excellency of power:

4 Unstable as water, thou shalt not excel; because thou wentest up to thy father's bed; then defiledst thou it: he went up to my couch.

5 Simeon and Levi are brethren; instruments of cruelty are in their habitations.

6 O my soul, come not thou into their secret; unto their assembly, mine honour, be not thou united: for in their anger they slew a man, and in their selfwill they digged down a wall.

7 Cursed be their anger, for it was fierce; and their wrath, for it was cruel: I will divide them in Jacob, and scatter them in Israel.

8 Judah, thou art he whom thy brethren shall praise: thy hand shall be in the neck of thine enemies; thy father's children shall bow down before thee.

9 Judah is a lion's whelp: from the prey, my son, thou art gone up: he stooped down, he couched as a lion, and as an old lion; who shall rouse him up?

10 The sceptre shall not depart from Judah, nor a lawgiver from between his feet, until Shiloh come; and unto him shall the gathering of the people be.

11 Binding his foal unto the vine, and his ass's colt unto the choice vine; he washed his garments in wine, and his clothes in the blood of grapes:

12 His eyes shall be red with wine, and his teeth white with milk.

13 Zebulun shall dwell at the haven of the sea; and he shall be for an haven of ships; and his border shall be unto Zidon.

14 Issachar is a strong ass couching down between two burdens:

15 And he saw that rest was good, and the land that it was pleasant; and bowed his shoulder to bear, and became a servant unto tribute.

16 Dan shall judge his people, as one of the tribes of Israel.

17 Dan shall be a serpent by the way, an adder in the path, that biteth the horse heels, so that his rider shall fall backward.

18 I have waited for thy salvation, O LORD.

19 Gad, a troop shall overcome him: but he shall overcome at the last.

20 Out of Asher his bread shall be fat, and he shall yield royal dainties.

21 Naphtali is a hind let loose: he giveth goodly words.

22 Joseph is a fruitful bough, even a fruitful bough by a well; whose branches run over the wall:

23 The archers have sorely grieved him, and shot at him, and hated him:

24 But his bow abode in strength, and the arms of his hands were made strong by the hands of the mighty God of Jacob; (from thence is the shepherd, the stone of Israel:)

25 Even by the God of thy father, who shall help thee; and by the Almighty, who shall bless thee with blessings of heaven above, blessings of the deep that lieth under, blessings of the breasts, and of the womb:

26 The blessings of thy father have prevailed above the blessings of my progenitors unto the utmost bound of the everlasting hills: they shall be on the head of Joseph, and on the crown of the head of him that was separate from his brethren.

27 Benjamin shall ravin as a wolf: in the morning he shall devour the prey, and at night he shall divide the spoil.

28 All these are the twelve tribes of Israel: and this is it that their father spake unto them, and blessed them; every one according to his blessing he blessed them.

29 And he charged them, and said unto them, I am to be gathered unto my people: bury me with my fathers in the cave that is in the field of Ephron the Hittite,

30 In the cave that is in the field of Machpelah, which is before Mamre, in the land of Canaan, which Abraham bought with the field of Ephron the Hittite for a possession of a buryingplace.

31 There they buried Abraham and Sarah his wife; there they buried Isaac and Rebekah his wife; and there I buried Leah.

32 The purchase of the field and of the cave that is therein was from the children of Heth.

33 And when Jacob had made an end of commanding his sons, he gathered up his feet into the bed, and yielded up the ghost, and was gathered unto his people.

(Genesis 49:1-33).

1635/2587

Gen. 50:26 Joseph died in the land of Egypt at the age of 110. NOTE: Approximately 2600 years have gone by now, and still no mention or history of the existence of 'new folks'. (white folks).)

1573/2649

Ex. 1:8-14 So now the Children of Israel are in the land of Egypt. God placed them there so that He could shew them, and the "Gentile Africans' of Egypt, His power and His might. God made the African Hebrew Israelites fruitful, and they increased so abundantly, that in order to control them, the African Gentile king of Egypt, who was called "Pharaoh", placed taskmasters over the Children of Israel, and subjected them to hard labour. But the more 'Pharaoh' punished them, the more God made the Children of Israel grow.

8 Now there arose up a new king over Egypt, which knew not Joseph.

9 And he said unto his people, Behold, the people of the children of Israel are more and mightier than we:

10 Come on, let us deal wisely with them; lest they multiply, and it come to pass, that, when there falleth out any war, they join also unto our enemies, and fight against us, and so get them up out of the land.

11 Therefore they did set over them taskmasters to afflict them with their burdens. And they built for Pharaoh treasure cities, Pithom and Raamses.

12 But the more they afflicted them, the more they multiplied and grew. And they were grieved because of the children of Israel.

13 And the Egyptians made the children of Israel to serve with rigour:

14 And they made their lives bitter with hard bondage, in morter, and

> in brick, and in all manner of service in the field: all their service, wherein they made them serve, was with rigour.

(Exodus 1:8-14).

<u>"VITAL"</u>

The African Children of Israel were in bondage in the land of Egypt for 266 years. The African Children of Israel's captivity in America is 400 years, and it is almost over. God said HE will deliver the Children of Israel from America, similar to the way He delivered their forefathers from the land of Egypt. (Please read Gen. 15:13-14 and Jer. 16:14-15.) It's time now for the next part of God's plan. The name that we call the 'CREATOR', is 'GOD', but we must understand that 'GOD' is a 'SPIRIT', not a 'human'. (Please read Amos 3:7). This is why a 'person' is always used to represent and present the "Will" of God to the people. Abraham worked for God, Isaac and Jacob worked for GOD, and now GOD needed someone else to do a job for HIM. (Remember Amos 3:7)

1571/2651

Exodus 2:1-10 The birth of Moses.

1531/2691

Exodus Chapter 3. God chose Moses to deliver the African Children of Isarel from the land of Egypt. Moses was just a normal African like everyone else, a shepherd, minding his own business. God came to Moses and said, Moses, I have heard my people crying, and I have seen their affliction. I am ready to deliver them from the land of Egypt, and place them in a good land, and I want you to lead them.

1520/2702

The life and experiences of the book of "JOB".

1491/2731

Exodus Chapter 4 : 1-3. Moses was very uncomfortable being chosen to deliver and lead the African Hebrew Israelites from the land of Egypt. Moses said unto God, 'Those folks won't believe that You sent me unto them, they won't listen to me." Moses could not see God, so like many of us, Moses was reluctant. So God turned a stick into a snake which scared Moses so much that he ran. But God turned the snake back into a stick.

1 And Moses answered and said, But, behold, they will not believe me, nor hearken unto my voice: for they will say, The LORD hath not appeared unto thee.

2 And the LORD said unto him, What is that in thine hand? And he said, A rod.

3 And he said, Cast it on the ground. And he cast it on the ground, and it became a serpent; and Moses fled from before it.

(Exodus 4:1-3).

1491/2731

Exodus 4:6-7 . MOSES COLOR IS DEFINED. To further convince Moses that he was dealing with the one and only "Almighty God", God turned Moses's hand from 'black' to 'white', then back to black again.

6 And the LORD said furthermore unto him, Put now thine hand into thy bosom. And he put his hand into his bosom: and when he took it out, behold, his hand was leprous as snow.

7 And he said, Put thine hand into thy bosom again. And he put his hand into his bosom again; and plucked it out of his bosom, and, behold, it was turned again as his other flesh.

(Exodus 4:6-7).

<u>"VITAL"</u>

If Moses was a white man (Caucasian or 'new folk') what difference would it have made to him when God turned his hand white as snow? If Moses was a 'white man' (new folks), it would seem more logical for God to turn his hand 'black as the earth', instead of "white as snow." <u>THINK ABOUT IT.</u>

1491/2731

Exodus 12:1-2 Many people today have been taught that January is the first month of the year, (New Year), but Abib (April) is the first month of the 'New Year'. Have you ever noticed what takes place in 'April" (Abib)? Everything is 'new'. Spring-time. January 1st brings nothing new. It's cold. The ground is frozen and hard, and nothing 'natural' grows.

1 And the LORD spake unto Moses and Aaron in the land of Egypt, saying,

2 This month shall be unto you the beginning of months: it shall be the first month of the year to you.

(Exodus 12:1-2).

1491/2731

Exodus 13:4 The African Children of Israel were brought out of the land of Egypt in the month of Abib (April, the first month of the 'NEW YEAR'), in the year of 1491, BCE, or 2731 which was the 'actual' year. The 'Exodus' from Egypt concluded the 430 year sojourn for the Children of Israel, not the fulfillment of Genesis 15:13-14.

4 This day came ye out in the month Abib.

(Exodus 13:4).

1491/2731

Exodus Chapters 13 and 14. God delivered the African Children of Israel from the land of Egypt with a mighty hand. We all know the story, so I won't repeat it. If you don't know the story, please read it so you can understand the 'power' and the 'might' of the

Almighty God. The day is coming fast upon us, when we in this present day, will see God's mighty powerful, strange and terrible acts. We better get ready, because the 400 year captivity of the African Children of Israel in America is almost over.

So God's plan was working. He had chosen and set apart, one African nation from all of the nations in Africa, neither numerous, nor powerful, to be the recipient of His laws, statutes and judgements and by obeying God's laws, would be a nation living in perfect obedience and harmony to the 'Will' of God.

1491/2731

Exodus 20: 1-18. God gave the Children of Israel the Ten Commandments to live by. During the time of Moses and Aaron, the Children of Israel were warned of what would happen to them if they did not obey the Ten Commandments. This warning was repeated all thru the 'TORAH'. (The first five books of the Old Testament.)

1 And God spake all these words, saying,

2 I am the LORD thy God, which have brought thee out of the land of Egypt, out of the house of bondage.

3 Thou shalt have no other gods before me.

4 Thou shalt not make unto thee any graven image, or any likeness of any thing that is in heaven above, or that is in the earth beneath, or that is in the water under the earth:

5 Thou shalt not bow down thyself to them, nor serve them: for I the LORD thy God am a jealous God, visiting the iniquity of the fathers upon the children unto the third and fourth generation of them that hate me;

6 And shewing mercy unto thousands of them that love me, and keep my commandments.

7 Thou shalt not take the name of the LORD thy God in vain; for the LORD will not hold him guiltless that taketh his name in vain.

8 Remember the sabbath day, to keep it holy.

9 Six days shalt thou labour, and do all thy work:

10 But the seventh day is the sabbath of the LORD thy God: in it thou shalt not do any work, thou, nor thy son, nor thy daughter, thy manservant, nor thy maidservant, nor thy cattle, nor thy stranger that is within thy gates:

11 For in six days the LORD made heaven and earth, the sea, and all that in them is, and rested the seventh day: wherefore the LORD blessed the sabbath day, and hallowed it.

12 Honour thy father and thy mother: that thy days may be long upon the land which the LORD thy God giveth thee.

13 Thou shalt not kill.

14 Thou shalt not commit adultery.

15 Thou shalt not steal.

16 Thou shalt not bear false witness against thy neighbour.

17 Thou shalt not covet thy neighbour's house, thou shalt not covet thy neighbour's wife, nor his manservant, nor his maidservant, nor his ox, nor his ass, nor any thing that is thy neighbour's.

18 And all the people saw the thunderings, and the lightnings, and the noise of the trumpet, and the mountain smoking: and when the people saw it, they removed, and stood afar off.

(Exodus 20:1-18).

1453/2769

Numbers 20:28; Numbers 33:39 Aaron died at 123 years old, 40 years after the 'Exodus' from the land of Egypt.

1452/2770

Numbers 27:18 When Moses became old, God chose Joshua to lead the African Children of Israel.

1451/2771

Deuteronomy 18:15-22 It is important to realize and to remember that God is a 'spirit', and not a 'human'. Therefore, a human had to be used by the 'Spirit-God' to magnify God's law and make it honorable. (Amos 3:7 Surely the Lord GOD will do nothing, but he revealeth his secret unto his servants the prophets.)

God will always provide a prophet/prophetess, a priest, a king, a ruler, a judge, or a leader, to comfort, lead, judge, to direct and rule over His chosen people, the African Children of Israel. This is necessary to prevent them from straying away from the Ten Commandments. God also prepared someone to deliver the Children of Israel from their many battles with the 'African Gentiles'. Over the years, the term 'Spirit of Prophecy' has been used to identify this transaction between man and God.

15 The LORD thy God will raise up unto thee a Prophet from the midst of thee, of thy brethren, like unto me; unto him ye shall hearken;

16 According to all that thou desiredst of the LORD thy God in Horeb in the day of the assembly, saying, Let me not hear again the voice of the LORD my God, neither let me see this great fire any more, that I die not.

17 And the LORD said unto me, They have well spoken that which they have spoken.

18 I will raise them up a Prophet from among their brethren, like unto thee, and will put my words in his mouth; and he shall speak unto them all that I shall command him.

19 And it shall come to pass, that whosoever will not hearken unto my words which he shall speak in my name, I will require it of him.

20 But the prophet, which shall presume to speak a word in my name, which I have not commanded him to speak, or that shall speak in the name of other gods, even that prophet shall die.

21 And if thou say in thine heart, How shall we know the word which the LORD hath not spoken?

22 When a prophet speaketh in the name of the LORD, if the thing follow not, nor come to pass, that is the thing which the LORD hath not spoken, but the prophet hath spoken it presumptuously: thou shalt not be afraid of him.

(Deuteronomy 18:15-22).

1451/2771

Throughout the book of Deuteronomy, we find Moses exhorting the African Children of Israel to obey God's Commandments. They were warned against 'idolatry', against self-righteousness, against religious seducers, false prophets and the many crimes that would cause their downfall. Moses also exhorted and emphasized the blessings and rewards that the Children of Israel would receive by keeping God's Commandments. Discourse after discourse was rendered unto the African Children of Israel so that they would understand that they were an 'holy people' unto the Lord God, and that God had chosen them to be a special people unto HIMSELF, above all the people that were upon the face of Africa. Moses worked very hard trying to make the Children of Israel realize that everything in the Universe is governed by a Law that controls Human Behavior, and only by applying the Ten Commandments could they realize their greatest joys and expectations. Although the Ten Commandments were given to the African Children of Israel, this Law determines the fate and destiny of all mankind, and only by living in harmony with this perfect Law, can all people of the earth find true peace and happiness in life.

<u>"VITAL"</u>

1451/2771

Deuternonomy Chapter 28 clearly explained what would happen if the African people kept God's Commandments, and what would happen if they did not keep God's Commandments. Check it out, and you will understand why life for the African Children of Israel (Black folks) that reside in America, is full of sorrow, grief and disappointment. The condition of black folks in America was clearly foretold by Abraham in Genesis 15:13-14. Deuteronomy Chapter 28 shews the power and the might of God's Universal Law thru the Ten Commandments. This chapter does not only apply to the days of old when the Children of Israel lived in Africa,, but also to these present days. For example, everything that is written from the 15th verse on, has been, and still being experienced by the African Children of Israel (Black Folks). WHY? Because the Children of Israel (Black Folks) broke the Ten Commandments of God, while in Africa and caused the whole world to go astray and live contrary to God's Universal Law. Even today, America is 'upside down' because due to mis-education and falsehoods, the African American don't know that they are the Children of Israel.

1451/2771

<u>"VITAL"</u> The first 15 verses of Deuteronomy Chapter 28 shews the blessings that the African Children of Israel would receive if they kept the Commandments of God. The last 53 verses identify the many curses inflicted and the perils of disobedience. Ever since GOD placed the African Children of Israel (Black Folks) in America for 400 years, they have been blaming the 'New Folks' (White Folks) for their oppression, their downfall, their shame, their reproach, their poverty, their lack of self-determination, their lack of growth and development. You name it, and 'Black folks' have blamed someone for it. The African Children of Israel (Old Folks) have charged the 'New Folks' (White Folks) with 'racism', prejudice, discrimination and every other act that could cause someone to fall. The Ten Commandments is the 'cause' of the downfall of the Black folks.. In order for 'Old Folks' (Black Folks) to understand what happened to them, they must have a complete understanding of their "True History". The "TRUE HISTORY" of "Black Folks" is the "OLD TESTAMENT", The World's Best Kept Secret. Read Malachi 3:16

16 Then they that feared the LORD spake often one to another: and the LORD hearkened, and heard it, and a book of remembrance was written before him for them that feared the LORD, and that thought upon his name.

(Malachi 3:16).

As we continue this 'Revelation', all aspects of this 'Secret' will be revealed. Let's continue with Deuteronomy Chapter 28. I will not try to explain every verse in this chapter, but point out a few very significant ones that clearly shew graphically the relationship between God's Commandments and HIS chosen people, the African Children of Israel. (Black Folks) Verses 16-29 These verses shew the many curses and punishments that the African Children of Israel would receive in the cities of America once GOD destroyed them from Africa for breaking the Ten Commandments.

16 Cursed shalt thou be in the city, and cursed shalt thou be in the field.

17 Cursed shall be thy basket and thy store.

18 Cursed shall be the fruit of thy body, and the fruit of thy land, the increase of thy kine, and the flocks of thy sheep.

19 Cursed shalt thou be when thou comest in, and cursed shalt thou be when thou goest out.

20 The LORD shall send upon thee cursing, vexation, and rebuke, in all that thou settest thine hand unto for to do, until thou be destroyed, and until thou perish quickly; because of the wickedness of thy doings, whereby thou hast forsaken me.

21 The LORD shall make the pestilence cleave unto thee, until he have consumed thee from off the land, whither thou goest to possess it.

22 The LORD shall smite thee with a consumption, and with a fever, and with an inflammation, and with an extreme burning, and with the sword, and with blasting, and with mildew; and they shall pursue thee until thou perish.

23 And thy heaven that is over thy head shall be brass, and the earth that is under thee shall be iron.

24 The LORD shall make the rain of thy land powder and dust: from heaven shall it come down upon thee, until thou be destroyed.

25 The LORD shall cause thee to be smitten before thine enemies: thou shalt go out one way against them, and flee seven ways before them: and shalt be removed into all the kingdoms of the earth.

26 And thy carcase shall be meat unto all fowls of the air, and unto the beasts of the earth, and no man shall fray them away.

27 The LORD will smite thee with the botch of Egypt, and with the emerods, and with the scab, and with the itch, whereof thou canst not be healed.

28 The LORD shall smite thee with madness, and blindness, and astonishment of heart:

29 And thou shalt grope at noonday, as the blind gropeth in darkness, and thou shalt not prosper in thy ways: and thou shalt be only oppressed and spoiled evermore, and no man shall save thee.

(Deuteronomy 28:16-29).

Verse 30 shews why the African Hebrew women were taken from their husbands during Slavery in North America, and used for the pleasure of the Slavemaster.

30 Thou shalt betroth a wife, and another man shall lie with her: thou shalt build an house, and thou shalt not dwell therein: thou shalt plant a vineyard, and shalt not gather the grapes thereof.

(Deuteronomy 28:30).

Verse 32 shews why the African Children of Israel families were split apart and sold on the Slave markets of America, and no one could do anything to prevent it.

32 Thy sons and thy daughters shall be given unto another people, and thine eyes shall look, and fail with longing for them all the day long: and there shall be no might in thine hand.

(Deuteronomy 28:32).

1451\2771

Verses 33-34 The ‘new folks’ (White Folks) would take over Africa, oppress the African people, and the only thing that ‘old folks’ would be able to do is ’get mad’.

33 The fruit of thy land, and all thy labours, shall a nation (America) which thou knowest not eat up; and thou shalt be only oppressed and crushed alway:

34 So that thou shalt be mad for the sight of thine eyes which thou shalt see.

(Deuteronomy 28:33-34).

Verse 36 The African Children of Israel would be brought to America according to Genesis Chapter 15:13-14, and how they would make gods out of ‘money’, ‘drugs’, ‘sex’ ‘material objects’ and other ‘graven images’ that would destroy them and keep them in poverty.

36 The LORD shall bring thee, and thy king which thou shalt set over thee, unto a nation (America, etc)which neither thou nor thy fathers have known; and there shalt thou serve other gods, wood and stone.

(Deuteronomy 28:36).

Verse 37, The African Children of Israel would be called ‘niggers’, ‘negroes’, ‘colored’, ’black’, and all of those other funny names that the ‘new folks’ (Caucasians) call them in order to harass and degrade them..

37 And thou shalt become an astonishment, a proverb, and a byword, among all nations whither the LORD shall lead thee.

(Deuteronomy 28:37).

Verse 41 The African Hebrew Israelites would have children, but they would be sold as slaves in America.

41 Thou shalt beget sons and daughters, but thou shalt not enjoy them; for they shall go into captivity.

(Deuteronomy 28:41).

Verses 43-44 Shews why 'old folks' (black folks) have no economic power in America, and will not have any until they return to God's Commandments.

43 The stranger that is within thee shall get up above thee very high; and thou shalt come down very low.

44 He shall lend to thee, and thou shalt not lend to him: he shall be the head, and thou shalt be the tail.

(Deuteronomy 28:43-44).

The 'sorrow', 'grief' and 'disappointment' experienced by 'old folks', in America, is due to the fact that their forefathers broke God's Ten Commandments when they were living in Africa. These verses clearly shew that until the African Children of Israel realize that the Ten Commandments is the only way to their peace and happiness, they will always live in poverty, be on welfare, suffer injustice in the workplace, have more 'old folks' in prison instead of in college, continue to experience more 'black on black' crime in the cities of America and face 'hopelessness' in all their endeavors. The saddest part of the 'African' experience in America, is that they lack the vital understanding of 'WHO' and 'WHAT' they truly are. (Please read Hosea 4:6

6 My people are destroyed for lack of knowledge: because thou hast rejected knowledge, I will also reject thee, that thou shalt be no priest to me: seeing thou hast forgotten the law of thy God, I will also forget thy children.

(Hosea 4:6).

and Isaiah 29:10

10 For the LORD hath poured out upon you the spirit of deep sleep, and hath closed your eyes: the prophets and your rulers, the seers hath he covered.

(Isaiah 29:10).

The worse is yet to come as the 400 year captivity for 'black folks' draws near to the end.

1451/2771

Verses 49-63 Shews how God would cause the 'new folks' (white folks) to invade Africa.

49 The LORD shall bring a nation (new folks) against thee from far, from the end of the earth, as swift as the eagle flieth; a nation whose tongue thou shalt not understand;

50 A nation of fierce countenance, which shall not regard the person of the old, nor shew favour to the young:

51 And he shall eat the fruit of thy cattle, and the fruit of thy land, until thou be destroyed: which also shall not leave thee either corn, wine, or oil, or the increase of thy kine, or flocks of thy sheep, until he have destroyed thee.

52 And he shall besiege thee in all thy gates, until thy high and fenced walls come down, wherein thou trustedst, throughout all thy land: and he shall besiege thee in all thy gates throughout all thy land, which the LORD thy God hath given thee.

53 And thou shalt eat the fruit of thine own body, the flesh of thy sons and of thy daughters, which the LORD thy God hath given thee, in the siege, and in the straitness, wherewith thine enemies shall distress thee:

54 So that the man that is tender among you, and very delicate, his eye shall be evil toward his brother, and toward the wife of his bosom, and toward the remnant of his children which he shall leave:

55 So that he will not give to any of them of the flesh of his children whom he shall eat: because he hath nothing left him in the siege, and in the straitness, wherewith thine enemies shall distress thee in all thy gates.

56 The tender and delicate woman among you, which would not adventure to set the sole of her foot upon the ground for delicateness and tenderness, her eye shall be evil toward the husband of her bosom, and toward her son, and toward her daughter,

57 And toward her young one that cometh out from between her feet, and toward her children which she shall bear: for she shall

eat them for want of all things secretly in the siege and straitness, wherewith thine enemy shall distress thee in thy gates.

58 If thou wilt not observe to do all the words of this law that are written in this book, that thou mayest fear this glorious and fearful name, THE LORD THY GOD;

59 Then the LORD will make thy plagues wonderful, and the plagues of thy seed, even great plagues, and of long continuance, and sore sicknesses, and of long continuance.

60 Moreover he will bring upon thee all the diseases of Egypt, which thou wast afraid of; and they shall cleave unto thee.

61 Also every sickness, and every plague, which is not written in the book of this law, them will the LORD bring upon thee, until thou be destroyed.

62 And ye shall be left few in number, whereas ye were as the stars of heaven for multitude; because thou wouldest not obey the voice of the LORD thy God.

63 And it shall come to pass, that as the LORD rejoiced over you to do you good, and to multiply you; so the LORD will rejoice over you to destroy you, and to bring you to nought; and ye shall be plucked from off the land whither thou goest to possess it.

(Deuteronomy 28:49-63).

God also speaks to the character of the 'new folks' in verse 50, and how easy it is for them to burn churches and kill babies and elderly African people.

1451/2771

Deut. 28:64-68 Shews why 'old folks' (Africans) were destroyed from Africa, and how they would be scattered throughout the world, be reduced to the level of a slave, and spend 400 years of the worse treatment ever known to mankind. This whole chapter should be read over and over again so that people can understand the retribution of God's Holy Ten Commandments, and understand why the African Hebrew Israelites (old folks) are living their "Hell", in America.

64 And the LORD shall scatter thee among all people, (new folks) from the one end of the earth even unto the other; and there thou shalt serve other gods, which neither thou nor thy fathers have known, even wood and stone.

65 And among these nations (America, etc) shalt thou find no ease, neither shall the sole of thy foot have rest: but the LORD shall give thee there a trembling heart, and failing of eyes, and sorrow of mind:

66 And thy life shall hang in doubt before thee; and thou shalt fear day and night, and shalt have none assurance of thy life: (American slavery)

67 In the morning thou shalt say, Would God it were even! and at even thou shalt say, Would God it were morning! for the fear of thine heart wherewith thou shalt fear, and for the sight of thine eyes which thou shalt see.

68 And the LORD shall bring thee into Egypt (anachronism for America) again with ships, by the way whereof I spake unto thee, Thou shalt see it (Africa) no more again: and there ye shall be sold unto your enemies (new folks) for bondmen and bondwomen,(slaves) and no man shall buy you.

(Deuteronomy 28:64-68).

1451/2771

Deut. Chapter 30. After Moses completed his third discourse to the Children of Israel, he gave them a final warning. Moses explained how God's Ten Commandments is an <u>everlasting</u> covenant between God and his chosen people, the African Children of Israel, who reside presently in America, and know not who they are.

1 And it shall come to pass, when all these things are come upon thee, the blessing and the curse, which I have set before thee, and thou shalt call them to mind among all the nations, (America, etc,.) whither the LORD thy God hath driven thee,

2 And shalt return unto the LORD thy God, and shalt obey his voice according to all that I command thee this day, thou and thy children, with all thine heart, and with all thy soul;

3 That then the LORD thy God will turn thy captivity, and have compassion upon thee, and will return and gather thee from all the nations, (America, etc) whither the LORD thy God hath scattered thee.

4 If any of thine be driven out unto the outmost parts of heaven, from thence will the LORD thy God gather thee, and from thence will he fetch thee:

5 And the LORD thy God will bring thee into the land which thy fathers possessed, (Africa) and thou shalt possess it; and he will do thee good, and multiply thee above thy fathers.

6 And the LORD thy God will circumcise thine heart, and the heart of thy seed, to love the LORD thy God with all thine heart, and with all thy soul, that thou mayest live.

7 And the LORD thy God will put all these curses upon thine enemies, and on them that hate thee, which persecuted thee.

8 And thou shalt return and obey the voice of the LORD, and do all his commandments which I command thee this day.

9 And the LORD thy God will make thee plenteous in every work of thine hand, in the fruit of thy body, and in the fruit of thy cattle, and in the fruit of thy land, for good: for the LORD will again rejoice over thee for good, as he rejoiced over thy fathers:

10 If thou shalt hearken unto the voice of the LORD thy God, to keep his commandments and his statutes which are written in this book of the law, and if thou turn unto the LORD thy God with all thine heart, and with all thy soul.

11 For this commandment which I command thee this day, it is not hidden from thee, neither is it far off.

12 It is not in heaven, that thou shouldest say, Who shall go up for us to heaven, and bring it unto us, that we may hear it, and do it?

13 Neither is it beyond the sea, that thou shouldest say, Who shall go over the sea for us, and bring it unto us, that we may hear it, and do it?

14 But the word is very nigh unto thee, in thy mouth, and in thy heart, that thou mayest do it.

15 See, I have set before thee this day life and good, and death and evil;

16 In that I command thee this day to love the LORD thy God, to walk in his ways, and to keep his commandments and his statutes and his judgments, that thou mayest live and multiply: and the LORD thy God shall bless thee in the land whither thou goest to possess it.

17 But if thine heart turn away, so that thou wilt not hear, but shalt be drawn away, and worship other gods, and serve them;

18 I denounce unto you this day, that ye shall surely perish, and that ye shall not prolong your days upon the land, whither thou passest over Jordan to go to possess it.

19 I call heaven and earth to record this day against you, that I have set before you life and death, blessing and cursing: therefore choose life, that both thou and thy seed may live:

20 That thou mayest love the LORD thy God, and that thou mayest obey his voice, and that thou mayest cleave unto him: for he is thy life, and the length of thy days: that thou mayest dwell in the land which the LORD sware unto thy fathers, to Abraham, to Isaac, and to Jacob, to give them.

(Deuteronomy 30:1-20).

1451/2771

Deut. Chapter 31. When Moses was 120 years old, God chose Joshua, and placed him in command over the Children of Israel. (Old Folks)

1451/2771

Deut. 34:7 Moses dies at 120 years old.

1427/2795

Joshua 24:29 Joshua led the African Hebrews for over two decades and died at the age of 110. His valiant and courageous acts are recorded in book of Joshua.

God will always provide a 'Prophet', a 'Prophetess', a 'Priest', a 'King', a 'Ruler', a 'Judge', or a 'Leader', to comfort, lead, judge, direct and rule over the Children of Israel, so that they won't stray away from HIS Commandments. God always prepared someone to deliver Israel from their many battles against the African Gentiles.

1425/2797

Judges 1:1-2 After the death of Joshua, the Children of Israel asked GOD for help against the African Gentile Canaanites. God chose Judah to be the leader over the African Hebrew Israelites. Judges 1:19 The Lord was with Judah and he was able to drive out many of the African Gentile nations from among the Children of Israel. This was important because God made a covenant with the Children of Israel and told them to separate themselves from the African Gentiles, and not partake of their sinful ways. Read Judges 2:1-5. After the death of Joshua, there were many attempts by the Children of Israel to drive the African Gentiles from among them, but they were not successful because they were disobedient to God's Law, and provoked God to anger. Judges 1:27-36.

27 Neither did Manasseh (African Hebrews) drive out the inhabitants of Bethshean (African gentiles) and her towns, nor Taanach and her towns, nor the inhabitants of Dor and her towns, nor the inhabitants of Ibleam and her towns, nor the inhabitants of Megiddo and her towns: but the Canaanites would dwell in that land.

28 And it came to pass, when Israel (African Hebrews) was strong, that they put the Canaanites (African gentiles) to tribute, and did not utterly drive them out.

29 Neither did Ephraim (African Hebrews) drive out the Canaanites that dwelt in Gezer; but the Canaanites dwelt in Gezer among them.

30 Neither did Zebulun (African Hebrews) drive out the inhabitants of Kitron, (African gentiles) nor the inhabitants of Nahalol; but the Canaanites dwelt among them, and became tributaries.

31 Neither did Asher (African Hebrews) drive out the inhabitants of Accho, (African gentiles) nor the inhabitants of Zidon, nor of Ahlab, nor of Achzib, nor of Helbah, nor of Aphik, nor of Rehob:

32 But the Asherites dwelt among the Canaanites, the inhabitants of the land: for they did not drive them out.

33 Neither did Naphtali (African Hebrews) drive out the inhabitants of Bethshemesh, (African gentiles) nor the inhabitants of Bethanath; but he dwelt among the Canaanites, the inhabitants of the land: nevertheless the inhabitants of Bethshemesh and of Bethanath became tributaries unto them.

34 And the Amorites (African gentiles) forced the children of Dan (African Hebrews) into the mountain: for they would not suffer them to come down to the valley:

35 But the Amorites would dwell in mount Heres in Aijalon, and in Shaalbim: yet the hand of the house of Joseph (African Hebrews) prevailed, so that they became tributaries.

36 And the coast of the Amorites was from the going up to Akrabbim, from the rock, and upward.

(Judges 1:27-36).

1425/2797

Judges 2:10-15. After the death of Joshua, a new generation of African Children of Israel emerged which did not know God, nor did they know the mighty acts and the work which God did for Israel. in the past. The Children of Israel did evil in His sight. Instead of leading the African Gentile back to God, Israel followed the African Gentiles. God was really angry at the Children of Israel. God was so mad that He stopped fighting Israel's battles, and delivered them into the hands of African Gentile Philistines, to see if Israel would still keep His Commandments. They didn't. The Children of Israel took the African Gentile's daughters to be their wives, and gave their daughters to their sons, and served their idol gods. This had the same impact in the days of old, (even though everyone was black), as it does today when 'Israel' marry 'Gentiles'. God wanted Israel to remain 'spotless' from the Gentile Africans. In the days of old, when the Children of Israel were living in Africa, the only people that they had to worry about, were the African Gentiles. But today, the Children of Israel must work hard to remain spotless from the African Gentiles, and the 'new folks'. This is why GOD placed the Children of Israel in America for 400 years; Not only because of their forefathers sins, but also to be 'tried', 'tested', and 'proven' to see whether or not they would be worthy enough to be selected for 'jewels' for God's kingdom.

10 And also all that generation were gathered unto their fathers: and there arose another generation after them, which knew not the LORD, nor yet the works which he had done for Israel.

11 And the children of Israel did evil in the sight of the LORD, and served Baalim:

12 And they forsook the LORD God of their fathers, which brought them out of the land of Egypt, and followed other gods, of the gods of the people that were round about them, and bowed themselves unto them, and provoked the LORD to anger.

13 And they forsook the LORD, and served Baal and Ashtaroth.

14 And the anger of the LORD was hot against Israel, and he delivered them into the hands of spoilers that spoiled them, and he sold them into the hands of their enemies round about, so that they could not any longer stand before their enemies.

15 Whithersoever they went out, the hand of the LORD was against them for evil, as the LORD had said, and as the LORD had sworn unto them: and they were greatly distressed.

(Judges 2:10-15).

1406/2816

Judges 2:16-23 As mentioned earlier, God chooses a person to rule over, or lead his chosen people. We now enter the 'era' of the 'JUDGES' that God chose to deliver the African Hebrew Israelites out of the hand of the African Gentiles. During these days, there was no king to judge the Children of Israel, so everyone did anything that they wanted to do, whether it was right or wrong. We can read about the wickedness that took place during this time in Judges 17:6; Micah's Idolatry, Judges 18:1; The Idolatry of the Danites, Judges 19:1. The Levite and his Concubine. There was no king over Israel, so they acted up. In Judges Chapters 19 thru 21 we find the tribe of Benjamin fighting a war against the other tribes of Israel, and had to be cut off from the Children of Israel.

16 Nevertheless the LORD raised up judges, which delivered them out of the hand of those that spoiled them.

17 And yet they would not hearken unto their judges, but they went

a whoring after other gods, and bowed themselves unto them: they turned quickly out of the way which their fathers walked in, obeying the commandments of the LORD; but they did not so.

18 And when the LORD raised them up judges, then the LORD was with the judge, and delivered them out of the hand of their enemies all the days of the judge: for it repented the LORD because of their groanings by reason of them that oppressed them and vexed them.

19 And it came to pass, when the judge was dead, that they returned, and corrupted themselves more than their fathers, in following other gods to serve them, and to bow down unto them; they ceased not from their own doings, nor from their stubborn way.

20 And the anger of the LORD was hot against Israel; and he said, Because that this people hath transgressed my covenant which I commanded their fathers, and have not hearkened unto my voice;

21 I also will not henceforth drive out any from before them of the nations which Joshua left when he died:

22 That through them I may prove Israel, whether they will keep the way of the LORD to walk therein, as their fathers did keep it, or not.

23 Therefore the LORD left those nations, without driving them out hastily; neither delivered he them into the hand of Joshua.

(Judges 2:16-23).

1394/2828

Judges 3:12-14 The Children of Israel became negligent in their mission, they broke God's Commandments, and did evil in the sight of God. God delivered Israel into the hand of "Eglon", who was the African gentile king of Moab. The African Hebrews Israelites served "Eglon" for 18 years for breaking God's Commandments.

12 And the children of Israel did evil again in the sight of the LORD: and the LORD strengthened Eglon the king of Moab against Israel, because they had done evil in the sight of the LORD.

13 And he gathered unto him the children of Ammon (gentiles)and Amalek, and went and smote Israel, and possessed the city of palm trees.

14 So the children of Israel served Eglon the king of Moab eighteen years.

(Judges 3:12-14).

1376/2846

Judges 3:15-30 When Israel cried unto God for help, God raised up 'Ehud', who made a two-edged dagger and thrusted it into the fat belly of the African king 'Eglon'. After that, the Children of Israel slew about 10,000 African Gentile men of Moab, and the land had rest for 80 years.

15 But when the children of Israel cried unto the LORD, the LORD raised them up a deliverer, Ehud the son of Gera, a Benjamite, (African Hebrews) a man lefthanded: and by him the children of Israel sent a present unto Eglon the king of Moab.

16 But Ehud made him a dagger which had two edges, of a cubit length; and he did gird it under his raiment upon his right thigh.

17 And he brought the present unto Eglon king of Moab: and Eglon was a very fat man.

18 And when he had made an end to offer the present, he sent away the people that bare the present.

19 But he himself turned again from the quarries that were by Gilgal, and said, I have a secret errand unto thee, O king: who said, Keep silence. And all that stood by him went out from him.

20 And Ehud came unto him; and he was sitting in a summer parlour, which he had for himself alone. And Ehud said, I have a message from God unto thee. And he arose out of his seat.

21 And Ehud put forth his left hand, and took the dagger from his right thigh, and thrust it into his belly:

22 And the haft also went in after the blade; and the fat closed upon the blade, so that he could not draw the dagger out of his belly; and the dirt came out.

23 Then Ehud went forth through the porch, and shut the doors of the parlour upon him, and locked them.

24 When he was gone out, his servants came; and when they saw that, behold, the doors of the parlour were locked, they said, Surely he covereth his feet in his summer chamber.

25 And they tarried till they were ashamed: and, behold, he opened not the doors of the parlour; therefore they took a key, and opened them: and, behold, their lord was fallen down dead on the earth.

26 And Ehud escaped while they tarried, and passed beyond the quarries, and escaped unto Seirath.

27 And it came to pass, when he was come, that he blew a trumpet in the mountain of Ephraim, and the children of Israel went down with him from the mount, and he before them.

28 And he said unto them, Follow after me: for the LORD hath delivered your enemies the Moabites into your hand. And they went down after him, and took the fords of Jordan toward Moab, and suffered not a man to pass over.

29 And they slew of Moab at that time about ten thousand men, all lusty, and all men of valour; and there escaped not a man.

30 So Moab was subdued that day under the hand of Israel. And the land had rest fourscore years.

(Judges 3:15-30).

1336/2886

Judges 3:7-11 The Children of Israel violated the universal law of God again and served an 8 year captivity under the African gentile king whose name was 'Chushanrishathaim'. When the African Hebrews cried unto the Lord, God raised up 'Othniel' to deliver Israel. God delivered 'Chushanrishathaim' into the hand of 'Othniel', and the Children of Israel lived in peace for 40 years.

7 And the children of Israel did evil in the sight of the LORD, and forgat the LORD their God, and served Baalim and the groves.

8 Therefore the anger of the LORD was hot against Israel, and he sold them into the hand of Chushanrishathaim king of Mesopotamia: and the children of Israel served Chushanrishathaim eight years.

9 And when the children of Israel cried unto the LORD, the LORD

raised up a deliverer to the children of Israel, who delivered them, even Othniel the son of Kenaz, Caleb's younger brother.

10 And the Spirit of the LORD came upon him, and he judged Israel, and went out to war: and the LORD delivered Chushanrishathaim king of Mesopotamia into his hand; and his hand prevailed against Chushanrishathaim.

11 And the land had rest forty years. And Othniel the son of Kenaz died.

(Judges 3:7-11).

1316/2906

Judges 4:1-24 The Children of Israel broke God's Commandments again, and did evil in His sight, and served a 20 year captivity under the African (gentile) king 'Jabin'. When Israel cried unto God for help, God raised up 'Deborah', who was a 'prophetess', and she delivered and judged Israel.

1256/2966

Judges Chapters 6, 7, & 8. The Children of Israel broke the Commandments again. They were punished and served the African Gentile king of Midian for 7 years. When Israel cried unto the Lord for help, God raised up 'Gideon' (Jerubbaal) to deliver Israel from the hand of King Midian.

1256/2966

Judges 8:32-35 After the death of Gideon, the Children of Israel turned to evil again, and went a whoring after the African Gentiles and made them their god.

32 And Gideon the son of Joash died in a good old age, and was buried in the sepulchre of Joash his father, in Ophrah of the Abiezrites.

33 And it came to pass, as soon as Gideon was dead, that the children of Israel turned again, and went a whoring after Baalim, and made Baalberith their god.

34 And the children of Israel remembered not the LORD their God, who had delivered them out of the hands of all their enemies on every side:

35 Neither shewed they kindness to the house of Jerubbaal, namely, Gideon, according to all the goodness which he had shewed unto Israel.

(Judges 8:32-35).

1206/3016

Judges Chapter 9 After Gideon died, the people made 'Abimelech', Gideon's son king over Israel. Abimelech was a wicked king, and reigned over Israel three years.

1183/3039

Judges 10:1-2 Tola judged the African Hebrews for 23 years and died.

1171/3051

This is the year that Samuel was born. See the 1st book of Samuel for his life and works.

1160/3062

Judges 10:3-5 Jair judged the African Hebrews for 22 years and died.

1138/3084

Judges 10:6-18 Chapter 11 and 12:1-7 The Children of Israel broke God's Commandments again, and were sold to the African Gentile Philistines for 18 years. They were delivered by Jephthah, who judged the African Hebrews 6 years.

1131/3091

Judges 12:8-10 Ibzan judged the African Hebrews for 7 years.

1124/3098

Judges 12:11-12 Elon judged the African Hebrews for 10 years.

1114/3108

Judges 12:13-15 Abdon judged the African Hebrews for 8 years.

1106/3116

Judges Chapter 13; Judges 15:20 The Children of Israel broke God's Commandments again, and were held captive by the African Gentile

Philistines for 40 years. The Children of Israel were delivered by Samson, who judged them for 20 years.

THUS ENDETH THE 'ERA' OF THE AFRICAN 'JUDGES' WHO JUDGED THE AFRICAN HEBREW ISRAELITES FOR OVER 329 YEARS WHILE IN AFRICA.

"NOTE" Since this Revelation is designed to shew forth the "TRUTH", and to eliminate as much confusion as possible, I will not cover every book and chapter in the Bible. I will shew the "TRUTH", not re-write the Bible. By the way, we have covered over three thousand years of African history now, and there is still no mention of the existence of 'new folks' (White Folks). The only reference thus far in the Bible, is their 'coming', in Deuteronomy Chapter 28. But hold on because God will speak to the creation of 'new folks', and their function when we address the 'Prophets", the last 17 books of the Old Testament.

So, the Children of Israel went on and on, keeping God's Commandments for a while, then breaking them. Each time they broke God's Commandments, God would punish them, they would cry out, God would have mercy on them, and then deliver them. This happened over and over again, and GOD was getting tired of it.,,, Israel was so wicked before GOD that GOD was beginning to dislike them. God selected this people to represent Him on earth, to be a pure and holy nation of people, but Israel did not take their mission seriously. God did everything possible to make the Children of Israel obey the Ten Commandments, but no matter how many times God placed Israel in captivity, they came out doing the same thing. No matter how many times God shewed mercy unto Israel and delivered them from their many captivities, they still violated God's Commandments. WHY?

<u>"VITAL"</u>

Because even though the Children of Israel were oppressed with hard labour, they were allowed to mingle with, communicate with, and even marry the people who held them captive, because everyone on the earth in Africa at that time was 'black', (old folks) and they were never oppressed or denied because of the color of their skin.

No matter how many captivities GOD placed Israel in, they came out, worshipping their same God, speaking their same native language, and maintaining their family ties. Only the captivity and slavery in 'North America', denied the Children of Israel, and the African Gentiles, their 'humanity and justice', and called them inferior because of the color of their skin. But the 'new folks' (white folks) are truly not the blame for this action. By understanding the true history of the African people in the Old Testament, everyone can receive an objective viewpoint of why things happened to Black folks, and why things are still happening to the Children of Israel and the African Gentiles that reside in North America.

After the era of the 'Judges', GOD chose Samuel to be a prophet. (1 Samuel 3:19-21) The life and works of Samuel are found throughout the book of 1 Samuel.

1100/3122

1 Samuel 8:1-5 When Samuel became old, he made his sons judges over Israel. The people rejected Samuel's sons and demanded a king to be their ruler like all of the African Gentile nations.

1 And it came to pass, when Samuel was old, that he made his sons judges over Israel.

2 Now the name of his firstborn was Joel; and the name of his second, Abiah: they were judges in Beersheba.

3 And his sons walked not in his ways, but turned aside after lucre, and took bribes, and perverted judgment.

4 Then all the elders of Israel gathered themselves together, and came to Samuel unto Ramah,

5 And said unto him, Behold, thou art old, and thy sons walk not in thy ways: now make us a king to judge us like all the nations.

(1Samuel 8:1-5).

WE NOW BEGIN THE ERA OF 'AFRICAN KINGS' THAT REIGNED OVER THE CHILDREN OF ISRAEL WHILE IN AFRICA. SAUL, DAVID, AND SOLOMON WERE THE FIRST THREE KINGS THAT RULED OVER THE TWELVE TRIBES OF ISRAEL. EACH OF THESE AFRICAN KINGS REIGNED FORTY YEARS, AND THE CHILDREN OF ISRAEL WERE UNITED AS ONE KINGDOM FOR 120 YEARS.

1100/3122

Saul, the son of Kish was the first African Hebrew king over the Children of Israel and this began the African Hebrew monarchy that ruled over all of the tribes of Israel. Saul reigned for 40 years and died in battle. The life and works of Saul are found in 1 Samuel Chapters 10 thru 31.

1060/3162

David, son of Jesse. Reigned 40 years. 1 Sam. 16:1-13

1 And the LORD said unto Samuel, How long wilt thou mourn for Saul, seeing I have rejected him from reigning over Israel? fill thine horn with oil, and go, I will send thee to Jesse the Bethlehemite: for I have provided me a king among his sons.

2 And Samuel said, How can I go? if Saul hear it, he will kill me. And the LORD said, Take an heifer with thee, and say, I am come to sacrifice to the LORD.

3 And call Jesse to the sacrifice, and I will shew thee what thou shalt do: and thou shalt anoint unto me him whom I name unto thee.

4 And Samuel did that which the LORD spake, and came to Bethlehem. And the elders of the town trembled at his coming, and said, Comest thou peaceably?

5 And he said, Peaceably: I am come to sacrifice unto the LORD: sanctify yourselves, and come with me to the sacrifice. And he sanctified Jesse and his sons, and called them to the sacrifice.

6 And it came to pass, when they were come, that he looked on Eliab,

and said, Surely the LORD'S anointed is before him.

7 But the LORD said unto Samuel, Look not on his countenance, or on the height of his stature; because I have refused him: for the LORD seeth not as man seeth; for man looketh on the outward appearance, but the LORD looketh on the heart.

8 Then Jesse called Abinadab, and made him pass before Samuel. And he said, Neither hath the LORD chosen this.

9 Then Jesse made Shammah to pass by. And he said, Neither hath the LORD chosen this.

10 Again, Jesse made seven of his sons to pass before Samuel. And Samuel said unto Jesse, The LORD hath not chosen these.

11 And Samuel said unto Jesse, Are here all thy children? And he said, There remaineth yet the youngest, and, behold, he keepeth the sheep. And Samuel said unto Jesse, Send and fetch him: for we will not sit down till he come hither.

12 And he sent, and brought him in. Now he was ruddy, and withal of a beautiful countenance, and goodly to look to. And the LORD said, Arise, anoint him: for this is he.

13 Then Samuel took the horn of oil, and anointed him in the midst of his brethren: and the Spirit of the LORD came upon David from that day forward. So Samuel rose up, and went to Ramah.

(1Samuel 16:1-13).

1 Kings 2:11;

11 And the days that David reigned over Israel were forty years: seven years reigned he in Hebron, and thirty and three years reigned he in Jerusalem.

(1Kings 2:11).

1 Chron. 11:1; 1 Chron 29:30

1060/3162

The death of Samuel. 1 Sam. 25:1

1023/3199

The time-frame of the book of Psalms.

1020/3202

I Chron 28 and 29 Solomon, the son of David was the third African Hebrew king that reigned over the African Hebrew Israelites for 40 years.

1 And David assembled all the princes of Israel, the princes of the tribes, and the captains of the companies that ministered to the king by course, and the captains over the thousands, and captains over the hundreds, and the stewards over all the substance and possession of the king, and of his sons, with the officers, and with the mighty men, and with all the valiant men, unto Jerusalem.

2 Then David the king stood up upon his feet, and said, Hear me, my brethren, and my people: As for me, I had in mine heart to build an house of rest for the ark of the covenant of the LORD, and for the footstool of our God, and had made ready for the building:

3 But God said unto me, Thou shalt not build an house for my name, because thou hast been a man of war, and hast shed blood.

4 Howbeit the LORD God of Israel chose me before all the house of my father to be king over Israel for ever: for he hath chosen Judah to be the ruler; and of the house of Judah, the house of my father; and among the sons of my father he liked me to make me king over all Israel:

5 And of all my sons, (for the LORD hath given me many sons,) he hath chosen Solomon my son to sit upon the throne of the kingdom of the LORD over Israel.

6 And he said unto me, Solomon thy son, he shall build my house and my courts: for I have chosen him to be my son, and I will be his father.

7 Moreover I will establish his kingdom for ever, if he be constant to do my commandments and my judgments, as at this day.

8 Now therefore in the sight of all Israel the congregation of the LORD, and in the audience of our God, keep and seek for all the commandments of the LORD your God: that ye may possess this

good land, and leave it for an inheritance for your children after you for ever.

9 And thou, Solomon my son, know thou the God of thy father, and serve him with a perfect heart and with a willing mind: for the LORD searcheth all hearts, and understandeth all the imaginations of the thoughts: if thou seek him, he will be found of thee; but if thou forsake him, he will cast thee off for ever.

10 Take heed now; for the LORD hath chosen thee to build an house for the sanctuary: be strong, and do it.

11 Then David gave to Solomon his son the pattern of the porch, and of the houses thereof, and of the treasuries thereof, and of the upper chambers thereof, and of the inner parlours thereof, and of the place of the mercy seat,

12 And the pattern of all that he had by the spirit, of the courts of the house of the LORD, and of all the chambers round about, of the treasuries of the house of God, and of the treasuries of the dedicated things:

13 Also for the courses of the priests and the Levites, and for all the work of the service of the house of the LORD, and for all the vessels of service in the house of the LORD.

14 He gave of gold by weight for things of gold, for all instruments of all manner of service; silver also for all instruments of silver by weight, for all instruments of every kind of service:

15 Even the weight for the candlesticks of gold, and for their lamps of gold, by weight for every candlestick, and for the lamps thereof: and for the candlesticks of silver by weight, both for the candlestick, and also for the lamps thereof, according to the use of every candlestick.

16 And by weight he gave gold for the tables of shewbread, for every table; and likewise silver for the tables of silver:

17 Also pure gold for the fleshhooks, and the bowls, and the cups: and for the golden basons he gave gold by weight for every bason; and likewise silver by weight for every bason of silver:

18 And for the altar of incense refined gold by weight; and gold for

the pattern of the chariot of the cherubims, that spread out their wings, and covered the ark of the covenant of the LORD.

19 All this, said David, the LORD made me understand in writing by his hand upon me, even all the works of this pattern.

20 And David said to Solomon his son, Be strong and of good courage, and do it: fear not, nor be dismayed: for the LORD God, even my God, will be with thee; he will not fail thee, nor forsake thee, until thou hast finished all the work for the service of the house of the LORD.

21 And, behold, the courses of the priests and the Levites, even they shall be with thee for all the service of the house of God: and there shall be with thee for all manner of workmanship every willing skilful man, for any manner of service: also the princes and all the people will be wholly at thy commandment.

(1Chronicles 28:1-21).

1014/3208

The time-frame of the book of 'Song of Solomon'. During this year King Solomon also received the wisdom of God's Law". (I Kings 3:3-14)

3 And Solomon loved the LORD, walking in the statutes of David his father: only he sacrificed and burnt incense in high places.

4 And the king went to Gibeon to sacrifice there; for that was the great high place: a thousand burnt offerings did Solomon offer upon that altar.

5 In Gibeon the LORD appeared to Solomon in a dream by night: and God said, Ask what I shall give thee.

6 And Solomon said, Thou hast shewed unto thy servant David my father great mercy, according as he walked before thee in truth, and in righteousness, and in uprightness of heart with thee; and thou hast kept for him this great kindness, that thou hast given him a son to sit on his throne, as it is this day.

7 And now, O LORD my God, thou hast made thy servant king instead of David my father: and I am but a little child: I know not

how to go out or come in.

8 And thy servant is in the midst of thy people which thou hast chosen, a great people, that cannot be numbered nor counted for multitude.

9 Give therefore thy servant an understanding heart to judge thy people, that I may discern between good and bad: for who is able to judge this thy so great a people?

10 And the speech pleased the Lord, that Solomon had asked this thing.

11 And God said unto him, Because thou hast asked this thing, and hast not asked for thyself long life; neither hast asked riches for thyself, nor hast asked the life of thine enemies; but hast asked for thyself understanding to discern judgment;

12 Behold, I have done according to thy words: lo, I have given thee a wise and an understanding heart; so that there was none like thee before thee, neither after thee shall any arise like unto thee.

13 And I have also given thee that which thou hast not asked, both riches, and honour: so that there shall not be any among the kings like unto thee all thy days.

14 And if thou wilt walk in my ways, to keep my statutes and my commandments, as thy father David did walk, then I will lengthen thy days.

(1Kings 3:3-14).

In order for the Children of Israel, and all of mankind to live the highest, richest, fullest life one is capable of living, they must live in harmony with God's Universal Law; which is the TEN COMMANDMENTS, and the only way that you can keep the TEN COMMANDMENTS, IS TO APPLY THE INSTRUCTIONS THAT KING SOLOMON RECEIVED FROM GOD THAT ARE RECORDED IN THE 'PROVERBS'.

1000/3222

The time-frame of the book of 'Proverbs', the first 29 chapters. For years, the book of Proverbs has been referred to as; poetry, poems, etc. This is absolutely false. In TRUTH, the Proverbs contain the ingredients that aid us in keeping the Ten Commandments of God. The Proverbs contain the specific rules that brings us in harmony with God's Universal Law. The Proverbs explains both sides of our 'free will'; the 'negative' and the 'positive'. The Proverbs shew us the results of the 'Golden Rule', and the recompense of 'human judgement'. As human beings, we can only perform three transactions; 'a thought', 'a statement', 'an act'. Each of these 'transactions' are 'deeds'. Each 'deed' is a 'seed' that we plant. There is a 'harvest' (Judgement) for each 'seed' that we plant. The 'harvest' results in either a 'blessing' or a 'curse'. We determine our own reward, fate and destiny. We punish ourselves or we bless ourselves depending on our 'deeds' and 'seeds. The Proverbs contains every condition that a human being will experience, or be subjected to, and the associated judgement. The Proverbs are our 'INSTRUCTIONS TO THE LAW OF LIFE'. Everything in the universe is governed by absolute, unfailing LAW. We can't get around it, we can't go over it, we can't go thru or under it. We must face it 'head-on' and not blame others for our downfall. We determine our 'HEAVEN or HELL' based on how well we 'TURN' to God's Instructions in Proverbs. We see HEAVEN and HELL throughout the Proverbs. HEAVEN and HELL are not geographical locations; they are conditions within our personal lives. HELL is 'sorrow', 'grief', and 'disappointment' HEAVEN is 'peace', 'joy' and 'love'. Where are you? No wonder the condition of God's world is so messed up. There is no 'Law' in the people, and people make the world go around. There is no such thing as 'luck', only 'LAW'. LAW is necessary to maintain 'order'. LAW was established during the 'creation'. Without LAW and order, the universe would have been in complete chaos. Mankind is not following God's universal LAW, therefore mankind is subjecting itself to complete human chaos. The LAW of "CAUSE and EFFECT" is in motion. It moves according to the Instructions outlined in the Proverbs. Consider this. What inventor, manufacturer or creator would make something without providing specific instructions???. Think about it. When you purchase an item, in most cases it contains instructions. Well consider the Creator of the universe. It would be strange and odd for the Creator to make us and not provide us with a set of 'specific instructions. Well, our instructions are in the Proverbs. This is how it works. There are about thirty//thirty-one days per month. There are thirty-one chapters in Proverbs. Read one chapter per day. Which ever day of the month it is, read that chapter. Example, if it is the 3rd day of the month, read the 3rd chapter, and so on. It works like magic if you do it right. If you miss a day <u>DO NOT</u> go back and try to recover, continue on with the balance of the month. If you are serious about improving your personal life, you will 'reset' and start over each month. The key is, read your instructions every day. You deserve peace of mind, and you owe it to yourself and to your loved ones, and you will help make this world a better place. The first 'REQUIREMENT' is 'TURN', Proverbs 1:23. "Turn you, at GOD's reproof (Correction), behold, GOD will pour out HIS spirit unto you, God will make known HIS words unto you. The prerequisite to 'HEAVEN' which is 'peace', 'joy' and 'love', is , turning to God's correction (reproof). Our body is the temple of God, but the spirit of God is lying dormant in most of us because we have not 'turned' to God's laws. If we turn and read God's instructions each day we will feel the spirit of God activate itself within us, and if we follow and do God's instructions (as written), God will speak to us from within our soul and direct our steps in this world of uncertainty. I will leave this subject with two 'critical' words; TURN (Pr. 1:23) and DAILY (Pr. 8:34). TURN to God's instructions EVERYDAY.

980/3242

After the death of King Solomon, Rehoboam was made king over the Children of Israel. Rehoboam ruled the Israelites with such cruelty, that the Children of Israel revolted and split into two separate African Hebrew Kingdoms. The African Hebrew kingdom of 'Judah' which consisted of two tribes, (Judah and Benjamin) was also known as the 'Southern Kingdom'. The African Hebrew kingdom of 'Israel' which consisted of 10 tribes, was also known as the 'Northern Kingdom'. The details of this 'split' are contained in II Chron. 10, 11,12. Rehoboam, the son of King Solomon ruled over the African Hebrew Kingdom of Judah for 17 years. He was evil. I Kings 11:43--14:31; II Chron. 9:31 - 12:16. Jeroboam, the son of Nebat ruled over the African Hebrew Kingdom of Israel for 22 years. He was evil. I Kings 12:20; I Kings 14:20 II; Chron. 10:2; Chron. 13-20

977/3245

The time-frame of the book of Ecclesiastes.

963/3259

Abijam was the African King that ruled over the African Hebrew Kingdom of Judah for 3 years. He was the son of King Rehoboam. He was Evil. I Kings 14:31 - 15:8 II Chron. 12:16 - 4:1

960/3262

Asa was the son of King Abijam. King Asa ruled the African Hebrew Kingdom of Judah for 41 years. He was Good. I Kings 15:8 - 24 II Chron. 14:1 - 16:14

958/3264

Nadab was the African king that ruled over the African Hebrew Kingdom of Israel. He was the son of King Jeroboam. He reigned 2 years and was killed by Baasha. King Nadab was Evil. I Kings 14:20 - 15:31

956/3266

Baasha, the son of Ahijah became the African king over the African Hebrew Kingdom of Israel. King Baasha reigned for 24 years. He was Evil. I Kings 15:16 - 16:6 II Chron. 16:1-6

932/3290

Elah, reigned 2 years over the African Hebrew

Kingdom of Israel. He was the son of King Baasha. King Elah was Evil and was killed by Zimri. I Kings 16:8-14.

930/3292

Zimri, was a Captain in King Elah's army. This African King reigned over the African Hebrew Kingdom of Israel for 7 days. He committed suicide when he realized that his cause was lost. I Kings 16:8-20

930/3292

Omri, also a Captain in King Elah's army ruled the African Hebrew Northern Kingdom for 12 years. He was Evil. I Kings 16:16-28

919/3303

Jehoshaphat, was the son of the African King Asa. King Jehoshaphat ruled the African Hebrew Southern Kingdom of Judah for 25 years. He was Good. I Kings 15:24, 22:50; II Chron. 17:1, 21:1

918/3304

Ahab, was the son of the African King Omri. Ahab ruled the African Hebrew Northern Kingdom of Israel for 22 years. He was killed in battle. He was Evil. I Kings 16:28; 22:40, II Chron. 18:1-34

896/3326

Ahaziah was the next African King that ruled over the African Hebrew Northern Kingdom of Israel. He was the son of King Ahab. He reigned for 2 years. He was Evil. I Kings 22:40, II Kings 1: 1-2 II Chron. 20:35-37

894/3328

Jehoram (Joram), the son of King Jehoshaphat, was King over the African Hebrew Southern Kingdom of Judah for 8 years. He was Evil. II Kings 8:16-24 II Chron. 21:'1-20

894/3328

Jehoram (Joram), the son of King Ahab, was King over the African Hebrew Northern Kingdom of Israel for 12 years. He was Evil and was slain by Jehu. 2 Kings 1:17-9:29 2 Chron. 22:5-7

886/3336

Ahaziah, the son of Jehoram, reigned 1 year over the African Hebrew Southern Kingdom of Judah. He was Evil and was slain by Jehu. 2 Kings 8-25 - 9:27-28

885/3337

Athaliah, was the daughter of Ahab, king of Israel and Jezebel; wife of Jehoram, former king of Judah and mother of Ahariah. When Ahaziah was slain by Jehu, she, as queen mother, usurped the throne of Judah. Queen Athaliah reigned over the African Hebrew Southern Kingdom of Judah for 7 years. She was slain by the people of Judah. She was Evil. 2 Kings 11: 1-20 2 Chron. 22:10 - 23:12-15.

882/3340

Jehu, the son of Nimshi, reigned 28 years over the African Hebrew Northern Kingdom of Israel. He was Evil. 2 Kings 9:11 - 10:36 2 Chron 22:7-9

878/3344

Jehoash (Joash) was the son of King Ahaziah. He escaped death at the hands of Queen Athaliah. Jehoash was put on the throne at age 7, thereby restoring the Davidic dynasty. The African King Jehoash ruled the African Hebrew Southern Kingdom of Israel for 40 years. King Jehoash was Good. He was slain by his servants. 2 Kings 11:21 - 12:19-21 2 Chron 24:1-27

862/3360

This is the time-frame for the book of 'JONAH'.

854/3368

Jehoahaz was the son of King Jehu. Jehoahaz ruled the African Hebrew Northern Kingdom of Israel for 17 years. He was EVIL. 2 Kings 10:35 - 13:9

838/3384

Amaziah, the son of King Jehoash, ruled over the African Hebrew Southern Kingdom of Judah for 29 years. He was GOOD. He was slain by conspirators. 2 Kings 14:1-20, 2 Chron 24:27 - 25:28

837/3385

Jehoash (Joash) the son of King Jehoahaz, reigned 16 years over the African Hebrew Northern Kingdom of Israel. He was EVIL. 2 Kings 13:9--14:16 2 Chron 25:17-25

821/3401

Jeroboam II, the son of King Jehoash, ruled over the African Hebrew Northern Kingdom of Israel for 41 years. He was EVIL. 2 Kings 13:13--14:29

809/3413

Uzziah (Azariah) was the son of Amaziah. He was the African King that reigned 52 years over the African Hebrew Southern Kingdom of Judah. He was GOOD. King Uzziah became a leper. 2 Kings 14:21 - 15:7, 2 Chron. 26:1-23

800/3422

The time-frame of the book of the Prophet Joel.

787/3435

Jotham, the son of King Uzziah, was king of the African Hebrew Southern Kingdom of Judah for 16 years. He was GOOD. 2 Kings 15:7 2 Chron 26:23--27:9

785/3437

The beginning of Hosea's 60 years of Prophecy.

780/3442

Zachariah (Zechariah), the son of Jeroboam II, was king over the African Hebrew Northern Kingdom of Israel for only 6 months. He was EVIL, and was slain by Shallum. 2 Kings 14:29--15:11-12

780/3442

Shallum, the son of Jabesh, reigned only 1 month over the African Hebrew Kingdom of Israel. He was EVIL, and was slain by Menahem. 2 Kings 15:10-15

780/3442

Menahem, the son of Gadi, reigned 10 years over the African Hebrew Kingdom of Israel. He was EVIL.. 2 Kings 15:14-22

WE PAUSE HERE TO MAKE A VERY IMPORTANT POINT. WE WILL CONTINUE THE 'ERA' OF THE AFRICAN KINGS OF ISRAEL AND JUDAH AFTER THIS POINT IS MADE.

If you remember the story, the Children of Israel asked for a king to rule over them. As you can see, many kings were placed over the African Children of Israel, but evil and wickedness was the behavior of the kings. Instead of leading the African Children of Israel with righteousness, the kings led them into 'Idolatry'' Adultery', and other acts that violated God's universal law.

After GOD saw that the kings would not magnify the Ten Commandments , and make the Law honorable, GOD decided to raise up 'Prophets'. God sent these prophets to the kings to warn them of the destruction that would come for breaking the Ten Commandments. The African Prophet Hosea warned King Zachariah, King Shallum and King Menahem in the year 780 BCE; 3442 ACTUAL YEAR , Hosea 4-8.

We now continue with the 'era' of the Kings of the African Children of Israel. We will also include the African Prophets that God sent to the kings to warn them of the dangers for breaking God's Ten Commandments and causing the Children of Israel to go astray from God's universal law.

770/3452

Pekahiah, the son of Menahem, reigned 2 years over the African Hebrew Kingdom of Israel. He was Evil, and was slain by Pekah. 2 Kings 15:22-26 King Pekahiah was warned by the Prophet Hosea in Hosea Chapters 9 thru 14.

768/3454

Pekah was the son of Remaliah. He reigned for 20 years over the African Hebrew Kingdom of Israel. He was EVIL and was slain by Hoshea. He was also warned by the Prophet Hosea.

"NOTE...God used 16 Prophets to warn and shew the African Children of Israel the destruction that would come upon them for not keeping the Ten Commandments. The 16 prophets were 'Isaiah' thru 'Malachi'. God shewed and explained to each of these prophets, what would happen to the Children of Israel in those days (In Africa), which would cause them to be punished and placed in America for 400 years. God also shewed these prophets the details of the curses and punishment that the African Children of Israel would experience while serving their 400 year affliction in America. Please read Genesis 15:13-14. and Deut. 28

God also shewed the prophets how He would create the 'new folks' (white folks), and the work that He created the 'new folks' to do to the African Children of Israel and all Black folks for breaking the Ten Commandments while in Africa.

"VITAL"

A 'Prophet' is defined as, one who utters divinely inspired revelations, or one gifted with more than ordinary spiritual and moral insights. This is mentioned because the readers need to understand the significance of 'Prophecy'. As you read the Old Testament, you will find that it contains 'Prophecy' exclusively, not 'Religion'. The 'SPIRIT-GOD' used certain individuals (called Prophets), to express GOD's 'WILL'. Again, this transaction between GOD and man is called the 'SPIRIT OF PROPHECY'. The following Scriptures confirm the existence of:

"THE SPIRIT OF PROPHECY' (AMOS 3:7)

GEN. 20:7

Where is the first Prophet mentioned? (Abraham)

7 Now therefore restore the man his wife; for he is a prophet, and he shall pray for thee, and thou shalt live: and if thou restore her not, know thou that thou shalt surely die, thou, and all that are thine.

(Genesis 20:7).

NUMB. 12:6

How are Prophets established? (Appointed)

6 And he said, Hear now my words: If there be a prophet among you, I the LORD will make myself known unto him in a vision, and will speak unto him in a dream.

(Numbers 12:6).

DUET. 13:1-11

A true Prophet forsakes all others.

1 If there arise among you a prophet, or a dreamer of dreams, and giveth thee a sign or a wonder,

2 And the sign or the wonder come to pass, whereof he spake unto thee, saying, Let us go after other gods, which thou hast not known, and let us serve them;

3 Thou shalt not hearken unto the words of that prophet, or that

dreamer of dreams: for the LORD your God proveth you, to know whether ye love the LORD your God with all your heart and with all your soul.

4 Ye shall walk after the LORD your God, and fear him, and keep his commandments, and obey his voice, and ye shall serve him, and cleave unto him.

5 And that prophet, or that dreamer of dreams, shall be put to death; because he hath spoken to turn you away from the LORD your God, which brought you out of the land of Egypt, and redeemed you out of the house of bondage, to thrust thee out of the way which the LORD thy God commanded thee to walk in. So shalt thou put the evil away from the midst of thee.

6 If thy brother, the son of thy mother, or thy son, or thy daughter, or the wife of thy bosom, or thy friend, which is as thine own soul, entice thee secretly, saying, Let us go and serve other gods, which thou hast not known, thou, nor thy fathers;

7 Namely, of the gods of the people which are round about you, nigh unto thee, or far off from thee, from the one end of the earth even unto the other end of the earth;

8 Thou shalt not consent unto him, nor hearken unto him; neither shall thine eye pity him, neither shalt thou spare, neither shalt thou conceal him:

9 But thou shalt surely kill him; thine hand shall be first upon him to put him to death, and afterwards the hand of all the people.

10 And thou shalt stone him with stones, that he die; because he hath sought to thrust thee away from the LORD thy God, which brought thee out of the land of Egypt, from the house of bondage.

11 And all Israel shall hear, and fear, and shall do no more any such wickedness as this is among you.

(Deuteronomy 13:1-11).

DUET. 18:15-22

A true Prophet is 'chosen'.

15 The LORD thy God will raise up unto thee a Prophet from the

midst of thee, of thy brethren, like unto me; unto him ye shall hearken;

16 According to all that thou desiredst of the LORD thy God in Horeb in the day of the assembly, saying, Let me not hear again the voice of the LORD my God, neither let me see this great fire any more, that I die not.

17 And the LORD said unto me, They have well spoken that which they have spoken.

18 I will raise them up a Prophet from among their brethren, like unto thee, and will put my words in his mouth; and he shall speak unto them all that I shall command him.

19 And it shall come to pass, that whosoever will not hearken unto my words which he shall speak in my name, I will require it of him.

20 But the prophet, which shall presume to speak a word in my name, which I have not commanded him to speak, or that shall speak in the name of other gods, even that prophet shall die.

21 And if thou say in thine heart, How shall we know the word which the LORD hath not spoken?

22 When a prophet speaketh in the name of the LORD, if the thing follow not, nor come to pass, that is the thing which the LORD hath not spoken, but the prophet hath spoken it presumptuously: thou shalt not be afraid of him.

(Deuteronomy 18:15-22).

JUDGES 4:4

Female Prophetess (Debroah)

4 And Deborah, a prophetess, the wife of Lapidoth, she judged Israel at that time.

(Judges 4:4).

II CHRON. 20:20

We must believe in Prophets.

20 And they rose early in the morning, and went forth into the wilderness of Tekoa: and as they went forth, Jehoshaphat stood and said, Hear me, O Judah, and ye inhabitants of Jerusalem; Believe in the LORD your God, so shall ye be established; believe his prophets, so shall ye prosper.

(2 Chronicles 20:20).

JERE. 1:5

Prophets are chosen before birth. No age limit.

5 Before I formed thee in the belly I knew thee; and before thou camest forth out of the womb I sanctified thee, and I ordained thee a prophet unto the nations.

(Jeremiah 1:5).

JOEL 2:28

Are Prophets obsolete?

28 And it shall come to pass afterward, that I will pour out my spirit upon all flesh; and your sons and your daughters shall prophesy, your old men shall dream dreams, your young men shall see visions:

(Joel 2:28).

AMOS 3:7

Why must there always be a Prophet?

7 Surely the Lord GOD will do nothing, but he revealeth his secret unto his servants the prophets. (The Lord God will do nothing because this God that we try to define and describe is 'something', not someone'...this Spirit can only manifest it's will through a human being)

(Amos 3:7).

ZECH. 7:7

A Prophet is the 'mouth-piece' of GOD.

7 Should ye not hear the words which the LORD hath cried by the

former prophets, when Jerusalem was inhabited and in prosperity, and the cities thereof round about her, when men inhabited the south and the plain?

(Zechariah 7:7).

MATT. 5:17

What did Jesus say about Prophets?

17 Think not that I am come to destroy the law, or the prophets: I am not come to destroy, but to fulfil.

(Matthew 5:17).

LUKE 13:33

There will always be a Prophet.

33 Nevertheless I must walk to day, and to morrow, and the day following: for it cannot be that a prophet perish out of Jerusalem.

(Luke 13:33).

ACTS 21:10

Was Jesus the only New Testament Prophet?

10 And as we tarried there many days, there came down from Judaea a certain prophet, named Agabus.

(Acts 21:10).

I COR. 12:28

Paul validates Prophets.

28 And God hath set some in the church, first apostles, secondarily prophets, thirdly teachers, after that miracles, then gifts of healings, helps, governments, diversities of tongues.

(1Corinthians 12:28).

EPHES. 4:11

Everyone has a job to do.

11 And he gave some, apostles; and some, prophets; and some, evangelists; and some, pastors and teachers;

(Ephesians 4:11).

I THESS. 5:20

Should we turn our back on the Spirit of Prophecy?

20 Despise not prophesyings.

(1Thessalonians 5:20).

II PETER 1:21

Did man create the Spirit of Prophecy?

21 For the prophecy came not in old time by the will of man: but holy men of God spake as they were moved by the Holy Ghost.

(2Peter 1:21).

JOHN 1:14

The Spirit of Prophecy was made flesh.

14 And the Word was made flesh, and dwelt among us, (and we beheld his glory, the glory as of the only begotten of the Father,) full of grace and truth.

(John 1:14).

REV. 19:10

Was Jesus a Prophet? Was Jesus a man? Let us review and consider the following references:

10 And I fell at his feet to worship him. And he said unto me, See thou do it not: I am thy fellowservant, and of thy brethren that have the testimony of Jesus: worship God: for the testimony of Jesus is the spirit of prophecy.

(Revelation 19:10).

REV. 22:16, states that Jesus was the offspring of David. David was a man.

16 I Jesus have sent mine angel to testify unto you these things in the churches. I am the root and the offspring of David, and the bright and morning star.

(Revelation 22:16).

MATT. 12:23 States that Jesus was the son of David.

23 And all the people were amazed, and said, Is not this the son of David?

(Matthew 12:23).

MATT. 13:55-58 States that Jesus was a carpenters son. Joseph was a man.

55 Is not this the carpenter's son? is not his mother called Mary? and his brethren, James, and Joses, and Simon, and Judas?

56 And his sisters, are they not all with us? Whence then hath this man all these things?

57 And they were offended in him. But Jesus said unto them, A prophet is not without honour, save in his own country, and in his own house.

58 And he did not many mighty works there because of their unbelief.

(Matthew 13:55-58).

MATT.15:21-28 States that Jesus was the son of David.

21 Then Jesus went thence, and departed into the coasts of Tyre and Sidon.

22 And, behold, a woman of Canaan came out of the same coasts, and cried unto him, saying, Have mercy on me, O Lord, thou Son of David; my daughter is grievously vexed with a devil.

23 But he answered her not a word. And his disciples came and besought him, saying, Send her away; for she crieth after us.

24 But he answered and said, I am not sent but unto the lost sheep of the house of Israel.

25 Then came she and worshipped him, saying, Lord, help me.

26 But he answered and said, It is not meet to take the children's bread, and to cast it to dogs.

27 And she said, Truth, Lord: yet the dogs eat of the crumbs which fall from their masters' table.

28 Then Jesus answered and said unto her, O woman, great is thy faith: be it unto thee even as thou wilt. And her daughter was made whole from that very hour.

(Matthew 15:21-28).

MATT. 16:13-14 People said that Jesus was a Prophet, and looked like the African Prophet Jeremiah.

13 When Jesus came into the coasts of Caesarea Philippi, he asked his disciples, saying, Whom do men say that I the Son of man am?

14 And they said, Some say that thou art John the Baptist: some, Elias; and others, Jeremias, or one of the prophets.

(Matthew 16:13-14).

JERE. 8:21 If Jesus looked like Jeremiah, that means, Jesus was an African , because Jeremiah said that he was black. (Think about all of this).

21 For the hurt of the daughter of my people am I hurt; I am black; astonishment hath taken hold on me.

(Jeremiah 8:21).

This concludes the brief summary of the 'SPIRIT OF PROPHECY'. It is important for the reader to be aware of this extraordinary transaction between GOD and man. (AMOS 3:7)

We will begin with Isaiah and review the 'TRUTH' that will hopefully explain why 'new folks' (white folks) were created, and why the African Children of Israel (black folks) are doing so bad in America.

"VITAL"

In order to understand what GOD is shewing us in Isaiah thru Malachi, GOD had to use, what is known as "ANACHRONISMS". Anachronism is a misplacement of persons, places, events, objects, or customs in regard to each other. In other words, we must change names and locations from 'African names and locations, to American names and locations. This is necessary because America and 'new folks' did not exist during the time of the Old Testament. 'Anachronisms' had to be used at the time of Isaiah thru Malachi so that the 'Scripture of Truth' could relate to the days of old (in Africa), and to this present day. (in America), The Old Testament is 'past', 'present' and 'future, all at the same time. Most people can not understand the Old Testament, especially the last 16 books, because they do not understand the definition of, and the use of 'ANACHRONISMS'.

"VITAL"

For proper understanding, refer only to the specific chapters and verses that are indicated. This is imperative in order to understand the TRUTH. Most people try to read the 'prophets' straight thru, line by line, verse by verse, until they complete the whole chapter. This is where most people get confused, because the placement of the verses in the last 16 books of the Old Testament, do not follow the exact sequence of events chronologically. For example, you could be reading a few verses of a chapter that relates to a particular timeframe, while the next 6 verses may address an event 40 to 80 years later. This is why this 'revelation' is presented in chronological order.

If you notice, we have merged the 'era' of Kings with the Prophets. This is important because we must understand the gravity of God's law. The African Children of Israel (black folks) were chosen by God to magnify God's universal law, and make it honorable before all the people of Africa. But the African Hebrew Kings did not take their responsibility too serious, and led the chosen people of God, astray. God raised up a series of African Prophets, who warned the African Hebrew Kings, and pleaded with them to stop breaking the Ten Commandments of God.

760/3462

Isaiah Chapter 1 --Isaiah's warning to the African Israelites to "clean up".

By this time, God was really sick of the African Hebrew Israelites. God sent the Prophet Isaiah to the Children of Israel to warn them of the coming destruction, and to shew Israel how God felt about them.

1 The vision of Isaiah the son of Amoz, which he saw concerning Judah and Jerusalem in the days of Uzziah, Jotham, Ahaz, and Hezekiah, kings of Judah.

2 Hear, O heavens, and give ear, O earth: for the LORD hath spoken, I have nourished and brought up children, and they have rebelled against me.

3 The ox knoweth his owner, and the ass his master's crib: but Israel (African Hebrews) doth not know, my people doth not consider.

4 Ah sinful nation, a people laden with iniquity, a seed of evildoers, children that are corrupters: they have forsaken the LORD, they have provoked the Holy One of Israel unto anger, they are gone away backward.

5 Why should ye be stricken any more? ye will revolt more and more: the whole head is sick, and the whole heart faint.

6 From the sole of the foot even unto the head there is no soundness in it; but wounds, and bruises, and putrifying sores: they have not been closed, neither bound up, neither mollified with ointment.

7 Your country is desolate, your cities are burned with fire: your land, strangers devour it in your presence, and it is desolate, as overthrown by strangers.

8 And the daughter of Zion is left as a cottage in a vineyard, as a lodge in a garden of cucumbers, as a besieged city.

9 Except the LORD of hosts had left unto us a very small remnant, we should have been as Sodom, and we should have been like unto Gomorrah.

10 Hear the word of the LORD, ye rulers of Sodom; give ear unto the law of our God, ye people of Gomorrah.

11 To what purpose is the multitude of your sacrifices unto me? saith the LORD: I am full of the burnt offerings of rams, and the fat of

fed beasts; and I delight not in the blood of bullocks, or of lambs, or of he goats.

12 When ye come to appear before me, who hath required this at your hand, to tread my courts?

13 Bring no more vain oblations; incense is an abomination unto me; the new moons and sabbaths, the calling of assemblies, I cannot away with; it is iniquity, even the solemn meeting.

14 Your new moons and your appointed feasts my soul hateth: they are a trouble unto me; I am weary to bear them.

15 And when ye spread forth your hands, I will hide mine eyes from you: yea, when ye make many prayers, I will not hear: your hands are full of blood.

16 Wash you, make you clean; put away the evil of your doings from before mine eyes; cease to do evil;

17 Learn to do well; seek judgment, relieve the oppressed, judge the fatherless, plead for the widow.

18 Come now, and let us reason together, saith the LORD: though your sins be as scarlet, they shall be as white as snow; though they be red like crimson, they shall be as wool.

19 If ye be willing and obedient, ye shall eat the good of the land:

20 But if ye refuse and rebel, ye shall be devoured with the sword: for the mouth of the LORD hath spoken it.

21 How is the faithful city become an harlot! it was full of judgment; righteousness lodged in it; but now murderers.

22 Thy silver is become dross, thy wine mixed with water:

23 Thy princes are rebellious, and companions of thieves: every one loveth gifts, and followeth after rewards: they judge not the fatherless, neither doth the cause of the widow come unto them.

24 Therefore saith the Lord, the LORD of hosts, the mighty One of Israel, Ah, I will ease me of mine adversaries, and avenge me of mine enemies:

25 And I will turn my hand upon thee, and purely purge away thy dross, and take away all thy tin:

26 And I will restore thy judges as at the first, and thy counsellors as at the beginning: afterward thou shalt be called, The city of righteousness, the faithful city.

27 Zion shall be redeemed with judgment, and her converts with righteousness.

28 And the destruction of the transgressors and of the sinners shall be together, and they that forsake the LORD shall be consumed.

29 For they shall be ashamed of the oaks which ye have desired, and ye shall be confounded for the gardens that ye have chosen.

30 For ye shall be as an oak whose leaf fadeth, and as a garden that hath no water.

31 And the strong shall be as tow, and the maker of it as a spark, and they shall both burn together, and none shall quench them.

(Isaiah 1:1-31).

760/3462

Isaiah 2:2-4....Nations pouring unto Israel. Not too many people today are aware that the Children of Israel are 'black folks', and that they reside in America under many different names. Once the TRUTH is revealed, and after the shock, God will cause all nations of the world to pour unto the African Hebrew Israelites so that may see, and understand, the true worship of GOD.

2 And it shall come to pass in the last days, that the mountain of the LORD'S house shall be established in the top of the mountains, and shall be exalted above the hills; and all nations shall flow unto it.

3 And many people shall go and say, Come ye, and let us go up to the mountain of the LORD, to the house of the God of Jacob; and he will teach us of his ways, and we will walk in his paths: for out of Zion (African Hebrews) shall go forth the law, and the word of the LORD from Jerusalem. (African Hebrews)

4 And he shall judge among the nations, and shall rebuke many

people: and they shall beat their swords into plowshares, and their spears into pruninghooks: nation shall not lift up sword against nation, neither shall they learn war any more.

(Isaiah 2:2-4).

760/3462

Isaiah 3:8-9....Why the African Children of Israel were destroyed. Many black folks (old folks) today feel that white folks (new folks) are responsible for their affliction and oppression. Not true. Once you understand the total TRUTH, you will find that it was the violation of God's law that punished the African American, and is still punishing them today for breaking God's holy Ten Commandments.

8 For Jerusalem (African Hebrews) is ruined, and Judah (African Hebrews) is fallen: because their tongue and their doings are against the LORD, to provoke the eyes of his glory.

9 The shew of their countenance doth witness against them; and they declare their sin as Sodom, they hide it not. Woe unto their soul! for they have rewarded evil unto themselves.

(Isaiah 3:8-9).

760/3462

Isaiah 3:13-15....God's judgement on the Oppressor for beating His people. God will bring judgement upon the people that afflicted the African Children of Israel during their 400 year captivity in America.

13 The LORD standeth up to plead, and standeth to judge the people.

14 The LORD will enter into judgment with the ancients of his people, and the princes thereof: for ye have eaten up the vineyard; the spoil of the poor is in your houses.

15 What mean ye that ye beat my people to pieces, and grind the faces of the poor? saith the Lord GOD of hosts.

(Isaiah 3:13-15).

760/3462

Isaiah 5:7....Israel is God's Vineyard. God regarded the African Children of Israel in such a special way, that |God called them, 'His Vineyard'. But God had to destroy His vineyard because of their sins.

7 For the vineyard of the LORD of hosts is the house of Israel, (African Hebrews) and the men of Judah (African Hebrews) his pleasant plant: and he looked for judgment, but behold oppression; for righteousness, but behold a cry.

(Isaiah 5:7).

760/3462

Isaiah 5:13...Why the African Hebrew Israelites went into captivity in America. The Children of Israel (black folks) have paid a terrible price for their fore-fathers sins, but God will reward them 'double' for their shame. But this cannot happen unless they have the knowledge to really understand the power of God's Ten Commandments. Without this knowledge of God, the Children of Israel will never be able to lead the rest of the world, back to the 'true' worship to GOD.

13 Therefore my people are gone into captivity, because they have no knowledge: and their honourable men are famished, and their multitude dried up with thirst.

(Isaiah 5:13).

760/3462

Isaiah 5:24-30....God angry with the Children of Israel, will bring 'new folks' (white folks) to Africa to destroy them. (Ensign=America, vs.26) Here we see that God has made up His mind to bring the 'new folks' (white folks) against Africa, and no matter how hard the people of Africa fought, God would cause the 'new folks' (white folks) to prevail. All because 'old folks' (black folks) broke the Ten Commandments of God.

24 Therefore as the fire devoureth the stubble, and the flame consumeth the chaff, so their root shall be as rottenness, and their blossom shall go up as dust: because they have cast away the law

of the LORD of hosts, and despised the word of the Holy One of Israel.

25 Therefore is the anger of the LORD kindled against his people, and he hath stretched forth his hand against them, and hath smitten them: and the hills did tremble, and their carcases were torn in the midst of the streets. For all this his anger is not turned away, but his hand is stretched out still.

26 And he will lift up an ensign (new folks) to the nations from far, and will hiss unto them from the end of the earth: and, behold, they shall come with speed swiftly:

27 None shall be weary nor stumble among them; none shall slumber nor sleep; neither shall the girdle of their loins be loosed, nor the latchet of their shoes be broken:

28 Whose arrows are sharp, and all their bows bent, their horses' hoofs shall be counted like flint, and their wheels like a whirlwind:

29 Their roaring shall be like a lion, they shall roar like young lions: yea, they shall roar, and lay hold of the prey, and shall carry it away safe, and none shall deliver it.

30 And in that day they shall roar against them like the roaring of the sea: and if one look unto the land, behold darkness and sorrow, and the light is darkened in the heavens thereof.

(Isaiah 5:24-30).

760/3462

The events in Hosea Chapter 9 took place in this year. GOD sent the Prophet Hosea to the Children of Israel to advise them of the distress and captivity that would overtake them because of their sins.

757/3465

Jotham, the son of King Uzziah, reigned for 16 years. He was good. He was king over the African Kingdom of Judah. II Kings 15:7; II Chron. 26:23, 27:9

750/3472

The beginning of Micah's 40 years of Prophecy.

GOD sent the Prophet Micah to King Jotham, King Ahaz and King Hezekiah, who were Kings of Judah. The Prophet Micah warned these Kings of their Idolary and Oppression. The events in Micah Chapter 1 (only) took place during this timeframe.

748/3474

Hoshea, the son of Elah, ruled the African Hebrew Kingdom of Israel for 9 years. He was taken into captivity by Shalmaneser. King Hoshea was EVIL. 2 Kings 15:30, 18:9-12

741/3481

Ahaz, the son of Jotham, was the African king over the African Hebrew Kingdom of Judah for 16 years. He was EVIL. 2 Kings 15:38, 16:20; 2 Chron. 27:9, 28:27

740/3482

The events in Hosea Chapters 10 & 11 took place in this year. Hosea Chapter 10 reproves and threatens the Children of Israel for their Idolatry. Chapter 11 shews Israel's 'Ingratitude' to GOD.

730/3492

Micah 2:1-10---GOD explaining and preparing the African Children of Israel for their destruction from Africa.

1 Woe to them that devise iniquity, and work evil upon their beds! when the morning is light, they practise it, because it is in the power of their hand.

2 And they covet fields, and take them by violence; and houses, and take them away: so they oppress a man and his house, even a man and his heritage.

3 Therefore thus saith the LORD; Behold, against this family (African Hebrews)do I devise an evil, from which ye shall not remove your necks; neither shall ye go haughtily: for this time is evil.

4 In that day shall one take up a parable against you, and lament with a doleful lamentation, and say, We be utterly spoiled: he hath changed the portion of my people: how hath he removed it from me! turning away he hath divided our fields.

5 Therefore thou shalt have none that shall cast a cord by lot in the congregation of the LORD.

6 Prophesy ye not, say they to them that prophesy: they shall not prophesy to them, that they shall not take shame.

7 O thou that art named the house of Jacob, (African Hebrews) is the spirit of the LORD straitened? are these his doings? do not my words do good to him that walketh uprightly?

8 Even of late my people is risen up as an enemy: ye pull off the robe with the garment from them that pass by securely as men averse from war.

9 The women of my people have ye cast out from their pleasant houses; from their children have ye taken away my glory for ever.

10 Arise ye, and depart; for this is not your rest: because it is polluted, it shall destroy you, even with a sore destruction.

(Micah 2:1-10).

730-3492

Micah 2:12-13 How GOD will gather the remnant of Israel, and give them a King that will lead them through the gates of America, and back to Africa.

12 I will surely assemble, O Jacob, (African Hebrews) all of thee; I will surely gather the remnant of Israel; (African Americans) I will put them together as the sheep of Bozrah,(A city in Africa) as the flock in the midst of their fold: they shall make great noise by reason of the multitude of men.

13 The breaker is come up before them: they have broken up, and have passed through the gate, and are gone out by it: and their king shall pass before them, and the LORD on the head of them.

(Micah 2:12-13).

725/3497

Hezekiah was the son of Ahaz. King Hezekiah was the African king over the African Hebrew Kingdom of Judah. He reigned for 29 years. He was GOOD. 2 Kings 16:20, 20:21; 2 Chron. 29:1-11, 32:33

725/3497

This is the timeframe for Hosea Chapters 12, 13, 14. In these chapters, GOD warns the African Children of Israel of their coming destruction, and how GOD will turn HIS back on them for breaking the TEN COMMANDMENTS.

722/3500

The fall of Samaria and the Assyrian Captivity. Samaria was the Capital of the Northern Kingdom, occupied by the Ten Tribes. It was purchased by the African King Omri, and fell, because King Omri was a wicked king, and did not keep GOD's Ten Commandments. When the African Children of Israel continued to break GOD's Ten Comandments, GOD placed the Ten Tribes in captivity under the hand of the Assyrians.

714/3508

Isaiah 19:1-4---- God bringing 'new folks' (white folks) to destroy the people of Africa. Egypt is the 'anachronism' for Africa or 'old folks.

1 The burden of Egypt.(Africa) Behold, the LORD rideth upon a swift cloud, and shall come into Egypt: and the idols of Egypt shall be moved at his presence, and the heart of Egypt shall melt in the midst of it.

2 And I will set the Egyptians (Africans) against the Egyptians: and they shall fight every one against his brother, and every one against his neighbour; city against city, and kingdom against kingdom.

3 And the spirit of Egypt (Africa) shall fail in the midst thereof; and I will destroy the counsel thereof: and they shall seek to the idols, and to the charmers, and to them that have familiar spirits, and to the wizards.

4 And the Egyptians (Africans) will I give over into the hand of a cruel lord;(new folks-white folks) and a fierce king (new folks) shall rule over them, saith the Lord, the LORD of hosts.

(Isaiah 19:1-4).

714/3508

Isaiah 19:16-25...GOD explaining what will happen to Africa in the coming days. Verse. 21 The 'old folks' (black folks) that are in Africa today, will also understand that it was Almighty God that caused 'apartheid', 'famine', 'pestilence and all other afflictions. Once they understand the 'cause', they will return and fear GOD and keep the Ten Commandments.

16 In that day shall Egypt (Africa) be like unto women: and it shall be afraid and fear because of the shaking of the hand of the LORD of hosts, which he shaketh over it.

17 And the land of Judah (Africa) shall be a terror unto Egypt,(Africa) every one that maketh mention thereof shall be afraid in himself, because of the counsel of the LORD of hosts, which he hath determined against it.

18 In that day shall five cities in the land of Egypt (Africa) speak the language of Canaan, and swear to the LORD of hosts; one shall be called, The city of destruction.

19 In that day shall there be an altar to the LORD in the midst of the land of Egypt,(Africa) and a pillar at the border thereof to the LORD.

20 And it shall be for a sign and for a witness unto the LORD of hosts in the land of Egypt:(Africa) for they shall cry unto the LORD because of the oppressors, and he shall send them a saviour, and a great one, and he shall deliver them.

21 And the LORD shall be known to Egypt, (Africa) and the Egyptians (Africans) shall know the LORD in that day, and shall do sacrifice and oblation; yea, they shall vow a vow unto the LORD, and perform it.

22 And the LORD shall smite Egypt:(Africa) he shall smite and heal it: and they shall return even to the LORD, and he shall be intreated of them, and shall heal them.

23 In that day shall there be a highway out of Egypt (Africa) to Assyria,(America) and the Assyrian (Americans) shall come into Egypt,(Africa) and the Egyptian(Africans) into Assyria,(America) and the Egyptians (old folks) shall serve with the Assyrians.(new

folks)

24 In that day shall Israel (African Hebrews) be the third with Egypt (Gentile old folks) and with Assyria,(new folks) even a blessing in the midst of the land:

25 Whom the LORD of hosts shall bless, saying, Blessed be Egypt (Gentile old folks) my people, and Assyria (new folks) the work of my hands, and Israel (African Hebrews) mine inheritance.

(Isaiah 19:16-25).

Verse 23

God will prepare a highway between Africa and America so that the 'Gentiles' can travel back and forth to observe, learn and serve God properly Egypt= Africa...Assyria is the 'anachronism for America.

Verse 24

Although the 'true' Children of Israel are unknown to most people today, God will increase them in size. They will be equal in size to all of the 'gentile old folks', and equal in size to all of the 'new folks' (white folks) in America. God said, the whole world will know who the 'chosen people' are. Anachronisms in this verse are: Egypt='gentile old folks. Assyrians= new folks or white folks.

Verse 25

God shewing us the types of people that He created and how He regards them today. "Egypt my people"= the old folks (black folks)that God created in the beginning...'gentile old folks' today. "Assyria", the work of My hand= the 'new folks' or (white folks) that God had to create thousands of years after the creation of the black man. God said He created 'new folks' (white folks) and has used them as a 'tool' to prove, try, test, and afflict the African Children of Israel for breaking the Ten Commandments of GOD. "Israel", mine inheritance'= the African Children of Israel that God selected from the rest of the black folks in Africa to represent and implement God's universal law. (African Americans today)

713/3509

Isaiah 10:5-6...God considers America, 'The Rod Of His Anger. Assyrian is the anachronism for America. God gave the new folks (white folks) complete charge over the African Children of Israel because they broke the Ten Commandments.

5 O Assyrian,(America) the rod of mine anger, and the staff in their hand is mine indignation.

6 I will send him (new folks) against an hypocritical nation, and against the people of my wrath (old folks) will I give him a charge, to take the spoil, and to take the prey, and to tread them down like the mire of the streets.

(Isaiah 10:5-6).

713/3509

Isaiah 10:20-27...The African Hebrew Israelites rescued from America. The African Hebrews are being punished in America for 400 years. In these verses, God is telling the Prophet Isaiah how He will rescue the African Hebrews from America. Assyrian= America in verse 24.

20 And it shall come to pass in that day, that the remnant of Israel, (African Hebrews) and such as are escaped of the house of Jacob, (African Hebrews) shall no more again stay upon him that smote them; but shall stay upon the LORD, the Holy One of Israel, in **TRUTH** .

21 The remnant shall return, even the remnant of Jacob, unto the mighty God.

22 For though thy people Israel be as the sand of the sea, yet a remnant of them shall return: the consumption decreed shall overflow with righteousness.

23 For the Lord GOD of hosts shall make a consumption, even determined, in the midst of all the land.

24 Therefore thus saith the Lord GOD of hosts, O my people (African Hebrews) that dwellest in Zion, be not afraid of the Assyrian:(American new folks) he shall smite thee with a rod, and shall lift up his staff against thee, after the manner of Egypt.(Africa)

25 For yet a very little while, and the indignation shall cease, and mine anger in their destruction.

26 And the LORD of hosts shall stir up a scourge for him according to the slaughter of Midian at the rock of Oreb: and as his rod was upon the sea, so shall he lift it up after the manner of Egypt.

27 And it shall come to pass in that day, that his (new folks)burden shall be taken away from off thy shoulder, and his yoke from off thy neck, and the yoke shall be destroyed because of the anointing.

(Isaiah 10:20-27).

713/3509

Isaiah 11:11-16...The African Hebrew Israelites will be going back to Africa. God said 'envy and jealousy' will no longer be a destructive element among black folks.

11 And it shall come to pass in that day, that the Lord shall set his hand again the second time to recover the remnant of his people, (African Hebrews) which shall be left, from Assyria,(America) and from Egypt,(Africa) and from Pathros,(Jamacia) and from Cush,(Hatia) and from Elam,(West Indies) and from Shinar, and from Hamath, and from the islands of the sea.

12 And he shall set up an ensign for the nations, and shall assemble the outcasts of Israel, (African Hebrews) and gather together the dispersed of Judah (African Hebrews) from the four corners of the earth.

13 The envy also of Ephraim shall depart, and the adversaries of Judah shall be cut off: Ephraim shall not envy Judah, and Judah shall not vex Ephraim. (All African Hebrews)

14 But they shall fly upon the shoulders of the Philistines (new folk airplanes)) toward the west;(Western civilization-America) they shall spoil them of the east together: they shall lay their hand upon Edom and Moab;(new folks) and the children of Ammon (new folks) shall obey them.

15 And the LORD shall utterly destroy the tongue of the Egyptian sea; (Atlantic Ocean)and with his mighty wind shall he shake his hand over the river, and shall smite it in the seven streams, and make men go over dryshod.

16 And there shall be an highway for the remnant of his people,

(African Hebrews) which shall be left, from Assyria;(America) like as it was to Israel (African Hebrews) in the day that he came up out of the land of Egypt.

(Isaiah 11:11-16).

Verse 11

Similar to the Exodus from Egypt, God will again rescue the African Hebrews from all of the lands that hold them captive. Ananchronisms are: Assyria=America, Egypt=Africa, Pathros=Jamaica Cush=West Indies, Elam, Shinar and Hamath=the other Islands where 'black' folks presently reside..

Verse 12

Once all African Children of Israel are gathered together, a national standard will be established, and the whole world will follow it. Judah of course= The Children of Israel. The 'National Standard' is the TEN COMMANDMENTS.

Verse 13

Envy and jealousy will cease between 'black folks because their adversaries will be cut off. Black folks will dwell together in unity. Ephraim also= The Children of Israel.

Verse 14

The Africans that reside in Africa will use the airplanes of the 'new folks' (Philistines) and fly to America (the West). Before they leave Africa to unite with the African Hebrews in America, GOD will destroy the oppressor that raped Africa and it's people. Edom and Moab are Anachronisms for African locations that are presently ruled by 'new folks'.(white folks)

Verse 15

God will cause the Atlantic Ocean to be as an open highway so that the African Children of Israel can commute to and fro from Africa to America. This will be similar to the opening of the Red Sea in Africa when God delivered the African Hebrew Israelites from the land of Egypt.

713/3509

Isaiah 30:1-3...God addressing the 1st Commandment . In the days of old, the African Children of Israel turned to the 'gentile old folks for help, but only God could help them. Today, the African Children of Israel and the 'Gentile old folks' are turning to false religions and 'new folks' and begging them for help; but God did not create 'new folks' to help 'old folks'. God created 'new folks' (white folks) to afflict the African Children of Israel and the "gentile old folks' for 400 years. Only GOD can help them, no one else. This is why black folks are doing so bad in America, and it will only get worse until they turn and keep the Ten Commandments. This is why GOD created the 'new folks' and placed 'old folks' in America...so they could be tried; tested; and proven. The day is coming when black folks will have to prove to GOD, that they are worthy of the blessing that He has promised. In order for black folks (old folks) to prepare themselves for God's final test, they must free themselves from their 'slave-mentality'.

1 Woe to the rebellious children, (African Hebrews) saith the LORD, that take counsel, but not of me; and that cover with a covering, but not of my spirit, that they may add sin to sin:

2 That walk to go down into Egypt,(Gentiles) and have not asked at my mouth; to strengthen themselves in the strength of Pharaoh, (new folks) and to trust in the shadow of Egypt! (Gentiles)

3 Therefore shall the strength of Pharaoh (new folks) be your shame, and the trust in the shadow of Egypt (Gentiles) your confusion.

(Isaiah 30:1-3).

713/3509

During this same timeframe while GOD sent the Prophet Isaiah to warn the Kings of Israel of their sins, GOD also sent the Prophet Nahum to the city of Nineveh to warn them of their many sins. The 3 Chapters of Nahum took place during this time period.

712/3510

Isaiah 13.....The destruction of America. This whole chapter speaks to the fall of America. Anachronisms are used throughout this chapter ie., Babylon=America, Medes=Allies of America. Verse 17 speaks to how the 'Allies' of America, will turn against them. Verse 19 compares the destruction of America to Sodom and Gomorrah.

1 The burden of Babylon,(America) which Isaiah the son of Amoz did see.

2 Lift ye up a banner upon the high mountain, exalt the voice unto them, shake the hand, that they may go into the gates of the nobles.

3 I have commanded my sanctified ones, I have also called my mighty ones for mine anger, even them that rejoice in my highness.

4 The noise of a multitude in the mountains, like as of a great people; a tumultuous noise of the kingdoms of nations gathered together: the LORD of hosts mustereth the host of the battle.

5 They come from a far country, from the end of heaven, even the LORD, and the weapons of his indignation, to destroy the whole land.

6 Howl ye; for the day of the LORD is at hand; it shall come as a destruction from the Almighty.

7 Therefore shall all hands be faint, and every man's heart shall melt:

8 And they shall be afraid: pangs and sorrows shall take hold of them; they shall be in pain as a woman that travaileth: they shall be amazed one at another; their faces shall be as flames.

9 Behold, the day of the LORD cometh, cruel both with wrath and fierce anger, to lay the land desolate: and he shall destroy the sinners thereof out of it.

10 For the stars of heaven and the constellations thereof shall not give their light: the sun shall be darkened in his going forth, and the moon shall not cause her light to shine.

11 And I will punish the world for their evil, and the wicked for their iniquity; and I will cause the arrogancy of the proud to cease, and will lay low the haughtiness of the terrible.

12 I will make a man more precious than fine gold; even a man than the golden wedge of Ophir.

13 Therefore I will shake the heavens, and the earth shall remove out of her place, in the wrath of the LORD of hosts, and in the day of his fierce anger.

14 And it shall be as the chased roe, and as a sheep that no man taketh up: they shall every man turn to his own people, and flee every one into his own land. (There will be an American Exodus)

15 Every one that is found shall be thrust through; and every one that is joined unto them shall fall by the sword.

16 Their children also shall be dashed to pieces before their eyes; their houses shall be spoiled, and their wives ravished.

17 Behold, I will stir up the Medes against them, which shall not regard silver; and as for gold, they shall not delight in it.

18 Their bows also shall dash the young men to pieces; and they shall have no pity on the fruit of the womb; their eye shall not spare children.

19 And Babylon,(America) the glory of kingdoms, the beauty of the Chaldees'(new folks) excellency, shall be as when God overthrew Sodom and Gomorrah.

20 It shall never be inhabited, neither shall it be dwelt in from generation to generation: neither shall the Arabian (Imigrants) pitch tent there; neither shall the shepherds make their fold there.

21 But wild beasts of the desert shall lie there; and their houses shall be full of doleful creatures; and owls shall dwell there, and satyrs shall dance there.

22 And the wild beasts of the islands shall cry in their desolate houses, and dragons in their pleasant palaces: and her time is near to come, and her days shall not be prolonged.

(Isaiah 13:1-22).

712/3510

Isaiah 14:1-3... When GOD delivers the African Children of Israel from their 400 year captivity in America, He will take them back to Africa, and some 'new folks' (white folks) will be going along to be Israel's servants and handmaids.

1 For the LORD will have mercy on Jacob, (African Hebrews) and will yet choose Israel, (African Hebrews) and set them in their own land: (Africa) and the strangers(new folks) shall be joined with them, and they shall cleave to the house of Jacob.

2 And the people (African Hebrews) shall take them, and bring them to their place:(Africa) and the house of Israel (African Hebrews) shall possess them in the land of the LORD for servants and handmaids: and they shall take them captives, whose captives they were; and they shall rule over their oppressors.

3 And it shall come to pass in the day that the LORD shall give thee rest from thy sorrow, and from thy fear, and from the hard bondage wherein thou wast made to serve. (

(Isaiah 14:1-3).

712/3510

Isaiah 14:4-27 . The African Children of Israel will sing a 'song of triumph' when God causes America to fall.

4 That thou shalt take up this proverb against the king of Babylon,(America) and say, How hath the oppressor ceased! the golden city ceased!

5 The LORD hath broken the staff of the wicked, and the sceptre of the rulers.

6 He who smote the people in wrath with a continual stroke, he that ruled the nations in anger, is persecuted, and none hindereth.

7 The whole earth is at rest, and is quiet: they break forth into singing.

8 Yea, the fir trees rejoice at thee, and the cedars of Lebanon, saying, Since thou art laid down, no feller is come up against us.

9 Hell from beneath is moved for thee to meet thee at thy coming: it stirreth up the dead for thee, even all the chief ones of the earth; it hath raised up from their thrones all the kings of the nations.

10 All they shall speak and say unto thee, Art thou also become weak as we? art thou become like unto us?

11 Thy pomp is brought down to the grave, and the noise of thy viols: the worm is spread under thee, and the worms cover thee.

12 How art thou fallen from heaven, O Lucifer,(America) son of the morning! how art thou cut down to the ground, which didst weaken the nations!

13 For thou hast said in thine heart, I will ascend into heaven, I will exalt my throne above the stars of God: I will sit also upon the mount of the congregation, in the sides of the north:North America)

14 I will ascend above the heights of the clouds; I will be like the most High.

15 Yet thou shalt be brought down to hell, to the sides of the pit.

16 They that see thee shall narrowly look upon thee, and consider thee, saying, Is this the man that made the earth to tremble, that did shake kingdoms;

17 That made the world as a wilderness, and destroyed the cities thereof; that opened not the house of his prisoners?

18 All the kings of the nations, even all of them, lie in glory, every one in his own house.

19 But thou art cast out of thy grave like an abominable branch, and as the raiment of those that are slain, thrust through with a sword, that go down to the stones of the pit; as a carcase trodden under feet.

20 Thou shalt not be joined with them in burial, because thou hast destroyed thy land, and slain thy people: the seed of evildoers shall never be renowned.

21 Prepare slaughter for his children for the iniquity of their fathers; that they do not rise, nor possess the land, nor fill the face of the world with cities.

22 For I will rise up against them, saith the LORD of hosts, and cut off from Babylon (America) the name, and remnant, and son, and nephew, saith the LORD.

23 I will also make it a possession for the bittern, and pools of water:

and I will sweep it with the besom of destruction, saith the LORD of hosts.

24 The LORD of hosts hath sworn, saying, Surely as I have thought, so shall it come to pass; and as I have purposed, so shall it stand:

25 That I will break the Assyrian (American new folks) in my land,(Africa) and upon my mountains tread him under foot: then shall his yoke depart from off them,(African Americans) and his burden depart from off their shoulders.

26 This is the purpose that is purposed upon the whole earth: and this is the hand that is stretched out upon all the nations.

27 For the LORD of hosts hath purposed, and who shall disannul it? and his hand is stretched out, and who shall turn it back?

(Isaiah 14:4-27).

712/3510

Isaiah 22:17-25 . God placing the African Children of Israel and 'Gentile old folks' in America, and how the 'new folks' (white folks) would control them for 400 years. 'Eliakim and Hilkiah are 'anachronisms' for 'new folks'. The 'new folks' will call themselves 'Jews", take the African Hebrew's heritage, wear their Hebrew clothing and ornaments, and take a part of Africa and call it Israel...But in TRUTH, Israel is not a piece of land, it is a nation of African people. Even though new folks stole the African Hebrew's name while they serve their 400 year captivity in Americia and other strange lands, GOD will remove the LIE and re-establish the TRUTH.

17 Behold, the LORD will carry thee away with a mighty captivity, and will surely cover thee.

18 He will surely violently turn and toss thee like a ball into a large country: (America) there shalt thou die, and there the chariots of thy glory shall be the shame of thy lord's house.

19 And I will drive thee from thy station, (Africa) and from thy state shall he pull thee down.

20 And it shall come to pass in that day, that I will call my servant Eliakim (new folks) the son of Hilkiah:

21 And I will clothe him (new folks) with thy robe, and strengthen him with thy girdle, and I will commit thy government into his hand: and he shall be a father to the inhabitants of Jerusalem, (Africa) and to the house of Judah.

22 And the key of the house of David will I lay upon his shoulder; so he shall open, and none shall shut; and he shall shut, and none shall open.

23 And I will fasten him as a nail in a sure place; and he shall be for a glorious throne to his father's house.

24 And they shall hang upon him all the glory of his father's house, the offspring and the issue, all vessels of small quantity, from the vessels of cups, even to all the vessels of flagons.

What GOD is saying here is, the new folks will possess the land of Africa and everything that the African people had, will be given over into the hands of the new folks for 400 years. This happened because the African people broke the Ten Commandments of GOD while in Africa. The next verse shews you what will happen after the African Hebrews serves their 400 year punishment in America.

25 In that day, saith the LORD of hosts, shall the nail that is fastened in the sure place be removed, and be cut down, and fall; and the burden that was upon it shall be cut off: for the LORD hath spoken it.

(Isaiah 22:17-25).

712/3510

Isaiah 27:12-13 . God will gather the African Children of Israel, one by one, and lead them back to their original home in Africa. (Egypt=Africa, Assyria= America, Jerusalem=The new location in Africa for the African Hebrew Israelites.)

12 And it shall come to pass in that day, that the LORD shall beat off from the channel of the river (Atlantic Ocean) unto the stream of Egypt,(Africa) and ye shall be gathered one by one, O ye children of Israel. (African Hebrews)

13 And it shall come to pass in that day, that the great trumpet shall

be blown, and they (African Hebrews) shall come which were ready to perish in the land of Assyria, (America) and the outcasts in the land of Egypt, (Africa) and shall worship the LORD in the holy mount at Jerusalem. (Africa)

(Isaiah 27:12-13).

712/3510

Isaiah 29:9-16 . God explaining why the 'TRUTH' to the Bible was hidden, and why the mentality of 'old folk' (black folks), was reduced to the level of a slave. Verse 10 speaks to the condition of many black folks today. Regardless of their high educational achievements, black folks are still walking around in a 'deep sleep' because they are unaware of their 'TRUE' history, which is the 'OLD TESTAMENT'.

9 Stay yourselves, and wonder; cry ye out, and cry: they are drunken, but not with wine; they stagger, but not with strong drink.

10 For the LORD hath poured out upon you the spirit of deep sleep, and hath closed your eyes: the prophets and your rulers, the seers hath he covered.

11 And the vision of all is become unto you as the words of a book that is sealed, which men deliver to one that is learned, saying, Read this, I pray thee: and he saith, I cannot; for it is sealed:

12 And the book is delivered to him that is not learned, saying, Read this, I pray thee: and he saith, I am not learned.

13 Wherefore the Lord said, Forasmuch as this people draw near me with their mouth, and with their lips do honour me, but have removed their heart far from me, and their fear toward me is taught by the precept of men:

14 Therefore, behold, I will proceed to do a marvellous work among this people, even a marvellous work and a wonder: for the wisdom of their wise men shall perish, and the understanding of their prudent men shall be hid.

15 Woe unto them that seek deep to hide their counsel from the LORD, and their works are in the dark, and they say, Who seeth us? and who knoweth us?

16 Surely your turning of things upside down shall be esteemed as the potter's clay: for shall the work say of him that made it, He made me not? or shall the thing framed say of him that framed it, He had no understanding?

(Isaiah 29:9-16).

712/3510

Isaiah 29:18-24 . God shewing what will happen when the "TRUTH' to the Bible is revealed. The TRUTH to the Bible will free 'black folks' (old folks) from their reproach and shame, and give them the necessary hope and strength, to endure the trials and tribulations of America.

18 And in that day shall the deaf hear the words of the book, and the eyes of the blind shall see out of obscurity, and out of darkness.

19 The meek also shall increase their joy in the LORD, and the poor among men shall rejoice in the Holy One of Israel.

20 For the terrible one (new folks/America) is brought to nought, and the scorner is consumed, and all that watch for iniquity are cut off:

21 That make a man an offender for a word, and lay a snare for him that reproveth in the gate, and turn aside the just for a thing of nought.

22 Therefore thus saith the LORD, who redeemed Abraham, concerning the house of Jacob, (African Hebrews) Jacob shall not now be ashamed, neither shall his face now wax pale.

23 But when he seeth his children, the work of mine hands, (new folks) in the midst of him, they shall sanctify my name, and sanctify the Holy One of Jacob, and shall fear the God of Israel.

24 They also that erred in spirit shall come to understanding, and they that murmured shall learn doctrine.

(Isaiah 29:18-24).

712/3510

Isaiah 42:22-25 . God explaining the condition of 'old folks' (black folks) while in America, and why God punished them.

22 But this is a people robbed and spoiled; they (African Americans)are all of them snared in holes, and they are hid in prison houses: they are for a prey, and none delivereth; for a spoil, and none saith, Restore.

23 Who among you will give ear to this? who will hearken and hear for the time to come?

24 Who gave Jacob (African Hebrews) for a spoil, and Israel (African Hebrews)to the robbers? did not the LORD, he against whom we have sinned? for they would not walk in his ways, neither were they obedient unto his law.

25 Therefore he hath poured upon him the fury of his anger, and the strength of battle: and it hath set him on fire round about, yet he knew not; and it burned him, yet he laid it not to heart.

(Isaiah 42:22-25).

712/3510

Isaiah 43:1-7 . God will be with the African people when He gathers them from the many African lands that are presently controlled by "new folks" (Egypt, Ethiopia, and Seba=Africa).

1 But now thus saith the LORD that created thee, O Jacob,(African Hebrews) and he that formed thee, O Israel,(African Hebrews) Fear not: for I have redeemed thee, I have called thee by thy name; thou art mine.

2 When thou passest through the waters, I will be with thee; and through the rivers, they shall not overflow thee: when thou walkest through the fire, thou shalt not be burned; neither shall the flame kindle upon thee.

3 For I am the LORD thy God, the Holy One of Israel, thy Saviour: I gave Egypt (Africa) for thy ransom, Ethiopia and Seba for thee.

4 Since thou wast precious in my sight, thou hast been honourable, and I have loved thee: therefore will I give men for thee, and

people for thy life.

5 Fear not: for I am with thee: I will bring thy seed from the east, and gather thee from the west;

6 I will say to the north, (North America) Give up; and to the south, Keep not back: bring my sons from far, and my daughters from the ends of the earth;

7 Even every one that is called by my name: for I have created him for my glory, I have formed him; yea, I have made him.

(Isaiah 43:1-7).

712/3510

Isaiah 43:8-13. The African Children of Israel are GOD's only witnesses that "there is only One GOD", and that God is our saviour, and no one else.

8 Bring forth the blind people that have eyes, and the deaf that have ears.

9 Let all the nations be gathered together, and let the people be assembled: who among them can declare this, and shew us former things? let them bring forth their witnesses, that they may be justified: or let them hear, and say, It is truth.

10 Ye are my witnesses, saith the LORD, and my servant whom I have chosen: that ye may know and believe me, and understand that I am he: before me there was no God formed, neither shall there be after me.

11 I, even I, am the LORD; and beside me there is no saviour.

12 I have declared, and have saved, and I have shewed, when there was no strange god among you: therefore ye are my witnesses, saith the LORD, that I am God.

13 Yea, before the day was I am he; and there is none that can deliver out of my hand: I will work, and who shall let it?

(Isaiah 43:8-13).

712/3510

Isaiah 43:15-21. The African Children of Israel will shew forth GOD's praise when GOD does HIS 'new thing'.

15 I am the LORD, your Holy One, the creator of Israel, (African Hebrews) your King.

16 Thus saith the LORD, which maketh a way in the sea, and a path in the mighty waters;

17 Which bringeth forth the chariot and horse, the army and the power; they shall lie down together, they shall not rise: they are extinct, they are quenched as tow.

18 Remember ye not the former things, neither consider the things of old.

19 Behold, I will do a new thing; now it shall spring forth; shall ye not know it? I will even make a way in the wilderness, and rivers in the desert.

20 The beast of the field shall honour me, the dragons and the owls: because I give waters in the wilderness, and rivers in the desert, to give drink to my people, (African Hebrews) my chosen.

21 This people have I formed for myself; they shall shew forth my praise.

(Isaiah 43:15-21).

712/3510

Isaiah 43:22-28 . God's appeal to the African Children of Israel for honor, and explains why HE punished and cursed them.

22 But thou hast not called upon me, O Jacob;(African Hebrews) but thou hast been weary of me, O Israel. (African Hebrews)

23 Thou hast not brought me the small cattle of thy burnt offerings; neither hast thou honoured me with thy sacrifices. I have not caused thee to serve with an offering, nor wearied thee with incense.

24 Thou hast bought me no sweet cane with money, neither hast thou filled me with the fat of thy sacrifices: but thou hast made me to serve with thy sins, thou hast wearied me with thine iniquities.

25 I, even I, am he that blotteth out thy transgressions for mine own sake, and will not remember thy sins.

26 Put me in remembrance: let us plead together: declare thou, that thou mayest be justified.

27 Thy first father hath sinned, and thy teachers have transgressed against me.

28 Therefore I have profaned the princes of the sanctuary, and have given Jacob to the curse, and Israel to reproaches.

(Isaiah 43:22-28).

712/3510

Isaiah Chapter 44:1-20. GOD speaking to the many 'false' religions.

1 Yet now hear, O Jacob (African Hebrews) my servant; and Israel,(African Hebrews) whom I have chosen:

2 Thus saith the LORD that made thee, and formed thee from the womb, which will help thee; Fear not, O Jacob, my servant; and thou, Jesurun, whom I have chosen.

3 For I will pour water upon him that is thirsty, and floods upon the dry ground: I will pour my spirit upon thy seed, and my blessing upon thine offspring:

4 And they shall spring up as among the grass, as willows by the water courses.

5 One shall say, I am the LORD'S; and another shall call himself by the name of Jacob; and another shall subscribe with his hand unto the LORD, and surname himself by the name of Israel.

6 Thus saith the LORD the King of Israel, and his redeemer the LORD of hosts; I am the first, and I am the last; and beside me there is no God.

7 And who, as I, shall call, and shall declare it, and set it in order for me, since I appointed the ancient people? and the things that are coming, and shall come, let them shew unto them.

8 Fear ye not, neither be afraid: have not I told thee from that time, and have declared it? ye are even my witnesses. Is there a God beside me? yea, there is no God; I know not any.

9 They that make a graven image are all of them vanity; and their delectable things shall not profit; and they are their own witnesses; they see not, nor know; that they may be ashamed.

10 Who hath formed a god, or molten a graven image that is profitable for nothing?

11 Behold, all his fellows shall be ashamed: and the workmen, they are of men: let them all be gathered together, let them stand up; yet they shall fear, and they shall be ashamed together.

12 The smith with the tongs both worketh in the coals, and fashioneth it with hammers, and worketh it with the strength of his arms: yea, he is hungry, and his strength faileth: he drinketh no water, and is faint.

13 The carpenter stretcheth out his rule; he marketh it out with a line; he fitteth it with planes, and he marketh it out with the compass, and maketh it after the figure of a man, according to the beauty of a man; that it may remain in the house.

14 He heweth him down cedars, and taketh the cypress and the oak, which he strengtheneth for himself among the trees of the forest: he planteth an ash, and the rain doth nourish it.

15 Then shall it be for a man to burn: for he will take thereof, and warm himself; yea, he kindleth it, and baketh bread; yea, he maketh a god, and worshippeth it; he maketh it a graven image, and falleth down thereto.

16 He burneth part thereof in the fire; with part thereof he eateth flesh; he roasteth roast, and is satisfied: yea, he warmeth himself, and saith, Aha, I am warm, I have seen the fire:

17 And the residue thereof he maketh a god, even his graven image: he falleth down unto it, and worshippeth it, and prayeth unto it, and saith, Deliver me; for thou art my god.

18 They have not known nor understood: for he hath shut their eyes, that they cannot see; and their hearts, that they cannot

understand.

19 And none considereth in his heart, neither is there knowledge nor understanding to say, I have burned part of it in the fire; yea, also I have baked bread upon the coals thereof; I have roasted flesh, and eaten it: and shall I make the residue thereof an abomination? shall I fall down to the stock of a tree?

20 He feedeth on ashes: a deceived heart hath turned him aside, that he cannot deliver his soul, nor say, Is there not a lie in my right hand?

(Isaiah 44:1-20).

712/3510

Isaiah 44:21-28. Even though GOD punished the African Children of Israel for breaking the Ten Commandments, HE will have mercy on them after they serve their 400 year punishment. (Cyrus in verse 28, refers to 'forgiveness' and 'mercy'. Cyrus was a humane person who granted the African Hebrew Israelites the right to return to their homeland, and rebuild the temple.in Ezra 1:1-5).

21 Remember these, O Jacob and Israel;(African Hebrews) for thou art my servant: I have formed thee; thou art my servant: O Israel, thou shalt not be forgotten of me.

22 I have blotted out, as a thick cloud, thy transgressions, and, as a cloud, thy sins: return unto me; for I have redeemed thee.

23 Sing, O ye heavens; for the LORD hath done it: shout, ye lower parts of the earth: break forth into singing, ye mountains, O forest, and every tree therein: for the LORD hath redeemed Jacob, and glorified himself in Israel.

24 Thus saith the LORD, thy redeemer, and he that formed thee from the womb, I am the LORD that maketh all things; that stretcheth forth the heavens alone; that spreadeth abroad the earth by myself;

25 That frustrateth the tokens of the liars, and maketh diviners mad; that turneth wise men backward, and maketh their knowledge foolish;

26 That confirmeth the word of his servant, and performeth the counsel of his messengers; that saith to Jerusalem, Thou shalt be inhabited; and to the cities of Judah, Ye shall be built, and I will raise up the decayed places thereof:

27 That saith to the deep, Be dry, and I will dry up thy rivers:

28 That saith of Cyrus, He is my shepherd, and shall perform all my pleasure: even saying to Jerusalem, Thou shalt be built; and to the temple, Thy foundation shall be laid.

(Isaiah 44:21-28).

712/3510

Isaiah 47:1-15 God explaining to 'new folks' (white folks) why HE punished 'old folks' (black folks), and what will happen to 'new folks' for beating and mistreating HIS chosen people..Babylon and Chaldeans=America and 'new folks'.

1 Come down, and sit in the dust, O virgin daughter of Babylon, (America) sit on the ground: there is no throne, O daughter of the Chaldeans:(Americans) for thou shalt no more be called tender and delicate.

2 Take the millstones, and grind meal: uncover thy locks, make bare the leg, uncover the thigh, pass over the rivers.

3 Thy nakedness shall be uncovered, yea, thy shame shall be seen: I will take vengeance, and I will not meet thee as a man.

4 As for our redeemer, the LORD of hosts is his name, the Holy One of Israel.

5 Sit thou silent, and get thee into darkness, O daughter of the Chaldeans:(Americans) for thou shalt no more be called, The lady of kingdoms.

6 I was wroth with my people, (African Hebrews) I have polluted mine inheritance, (African Hebrews) and given them into thine hand: thou didst shew them no mercy; upon the ancient (African Americans) hast thou very heavily laid thy yoke.

7 And thou saidst, I shall be a lady for ever: so that thou didst not lay these things to thy heart, neither didst remember the latter end of it.

8 Therefore hear now this, thou that art given to pleasures, that dwellest carelessly, that sayest in thine heart, I am, and none else beside me; I shall not sit as a widow, neither shall I know the loss of children:

9 But these two things shall come to thee in a moment in one day, the loss of children, and widowhood: they shall come upon thee in their perfection for the multitude of thy sorceries, and for the great abundance of thine enchantments.

10 For thou hast trusted in thy wickedness: thou hast said, None seeth me. Thy wisdom and thy knowledge, it hath perverted thee; and thou hast said in thine heart, I am, and none else beside me.

11 Therefore shall evil come upon thee; thou shalt not know from whence it riseth: and mischief shall fall upon thee; thou shalt not be able to put it off: and desolation shall come upon thee suddenly, which thou shalt not know.

12 Stand now with thine enchantments, and with the multitude of thy sorceries, wherein thou hast laboured from thy youth; if so be thou shalt be able to profit, if so be thou mayest prevail.

13 Thou art wearied in the multitude of thy counsels. Let now the astrologers, the stargazers, the monthly prognosticators, stand up, and save thee from these things that shall come upon thee.

14 Behold, they shall be as stubble; the fire shall burn them; they shall not deliver themselves from the power of the flame: there shall not be a coal to warm at, nor fire to sit before it.

15 Thus shall they be unto thee with whom thou hast laboured, even thy merchants, from thy youth: they shall wander every one to his quarter; none shall save thee.

(Isaiah 47:1-15).

712/3510

Isaiah 48:9-14...How GOD will refine the African Children of Israel, and punish America..Babylon and Chaldeans=America and 'New Folks' in vs. 14. God held back from destroying Africa the second time, because HE was determined that the Children of Israel would fulfill their mission. But the African Hebrews broke the Ten Commandments while in Africa. This is why GOD had to create 'new folks' and place 'old folks' in America for 400 years. In verse 10, GOD defines America as, 'the furnace of affliction'. God said, HE placed the Africa Hebrew Israelites in America to be refined. In other words, GOD wants to see if Israel can keep HIS Ten Commandments while living in a land that defiles GOD's Commandments.

9 For my name's sake will I defer mine anger, and for my praise will I refrain for thee, that I cut thee not off.

10 Behold, I have refined thee, but not with silver; I have chosen thee in the furnace of affliction. (America, the 'melting pot')

11 For mine own sake, even for mine own sake, will I do it: for how should my name be polluted? and I will not give my glory unto another.

12 Hearken unto me, O Jacob and Israel,(African Hebrews) my called; I am he; I am the first, I also am the last.

13 Mine hand also hath laid the foundation of the earth, and my right hand hath spanned the heavens: when I call unto them, they stand up together.

14 All ye, assemble yourselves, and hear; which among them hath declared these things? The LORD hath loved him: he will do his pleasure on Babylon,(America) and his arm shall be on the Chaldeans.(Americans)

(Isaiah 48:9-14).

712/3510

Isaiah 48:20...What the African Children of Israel must do to prove themselves to GOD.Babylon & Chaldeans= America and 'new folks'. The time is coming when African-Americans must seperate themselves from the way of 'new folks'. The African Hebrews must become a nation of people again as they were when they were in Africa. This is necessary because GOD is preparing to visit America soon, and unless the Children of Israel are assembled in the land that GOD's prophet purchased for them, they will perish along with many people who are violating the Ten Commandments of GOD.

20 Go ye forth of Babylon, (America) flee ye from the Chaldeans, (new folks) with a voice of singing declare ye, tell this, utter it even to the end of the earth; say ye, The LORD hath redeemed his servant Jacob. (African Hebrews)

(Isaiah 48:20).

712/3510

Isaiah 49:13-16..GOD has not forgotten HIS chosen people. Many 'old folks' (black folks) feel that there is no GOD because of the abuse that they have suffered since GOD place them in America for 400 years. Many 'old folks' feel that they will always be the 'underdog' on earth, and that they will get their reward in heaven. This is what the African Hebrews were taught when GOD placed them in American Slavery almost 400 years ago. The African-American must learn and remember that GOD placed them in America for a specific period of time..400 years, then they will be delivered by GOD 'only', from the 'furnace of affliction. (America)

13 Sing, O heavens; and be joyful, O earth; and break forth into singing, O mountains: for the LORD hath comforted his people, and will have mercy upon his afflicted.

14 But Zion (African Hebrews) said, The LORD hath forsaken me, and my Lord hath forgotten me.

15 Can a woman forget her sucking child, that she should not have compassion on the son of her womb? yea, they may forget, yet will I not forget thee.

16 Behold, I have graven thee upon the palms of my hands; thy walls are continually before me.

(Isaiah 49:13-16).

'VITAL'

Don't forget to refer often to, Genesis 15:13-14. Here we find GOD telling the African Prophet Abraham that the African Hebrew would serve America for 400 years, and what will happen when the 400 years are over. We better prepare ourselves folks, because GOD is just about ready to perform HIS mighty, terrible, strange acts. The 400 captivity for Israel is just about over, and GOD hasn't forgotten: (Isaiah 19:25)

* The African Hebrew Israelites - HIS inheritance,
* Gentile "old folks"--HIS people, or
* New folks - the work of HIS hands.

We all will get what GOD has promised.

712/3510

<u>Isaiah 49:22-26..How God will punish America, and cause the 'new folks' to worship at the African Hebrew's feet.</u> God will destroy the American way of life, and give the world a 'new standard' to live by. This 'new standard' will be governed by the African Hebrew Israelites, who are GOD's chosen people.

22 Thus saith the Lord GOD, Behold, I will lift up mine hand to the Gentiles, and set up my standard (TEN COMMANDMENTS) to the people: and they shall bring thy sons in their arms, and thy daughters shall be carried upon their shoulders.

23 And kings shall be thy nursing fathers, and their queens thy nursing mothers: they shall bow down to thee with their face toward the earth, and lick up the dust of thy feet; and thou shalt know that I am the LORD: for they shall not be ashamed that wait for me.

24 Shall the prey be taken from the mighty, or the lawful captive delivered?

25 But thus saith the LORD, Even the captives of the mighty shall be taken away, and the prey of the terrible shall be delivered: for I will contend with him that contendeth with thee, and I will save thy children.

26 And I will feed them that oppress thee with their own flesh; and they shall be drunken with their own blood, as with sweet wine: and all flesh shall know that I the LORD am thy Saviour and thy Redeemer, the mighty One of Jacob.

(Isaiah 49:22-26).

712/3510

Isaiah 51:17-23...GOD shewing us what HE will do to America after the African Children of Israel serves their 400 years...(Jerusalem=the African Hebrews. God will deliver and comfort the Children of Israel, and give the 'cup of trembling' to America and 'new folks' for their wickedness and evil ways.

17 Awake, awake, stand up, O Jerusalem, (African Hebrews) which hast drunk at the hand of the LORD the cup of his fury; thou hast drunken the dregs of the cup of trembling, and wrung them out.

18 There is none to guide her among all the sons whom she hath brought forth; neither is there any that taketh her by the hand of all the sons that she hath brought up.

19 These two things are come unto thee; who shall be sorry for thee? desolation, and destruction, and the famine, and the sword: by whom shall I comfort thee?

20 Thy sons have fainted, they lie at the head of all the streets, as a wild bull in a net: they are full of the fury of the LORD, the rebuke of thy God.

21 Therefore hear now this, thou afflicted, and drunken, but not with wine:

22 Thus saith thy Lord the LORD, and thy God that pleadeth the cause of his people, Behold, I have taken out of thine hand the cup of trembling, even the dregs of the cup of my fury; thou shalt no more drink it again:

23 But I will put it into the hand of them that afflict thee; which have said to thy soul, Bow down, that we may go over: and thou hast laid thy body as the ground, and as the street, to them that went over.

(Isaiah 51:17-23).

712/3510

<u>Isaiah 54:3-4...Israel to inherit the 'Gentiles.'</u> Although the African Children of Israel are small in number, and unknown to the world, GOD will cause them to rise, be known, and inherit the 'gentiles'.

3 For thou shalt break forth on the right hand and on the left; and thy seed shall inherit the Gentiles, and make the desolate cities to be inhabited.

4 Fear not; for thou shalt not be ashamed: neither be thou confounded; for thou shalt not be put to shame: for thou shalt forget the shame of thy youth, and shalt not remember the reproach of thy widowhood any more.

(Isaiah 54:3-4).

712/3510

<u>Isaiah 54:7-17...God will not forsake Israel forever.</u> The 400 years that Israel must serve in America must seem like forever, but unto GOD it is but a small moment. GOD won't be angry with Israel forever. Israel and 'gentile old folks' must understand that they are being punished for not keeping GOD's Ten Commandments, and unless they start keeping GOD's Commandments, it's going to be very difficult until they complete the 400 year captivity. The oppressed will be comforted, everyone will learn the 'TRUE' word of GOD, and there will be 'peace' in the earth. Once the African Children of Israel establishes themselves in righteousness, oppression, fear and terror will cease. Israel's reward for righteousness will be so great, that people will envy them and turn against them. People will gather themselves against the African Hebrew Israelites, but GOD will cause their weapons to fail.

7 For a small moment have I forsaken thee; but with great mercies will I gather thee.

8 In a little wrath I hid my face from thee for a moment; but with everlasting kindness will I have mercy on thee, saith the LORD thy Redeemer.

9 For this is as the waters of Noah unto me: for as I have sworn that

the waters of Noah should no more go over the earth; so have I sworn that I would not be wroth with thee, nor rebuke thee.

10 For the mountains shall depart, and the hills be removed; but my kindness shall not depart from thee, neither shall the covenant of my peace be removed, saith the LORD that hath mercy on thee.

11 O thou afflicted, tossed with tempest, and not comforted, behold, I will lay thy stones with fair colours, and lay thy foundations with sapphires.

12 And I will make thy windows of agates, and thy gates of carbuncles, and all thy borders of pleasant stones.

13 And all thy children shall be taught of the LORD; and great shall be the peace of thy children.

14 In righteousness shalt thou be established: thou shalt be far from oppression; for thou shalt not fear: and from terror; for it shall not come near thee.

15 Behold, they shall surely gather together, but not by me: whosoever shall gather together against thee shall fall for thy sake.

16 Behold, I have created the smith that bloweth the coals in the fire, and that bringeth forth an instrument for his work; and I have created the waster to destroy.

17 No weapon that is formed against thee shall prosper; and every tongue that shall rise against thee in judgment thou shalt condemn. This is the heritage of the servants of the LORD, and their righteousness is of me, saith the LORD.

(Isaiah 54:7-17).

712/3510

<u>Isaiah 55...God's plan of life must be fulfilled through the Children of Israel=(David)</u>. Every 'so-called' religion today feels that it is 'correct', but each one will find that it is 'wrong'. In Revelation Chapters 1, 2 and 3, you will find GOD performing an evaluation on the 7 most prominent religions. Can you identify yours? When you find it, you will find that according to GOD, it's not perfect. Moreover, it may not even be acceptable. Out

of the 7, you will find that there is one that is acceptable in the sight of GOD.....that one is the African Children of Israel, who are evaluated in Rev. 3:7-10. Isn't the "Philadelphia' paradox interesting in verse 7? Philadelphia was a landmark location' for the African Children of Israel when GOD re-established them in America in the year 1896/5656. In the whole Chapter of Isaiah 55, God is exhorting the 'gentiles' to seek HIM through the African Children of Israel (David). The day is upon us when all will know, that the only way to 'salvation', 'freedom', and 'mercy', is through the 'Children of Israel'. Everyone must understand and remember that GOD chose "ISRAEL", the African Hebrew Israelites, to be HIS 'witness' to the people', thousands of years ago, and GOD never changes HIS plan. GOD's word will never go forth without accomplishing the things that HE planned. When GOD redeems the Children of Israel, many nations will flow unto them, searching for the 'TRUE' worship to GOD, and for refuge. Look around you....can't you see GOD's spirit of judgement closing in?. It is time for us to come to the end of ourselves, and acknowledge the fact that, without the 'TRUE' word of GOD, we 'wander in darkness'.

1 Ho, every one that thirsteth, come ye to the waters, and he that hath no money; come ye, buy, and eat; yea, come, buy wine and milk without money and without price.

2 Wherefore do ye spend money for that which is not bread? and your labour for that which satisfieth not? hearken diligently unto me, and eat ye that which is good, and let your soul delight itself in fatness.

3 Incline your ear, and come unto me: hear, and your soul shall live; and I will make an everlasting covenant with you, even the sure mercies of David.

4 Behold, I have given him for a witness to the people, a leader and commander to the people.

5 Behold, thou shalt call a nation that thou knowest not, and nations that knew not thee shall run unto thee because of the LORD thy God, and for the Holy One of Israel; for he hath glorified thee.

6 Seek ye the LORD while he may be found, call ye upon him while he is near:

7 Let the wicked forsake his way, and the unrighteous man his thoughts: and let him return unto the LORD, and he will have mercy upon him; and to our God, for he will abundantly pardon.

8 For my thoughts are not your thoughts, neither are your ways my ways, saith the LORD.

9 For as the heavens are higher than the earth, so are my ways higher than your ways, and my thoughts than your thoughts.

10 For as the rain cometh down, and the snow from heaven, and returneth not thither, but watereth the earth, and maketh it bring forth and bud, that it may give seed to the sower, and bread to the eater:

11 So shall my word be that goeth forth out of my mouth: it shall not return unto me void, but it shall accomplish that which I please, and it shall prosper in the thing whereto I sent it.

12 For ye shall go out with joy, and be led forth with peace: the mountains and the hills shall break forth before you into singing, and all the trees of the field shall clap their hands.

13 Instead of the thorn shall come up the fir tree, and instead of the brier shall come up the myrtle tree: and it shall be to the LORD for a name, for an everlasting sign that shall not be cut off.

(Isaiah 55:1-13).

712/3510

Isaiah 56:1-8...GOD's Sabbath is the 7th Day... Constantine, Emperor of Rome changed GOD's Sabbath from Saturday to Sunday in 321 A.D., in order to gain political power. This change has caused many people to go astray, and has affected the balance of GOD's 'universal law'. The whole earth is in a state of discord and chaos, the curse of GOD's judgement is in every land, people are hopeless, hurting, and helplessly searching for 'grief relief'. It is all because people are not keeping the TEN COMMANDMENTS, especially the FOURTH COMMANDMENT. The 7th day of the week (Commonly Called Saturday) is the Sabbath of The Lord Thy God. We learn from the bible that we must cease from all work refrain from all our pleasures, and honor and worship God on this, God's Holy

Day. The Sabbath is in memory of God's great creative work--the Heavens and the Earth--the Seas, and all that is in them, including the whole Universe. The Almighty God, therefore, commands all mankind to pause and give respect unto the Creator and It's Creation. God's creation is the greatest of all It's works. When we pause on God's Sabbath Day (Saturday), We honor God and at the same time celebrate It's Creation. Some people may say "It is the Jewish Sabbath, therefore I am not dutybound to keep it". Well, the Sabbath was established long before there ever was a Jew on earth. For if the Sabbath Commandment is Jewish, then, "Thou shalt not steal", and Thou shalt not kill," etc,. would also have to be "Jewish". Nowhere in the Scripture is it referred to as "the Jewish Sabbath," but always as the "the Sabbath of the Lord thy God." Sunday as a day of rest and worship was signed into law by Constantine, Emperor of Rome, in the year 321 C.E. (A.D.) after Rome had become a world power. It was punishable by death if anyone was found observing Saturday (the Sabbath that Jesus taught) as a day of rest. We must remember that by the time Constantine came into power, Jesus had already made his impact on the people with his teachings of God's Commandmentrs. (St Matt. 5:17) Constantine's change of the Sabbath from Saturday to Sunday was his attempt to established power over the people. Over a period of hundreds of years, millions were murdered at Rome, in Palestine and throughout many other parts of the then known world for keeping the Sabbath on Saturday, which violated the decree of the Emperor. In order to keep all TEN COMMANDMENTS, we must keep the FOURTH. We can keep nine of them six days a week, but we can't keep the FOURTH until Saturday, which is the 7th day, which is GOD's HOLY SABBATH DAY. NOT SUNDAY--THE 1ST DAY. Mankind has, and is continually upsetting the balance of 'nature' by not keeping the TEN COMMANDMENTS, especially the FOURTH COMMANDMENT.

1 Thus saith the LORD, Keep ye judgment, and do justice: for my salvation is near to come, and my righteousness to be revealed.

2 Blessed is the man that doeth this, and the son of man that layeth hold on it; that keepeth the sabbath from polluting it, and keepeth his hand from doing any evil.

3 Neither let the son of the stranger, that hath joined himself to the LORD, speak, saying, The LORD hath utterly separated me from his people: neither let the eunuch say, Behold, I am a dry tree.

4 For thus saith the LORD unto the eunuchs that keep my sabbaths, and choose the things that please me, and take hold of my covenant;

5 Even unto them will I give in mine house and within my walls a place and a name better than of sons and of daughters: I will give them an everlasting name, that shall not be cut off.

6 Also the sons of the stranger, that join themselves to the LORD, to serve him, and to love the name of the LORD, to be his servants, every one that keepeth the sabbath from polluting it, and taketh hold of my covenant;

7 Even them will I bring to my holy mountain, and make them joyful in my house of prayer: their burnt offerings and their sacrifices shall be accepted upon mine altar; for mine house shall be called an house of prayer for all people.

8 The Lord GOD which gathereth the outcasts of Israel saith, Yet will I gather others to him, beside those that are gathered unto him.

(Isaiah 56:1-8).

712/3510

Isaiah 56:10-12...Most Ministers are not teaching GOD's TRUTH. **God is very displeased with the Ministers that are leading HIS people in darkness. These couple of verses express GOD's disturbance. There will be more references later expressing GOD's discontent with all of the 'preachers', pastors, and 'ministers', that are leading GOD's people astray.**

10 His watchmen (Ministers) are blind: they are all ignorant, they are all dumb dogs, they cannot bark; sleeping, lying down, loving to slumber.

11 Yea, they are greedy dogs which can never have enough, and they are shepherds that cannot understand: they all look to their own way, every one for his gain, from his quarter.

12 Come ye, say they, I will fetch wine, and we will fill ourselves with strong drink; and to morrow shall be as this day, and much more abundant.

(Isaiah 56:10-12).

710/3512

<u>Micah Chapter 3 .</u> GOD explaining to the leaders and the heads of the African Children of Israel, while in Africa, how they caused HIS people to err.

1 And I said, Hear, I pray you, O heads of Jacob, (African Hebrew leaders and ministers) and ye princes of the house of Israel; (African Hebrews) Is it not for you to know judgment?

2 Who hate the good, and love the evil; who pluck off their skin from off them, and their flesh from off their bones;

3 Who also eat the flesh of my people, and flay their skin from off them; and they break their bones, and chop them in pieces, as for the pot, and as flesh within the caldron.

4 Then shall they cry unto the LORD, but he will not hear them: he will even hide his face from them at that time, as they have behaved themselves ill in their doings.

5 Thus saith the LORD concerning the prophets that make my people err, that bite with their teeth, and cry, Peace; and he that putteth not into their mouths, they even prepare war against him.

6 Therefore night shall be unto you, that ye shall not have a vision; and it shall be dark unto you, that ye shall not divine; and the sun shall go down over the prophets, and the day shall be dark over them.

7 Then shall the seers be ashamed, and the diviners confounded: yea, they shall all cover their lips; for there is no answer of God.

8 But truly I am full of power by the spirit of the LORD, and of judgment, and of might, to declare unto Jacob (African Hebrews) his transgression, and to Israel (African Hebrews) his sin.

9 Hear this, I pray you, ye heads of the house of Jacob, and princes of the house of Israel, that abhor judgment, and pervert all equity.

10 They build up Zion (Africa) with blood, and Jerusalem with iniquity.

11 The heads thereof judge for reward, and the priests thereof teach for hire, and the prophets thereof divine for money: yet will they lean upon the LORD, and say, Is not the LORD among us? none evil can come upon us.

12 Therefore shall Zion (Africa) for your sake be plowed as a field, and Jerusalem (Africa) shall become heaps, and the mountain of the house as the high places of the forest.

(Micah 3:1-12).

710/3512

Micah Chapter 4 How GOD will assemble the remnant of the African Children of Israel (African Americans , and how nations of people shall flow unto them.

1 But in the last days it shall come to pass, that the mountain of the house of the LORD shall be established in the top of the mountains, and it shall be exalted above the hills; and people shall flow unto it.

2 And many nations shall come, and say, Come, and let us go up to the mountain of the LORD, (African Hebrews) and to the house of the God of Jacob; and he will teach us of his ways, and we will walk in his paths: for the law shall go forth of Zion, (African Hebrews) and the word of the LORD from Jerusalem.

3 And he shall judge among many people, and rebuke strong nations afar off; and they shall beat their swords into plowshares, and their spears into pruninghooks: nation shall not lift up a sword against nation, neither shall they learn war any more.

4 But they shall sit every man under his vine and under his fig tree; and none shall make them afraid: for the mouth of the LORD of hosts hath spoken it.

5 For all people will walk every one in the name of his god, and we will walk in the name of the LORD our God for ever and ever.

6 In that day, saith the LORD, will I assemble her that halteth, and I

will gather her that is driven out, and her that I have afflicted;

7 And I will make her that halted a remnant, and her that was cast far off a strong nation: and the LORD shall reign over them in mount Zion (Africa) from henceforth, even for ever.

8 And thou, O tower of the flock, the strong hold of the daughter of Zion, (Africa) unto thee shall it come, even the first dominion; the kingdom shall come to the daughter of Jerusalem. (African Hebrews).

9 Now why dost thou cry out aloud? is there no king in thee? is thy counsellor perished? for pangs have taken thee as a woman in travail.

10 Be in pain, and labour to bring forth, O daughter of Zion, (Africa) like a woman in travail: for now shalt thou go forth out of the city, and thou shalt dwell in the field, and thou shalt go even to Babylon; (America) there shalt thou be delivered; there the LORD shall redeem thee from the hand of thine enemies.

11 Now also many nations are gathered against thee, that say, Let her be defiled, and let our eye look upon Zion. (Africa)

12 But they know not the thoughts of the LORD, neither understand they his counsel: for he shall gather them as the sheaves into the floor.

13 Arise and thresh, O daughter of Zion: (Africa) for I will make thine horn iron, and I will make thy hoofs brass: and thou shalt beat in pieces many people: and I will consecrate their gain unto the LORD, and their substance unto the Lord of the whole earth.

(Micah 4:1-13).

710/3510

Micah 5:7-9.... The African Children of Israel (Black Folks) new position in America.

7 And the remnant of Jacob (African Hebrews) shall be in the midst of many people as a dew from the LORD, as the showers upon the grass, that tarrieth not for man, nor waiteth for the sons of men.

8 And the remnant of Jacob (African Hebrews) shall be among the

Gentiles in the midst of many people as a lion among the beasts of the forest, as a young lion among the flocks of sheep: who, if he go through, both treadeth down, and teareth in pieces, and none can deliver.

9 Thine hand shall be lifted up upon thine adversaries, and all thine enemies shall be cut off.

(Micah 5:7-9).

710/3510

Micah 5:10-15 How GOD will destroy America.

10 And it shall come to pass in that day, saith the LORD, that I will cut off thy horses (Weapons) out of the midst of thee, and I will destroy thy chariots: (Weapons)

11 And I will cut off the cities of thy land, and throw down all thy strong holds:

12 And I will cut off witchcrafts out of thine hand; and thou shalt have no more soothsayers:

13 Thy graven images also will I cut off, and thy standing images out of the midst of thee; and thou shalt no more worship the work of thine hands.

14 And I will pluck up thy groves out of the midst of thee: so will I destroy thy cities.

15 And I will execute vengeance in anger and fury upon the heathen, such as they have not heard.

(Micah 5:10-15).

710/3510

Micah Chapter 6 GOD pleading with the Children of Israel before HE placed HIS wrath upon them.

1 Hear ye now what the LORD saith; Arise, contend thou before the mountains, and let the hills hear thy voice.

2 Hear ye, O mountains, the LORD'S controversy, and ye strong foundations of the earth: for the LORD hath a controversy with

his people, and he will plead with Israel.

3 O my people, what have I done unto thee? and wherein have I wearied thee? testify against me.

4 For I brought thee up out of the land of Egypt, and redeemed thee out of the house of servants; and I sent before thee Moses, Aaron, and Miriam.

5 O my people, remember now what Balak (Gentile old folks) king of Moab consulted, and what Balaam the son of Beor answered him from Shittim unto Gilgal; that ye may know the righteousness of the LORD.

6 Wherewith shall I come before the LORD, and bow myself before the high God? shall I come before him with burnt offerings, with calves of a year old?

7 Will the LORD be pleased with thousands of rams, or with ten thousands of rivers of oil? shall I give my firstborn for my transgression, the fruit of my body for the sin of my soul?

8 He hath shewed thee, O man, what is good; and what doth the LORD require of thee, but to do justly, and to love mercy, and to walk humbly with thy God?

9 The LORD'S voice crieth unto the city, and the man of wisdom shall see thy name: hear ye the rod, and who hath appointed it.

10 Are there yet the treasures of wickedness in the house of the wicked, and the scant measure that is abominable?

11 Shall I count them pure with the wicked balances, and with the bag of deceitful weights?

12 For the rich men thereof are full of violence, and the inhabitants thereof have spoken lies, and their tongue is deceitful in their mouth.

13 Therefore also will I make thee sick in smiting thee, in making thee desolate because of thy sins.

14 Thou shalt eat, but not be satisfied; and thy casting down shall be in the midst of thee; and thou shalt take hold, but shalt not deliver; and that which thou deliverest will I give up to the sword.

15 Thou shalt sow, but thou shalt not reap; thou shalt tread the olives, but thou shalt not anoint thee with oil; and sweet wine, but shalt not drink wine.

16 For the statutes of Omri (The 6th African Hebrew king) are kept, and all the works of the house of Ahab,(Son of King Omri) and ye walk in their counsels; that I should make thee a desolation, and the inhabitants thereof an hissing: therefore ye shall bear the reproach of my people.

(Micah 6:1-16).

710/3510

Micah 7:15-20 How GOD will shew the world that the African Children of Israel (African Americans) are HIS chosen people.

15 According to the days of thy coming out of the land of Egypt will I shew unto him marvellous things.

16 The nations shall see and be confounded at all their might: they shall lay their hand upon their mouth, their ears shall be deaf.

17 They shall lick the dust like a serpent, they shall move out of their holes like worms of the earth: they shall be afraid of the LORD our God, and shall fear because of thee.

18 Who is a God like unto thee, that pardoneth iniquity, and passeth by the transgression of the remnant of his heritage? he retaineth not his anger for ever, because he delighteth in mercy.

19 He will turn again, he will have compassion upon us; he will subdue our iniquities; and thou wilt cast all their sins into the depths of the sea.

20 Thou wilt perform the truth to Jacob, (African Hebrews) and the mercy to Abraham, which thou hast sworn unto our fathers from the days of old.

(Micah 7:15-20).

700/3522

This is the timeframe for the book of 'PROVERBS'.

698/3524

Isaiah 57:16-21..GOD will not be mad at Israel forever. Although GOD withdrew Himself from the African Hebrew Israelites (African Americans) for 400 years, God will not hide Himself forever. GOD is still close enough to see and judge what they are doing in their daily lives. GOD knows that most folks are living wrong because there is no TRUE understanding of GOD's word being taught in the churches. The world is upside down because the African Hebrew Israelites forsook their 'mission'. GOD punished them, created 'new folks' to afflict them, and placed them on the bottom of life for 400 years. The time has finally come when GOD will forgive the Children of Israel for their sins, and will comfort their ways, and lead them back to AFRICA.

16 For I will not contend for ever, neither will I be always wroth: for the spirit should fail before me, and the souls which I have made.

17 For the iniquity of his covetousness was I wroth, and smote him: (African Hebrews) I hid me, and was wroth, and he went on frowardly in the way of his heart.

18 I have seen his ways, and will heal him: I will lead him also, and restore comforts unto him and to his mourners.

19 I create the fruit of the lips; Peace, peace to him that is far off, and to him that is near, saith the LORD; and I will heal him.

20 But the wicked are like the troubled sea, when it cannot rest, whose waters cast up mire and dirt.

21 There is no peace, saith my God, to the wicked.

(Isaiah 57:16-21).

698/3524

Isaiah 58:13-14.. How to keep GOD's Sabbath Day 'holy', and the reward for keeping the Sabbath. GOD never changed HIS Sabbath from Saturday to Sunday. This was done by man, and man will surely have to pay. That's why in most cities, there is a church sitting on every corner, stretching to the sky, but the streets of America, and the condition of the whole world is getting worse. This is because 'false' doctrine is being taught and preached in the churches, instead of GOD's Commandments, especially GOD's SABBATH.

13 If thou turn away thy foot from the sabbath, from doing thy pleasure on my holy day; and call the sabbath a delight, the holy of the LORD, honourable; and shalt honour him, not doing thine own ways, nor finding thine own pleasure, nor speaking thine own words:

14 Then shalt thou delight thyself in the LORD; and I will cause thee to ride upon the high places of the earth, and feed thee with the heritage of Jacob thy father: for the mouth of the LORD hath spoken it.

(Isaiah 58:13-14).

698/3524

Isaiah Chapter 59---Why African Americans are doing so bad in America. Although GOD placed the African people in America for 400 years, they further their affliction by not keeping GOD's TEN COMMANDMENTS. Chapter 59 explains why the African Americans are being oppressed, and why they are without unity.

1 Behold, the LORD'S hand is not shortened, that it cannot save; neither his ear heavy, that it cannot hear:

2 But your iniquities have separated between you and your God, and your sins have hid his face from you, that he will not hear.

3 For your hands are defiled with blood, and your fingers with iniquity; your lips have spoken lies, your tongue hath muttered perverseness.

4 None calleth for justice, nor any pleadeth for truth: they trust in vanity, and speak lies; they conceive mischief, and bring forth iniquity.

5 They hatch cockatrice' eggs, and weave the spider's web: he that eateth of their eggs dieth, and that which is crushed breaketh out into a viper.

6 Their webs shall not become garments, neither shall they cover themselves with their works: their works are works of iniquity,

and the act of violence is in their hands.

7 Their feet run to evil, and they make haste to shed innocent blood: their thoughts are thoughts of iniquity; wasting and destruction are in their paths.

8 The way of peace they know not; and there is no judgment in their goings: they have made them crooked paths: whosoever goeth therein shall not know peace.

9 Therefore is judgment far from us, neither doth justice overtake us: we wait for light, but behold obscurity; for brightness, but we walk in darkness.

10 We grope for the wall like the blind, and we grope as if we had no eyes: we stumble at noonday as in the night; we are in desolate places as dead men.

11 We roar all like bears, and mourn sore like doves: we look for judgment, but there is none; for salvation, but it is far off from us.

12 For our transgressions are multiplied before thee, and our sins testify against us: for our transgressions are with us; and as for our iniquities, we know them;

13 In transgressing and lying against the LORD, and departing away from our God, speaking oppression and revolt, conceiving and uttering from the heart words of falsehood.

14 And judgment is turned away backward, and justice standeth afar off: for truth is fallen in the street, and equity cannot enter.

15 Yea, truth faileth; and he that departeth from evil maketh himself a prey: and the LORD saw it, and it displeased him that there was no judgment.

16 And he saw that there was no man, and wondered that there was no intercessor: therefore his arm brought salvation unto him; and his righteousness, it sustained him.

17 For he put on righteousness as a breastplate, and an helmet of salvation upon his head; and he put on the garments of vengeance for clothing, and was clad with zeal as a cloke.

18 According to their deeds, accordingly he will repay, fury to his adversaries, recompence to his enemies; to the islands he will repay recompence.

19 So shall they fear the name of the LORD from the west, and his glory from the rising of the sun. When the enemy shall come in like a flood, the Spirit of the LORD shall lift up a standard against him.

20 And the Redeemer shall come to Zion, (African Hebrews) and unto them that turn from transgression in Jacob, (African Hebrews) saith the LORD.

21 As for me, this is my covenant with them, saith the LORD; My spirit that is upon thee, and my words which I have put in thy mouth, shall not depart out of thy mouth, nor out of the mouth of thy seed, nor out of the mouth of thy seed's seed, saith the LORD, from henceforth and for ever.

(Isaiah 59:1-21).

698/3524

<u>Isaiah Chapter 60.. All nations will serve the African Children of Israel.</u> Once again, GOD is shewing us that although HE punished the African Americans, HE will return, deliver them, and cause all nations to serve them.

1 Arise, shine; for thy light is come, and the glory of the LORD is risen upon thee. (African Hebrews)

2 For, behold, the darkness shall cover the earth, and gross darkness the people: but the LORD shall arise upon thee, and his glory shall be seen upon thee.

3 And the Gentiles shall come to thy light, and kings to the brightness of thy rising.

4 Lift up thine eyes round about, and see: all they gather themselves together, they come to thee: thy sons shall come from far, and thy daughters shall be nursed at thy side.

5 Then thou shalt see, and flow together, and thine heart shall fear, and be enlarged; because the abundance of the sea shall be converted

unto thee, the forces of the Gentiles shall come unto thee.

6 The multitude of camels shall cover thee, the dromedaries of Midian (A land named after the son of Abraham by Keturah) and Ephah; all they from Sheba shall come: they shall bring gold and incense; and they shall shew forth the praises of the LORD.

7 All the flocks of Kedar (One of the sons of the Muslim-Ishmael) shall be gathered together unto thee, (African Hebrews) the rams of Nebaioth (Son of Ishmael) shall minister unto thee: they shall come up with acceptance on mine altar, and I will glorify the house of my glory.

8 Who are these that fly as a cloud, and as the doves to their windows?

9 Surely the isles shall wait for me, and the ships of Tarshish (A son of Javan, great-grandson of Noah) first, to bring thy sons from far, their silver and their gold with them, unto the name of the LORD thy God, and to the Holy One of Israel, because he hath glorified thee.

10 And the sons of strangers shall build up thy walls, and their kings shall minister unto thee: for in my wrath I smote thee, but in my favour have I had mercy on thee.

11 Therefore thy gates shall be open continually; they shall not be shut day nor night; that men may bring unto thee the forces of the Gentiles, and that their kings may be brought.

12 For the nation and kingdom that will not serve thee shall perish; yea, those nations shall be utterly wasted.

13 The glory of Lebanon shall come unto thee, the fir tree, the pine tree, and the box together, to beautify the place of my sanctuary; and I will make the place of my feet glorious.

14 The sons also of them that afflicted thee shall come bending unto thee; and all they that despised thee shall bow themselves down at the soles of thy feet; and they shall call thee, The city of the LORD, The Zion of the Holy One of Israel.

15 Whereas thou hast been forsaken and hated, so that no man went through thee, I will make thee an eternal excellency, a joy of many

generations.

16 Thou shalt also suck the milk of the Gentiles, and shalt suck the breast of kings: and thou shalt know that I the LORD am thy Saviour and thy Redeemer, the mighty One of Jacob.

17 For brass I will bring gold, and for iron I will bring silver, and for wood brass, and for stones iron: I will also make thy officers peace, and thine exactors righteousness.

18 Violence shall no more be heard in thy land, wasting nor destruction within thy borders; but thou shalt call thy walls Salvation, and thy gates Praise.

19 The sun shall be no more thy light by day; neither for brightness shall the moon give light unto thee: but the LORD shall be unto thee an everlasting light, and thy God thy glory.

20 Thy sun shall no more go down; neither shall thy moon withdraw itself: for the LORD shall be thine everlasting light, and the days of thy mourning shall be ended.

21 Thy people also shall be all righteous: they shall inherit the land for ever, the branch of my planting, the work of my hands, that I may be glorified.

22 A little one shall become a thousand, and a small one a strong nation: I the LORD will hasten it in his time.

(Isaiah 60:1-22).

698/3524

Isaiah 61:4-11---The African Children of Israel shall have 'double' for their shame. Shame, Shame, Shame. There is no other way to describe the horrors that African people have experienced since GOD placed them in America. GOD will revenge the 'oppressor' for their evil against Israel, and GOD will give Israel, 'double' for their shame. The whole world will also acknowledge the fact that, ISRAEL ('black folks -the African Hebrew) are the 'chosen' people of GOD.

4 And they (African Hebrews) shall build the old wastes, they shall raise up the former desolations, and they shall repair the waste

cities, the desolations of many generations.

5 And strangers (new folks) shall stand and feed your flocks, and the sons of the alien (new folks) shall be your plowmen and your vinedressers.

6 But ye (African Hebrews) shall be named the Priests of the LORD: men shall call you the Ministers of our God: ye shall eat the riches of the Gentiles, and in their glory shall ye boast yourselves.

7 For your shame ye shall have double; and for confusion they shall rejoice in their portion: therefore in their land they shall possess the double: everlasting joy shall be unto them.

8 For I the LORD love judgment, I hate robbery for burnt offering; and I will direct their work in truth, and I will make an everlasting covenant with them.

9 And their seed shall be known among the Gentiles, and their offspring among the people: all that see them shall acknowledge them, that they are the seed which the LORD hath blessed.

10 I will greatly rejoice in the LORD, my soul shall be joyful in my God; for he hath clothed me with the garments of salvation, he hath covered me with the robe of righteousness, as a bridegroom decketh himself with ornaments, and as a bride adorneth herself with her jewels.

11 For as the earth bringeth forth her bud, and as the garden causeth the things that are sown in it to spring forth; so the Lord GOD will cause righteousness and praise to spring forth before all the nations.

(Isaiah 61:4-11).

698/3524

Isaiah Chapter 62..Israel, no more forsaken. The African Hebrew, or African American has been regarded as the 'dregs of civilization', from the first day GOD placed them in America. 'Old folks' were not even considered 'human beings' when America formed it's Constitution. This is why each time the African American (Old Folks) complain about injustice, the White House has to revise the Constitution to fit them in. But those days are just about over. In

Chapter 62, GOD is shewing us that after the African Hebrews serves their 400 year affliction in America, GOD will have mercy on them and redeem them. GOD will take the 'slave names' from the African Americans, and shew the whole world that the Children of Israel are HIS chosen people. (Heph-zi-bah in verse 4, was the mother of the African King Manasseh; 2 Kings 21:1 Beulah in verse 4, means "married"...Spiritually, the land of Africa was married to the GOD-Spirit because it was the first land of 'creation'. Beulah is referenced in this verse to shew how Africa will be re-married to GOD when 'old folks" are returned to Africa after their 400 years in America.)

1 For Zion's (African Hebrews) sake will I not hold my peace, and for Jerusalem's (African Hebrews) sake I will not rest, until the righteousness thereof go forth as brightness, and the salvation thereof as a lamp that burneth.

2 And the Gentiles shall see thy righteousness, and all kings thy glory: and thou shalt be called by a new name, which the mouth of the LORD shall name.

3 Thou shalt also be a crown of glory in the hand of the LORD, and a royal diadem in the hand of thy God.

4 Thou shalt no more be termed Forsaken; neither shall thy land any more be termed Desolate: but thou shalt be called Hephzibah, and thy land Beulah: for the LORD delighteth in thee, and thy land shall be married.

5 For as a young man marrieth a virgin, so shall thy sons marry thee: and as the bridegroom rejoiceth over the bride, so shall thy God rejoice over thee.

6 I have set watchmen upon thy walls, O Jerusalem, which shall never hold their peace day nor night: ye that make mention of the LORD, keep not silence,

7 And give him no rest, till he establish, and till he make Jerusalem a praise in the earth.

8 The LORD hath sworn by his right hand, and by the arm of his strength, Surely I will no more give thy corn to be meat for thine enemies; and the sons of the stranger (new folks) shall not drink thy wine, for the which thou hast laboured:

9 But they that have gathered it shall eat it, and praise the LORD; and they that have brought it together shall drink it in the courts of my holiness.

10 Go through, go through the gates; prepare ye the way of the people; cast up, cast up the highway; gather out the stones; lift up a standard for the people.

11 Behold, the LORD hath proclaimed unto the end of the world, Say ye to the daughter of Zion, Behold, thy salvation cometh; behold, his reward is with him, and his work before him.

12 And they shall call them, The holy people, The redeemed of the LORD: and thou shalt be called, Sought out, A city not forsaken.

(Isaiah 62:1-12).

698/3524

Isaiah 65:8-25...Israel's (Black Folks) new home. GOD is explaining what will take place when HE delivers the Children of Israel from America. GOD will join them with their brothers and sisters in Africa (Judah), and no more will they live in fear because of 'new folks'.

8 Thus saith the LORD, As the new wine is found in the cluster, and one saith, Destroy it not; for a blessing is in it: so will I do for my servants' sakes, that I may not destroy them all.

9 And I will bring forth a seed out of Jacob,(African Hebrews) and out of Judah (African Hebrews) an inheritor of my mountains: and mine elect shall inherit it, and my servants shall dwell there.

10 And Sharon (A coastal plain in Africa noted for it's fertility, paturage and beauty) shall be a fold of flocks, and the valley of Achor (This valley was named after Achan.. Achan's story is in Joshua Chapter 7. He broke the Ten Commandments of GOD by 'stealing', which cursed the African Hebrews. He and all that belonged to him was stoned to death. If you read the story in Joshua Chapter 7, you ;may get an appreciation of the power of GOD's Ten Commandments) a place for the herds to lie down in, for my people that have sought me.

11 But ye are they that forsake the LORD,(Gentiles) that forget my holy mountain, that prepare a table for that troop, and that furnish the drink offering unto that number.

12 Therefore will I number you to the sword, and ye shall all bow down to the slaughter: because when I called, ye did not answer; when I spake, ye did not hear; but did evil before mine eyes, and did choose that wherein I delighted not.

13 Therefore thus saith the Lord GOD, Behold, my servants shall eat, but ye shall be hungry: behold, my servants shall drink, but ye shall be thirsty: behold, my servants shall rejoice, but ye shall be ashamed:

14 Behold, my servants shall sing for joy of heart, but ye shall cry for sorrow of heart, and shall howl for vexation of spirit.

15 And ye (Gentiles) shall leave your name for a curse unto my chosen: for the Lord GOD shall slay thee, and call his servants by another name:

16 That he who blesseth himself in the earth shall bless himself in the God of TRUTH; and he that sweareth in the earth shall swear by the God of TRUTH; because the former troubles are forgotten, and because they are hid from mine eyes.

17 For, behold, I create new heavens and a new earth: and the former shall not be remembered, nor come into mind.

18 But be ye glad and rejoice for ever in that which I create: for, behold, I create Jerusalem (Africa) a rejoicing, and her people a joy.

19 And I will rejoice in Jerusalem,(Africa) and joy in my people: and the voice of weeping shall be no more heard in her, nor the voice of crying.

20 There shall be no more thence an infant of days, nor an old man that hath not filled his days: for the child shall die an hundred years old; but the sinner being an hundred years old shall be accursed.

21 And they (African Hebrews) shall build houses, and inhabit them; and they shall plant vineyards, and eat the fruit of them.

22 They shall not build, and another inhabit; they shall not plant, and another eat: for as the days of a tree are the days of my people, and mine elect shall long enjoy the work of their hands.

23 They shall not labour in vain, nor bring forth for trouble; for they are the seed of the blessed of the LORD, and their offspring with them.

24 And it shall come to pass, that before they call, I will answer; and while they are yet speaking, I will hear.

25 The wolf and the lamb shall feed together, and the lion shall eat straw like the bullock: and dust shall be the serpent's meat. They shall not hurt nor destroy in all my holy mountain, saith the LORD.

(Isaiah 65:8-25).

696/3526

Manasseh, the son of King Hezekiah, ruled over the African Hebrew Kingdom of Judah for 55 years. He was EVIL. He was punished and taken in chains to Babylon by the Assyrians. II Kings 20:21, 21:18 II Chron. 33:1-10, 33:20

641/3581

Amon ruled the African Hebrew Kingdom of Judah for 2 years. He was the son of Manasseh. He was EVIL and was killed by his servants. 2 Kings 21:19-22; 2 Chron. 33:20-25 King Amon was warned by the Prophets Jeremiah and Zephaniah.

639/3583

Josiah was the king of the African Hebrew Kingdom of Judah for 31 years. King Josiah was a GOOD king. He was slain in battle. 2 Kings 21:24, 23:30 2; Chron. 33:25, 35:25-27

639/3583

Jeremiah 32:37-44 The African Hebrew Israelites will possess Africa again. Many people today feel that because of the present conditon of Africa today, it could never be inhabited in an acceptable way. But in verse 43, GOD shews what will happen. Chaldeans='new folks'.

37 Behold, I will gather them (African Hebrews) out of all countries, whither I have driven them in mine anger, and in my fury, and in great wrath; and I will bring them again unto this place,(Africa) and I will cause them to dwell safely:

38 And they shall be my people, and I will be their God:

39 And I will give them one heart, and one way, that they may fear me for ever, for the good of them, and of their children after them:

40 And I will make an everlasting covenant with them,(African Hebrews) that I will not turn away from them, to do them good; but I will put my fear in their hearts, that they shall not depart from me.

41 Yea, I will rejoice over them to do them good, and I will plant them (African Hebrews)in this land (Africa) assuredly with my whole heart and with my whole soul.

42 For thus saith the LORD; Like as I have brought all this great evil upon this people,(African Hebrews) so will I bring upon them all the good that I have promised them.

43 And fields shall be bought in this land,(Africa) whereof ye say, It is desolate without man or beast; it is given into the hand of the Chaldeans.(new folks).

44 Men shall buy fields for money, and subscribe evidences, and seal them, and take witnesses in the land of Benjamin, (Africa) and in the places about Jerusalem,(Africa) and in the cities of Judah, (Africa) and in the cities of the mountains, and in the cities of the valley, and in the cities of the south: for I will cause their captivity to return, saith the LORD.

(Jeremiah 32:37-44).

Jeremiah 33:24-26 The African Hebrew Israelites are GOD's 'chosen people', no matter what people say or think.

24 Considerest thou not what this people have spoken, saying, The two families which the LORD hath chosen, (Israel and Judah-African Hebrews) he hath even cast them off? thus they have despised my people, that they should be no more a nation before them.

25 Thus saith the LORD; If my covenant be not with day and night, and if I have not appointed the ordinances of heaven and earth;

26 Then will I cast away the seed of Jacob,(African Hebrews) and David (African Hebrews) my servant, so that I will not take any of his seed to be rulers over the seed of Abraham, Isaac, and Jacob: for I will cause their captivity to return, and have mercy on them.

(Jeremiah 33:24-26).

630/3592

Zephaniah Chapter 1 GOD shewing Zephaniah how HE would destroy the African Hebrews and the African Gentiles from Africa for their sins.

1 The word of the LORD which came unto Zephaniah the son of Cushi, the son of Gedaliah, the son of Amariah, the son of Hizkiah, in the days of Josiah the son of Amon, king of Judah.

2 I will utterly consume all things from off the land, (Africa) saith the LORD.

3 I will consume man and beast; I will consume the fowls of the heaven, and the fishes of the sea, and the stumblingblocks with the wicked; and I will cut off man from off the land, (Africa) saith the LORD.

4 I will also stretch out mine hand upon Judah, (Africa) and upon all the inhabitants of Jerusalem; (Africa) and I will cut off the remnant of Baal (Gentile old folks) from this place, and the name of the Chemarims (Idolatrous Priest II Kings 23:5, Hos,. 10:5) with the priests;

5 And them that worship the host of heaven upon the housetops; and them that worship and that swear by the LORD, and that swear by Malcham; (Gentile idols of Moab)

6 And them that are turned back from the LORD; and those that have not sought the LORD, nor enquired for him.

7 Hold thy peace at the presence of the Lord GOD: for the day of the LORD is at hand: for the LORD hath prepared a sacrifice, he hath

bid his guests.

8 And it shall come to pass in the day of the LORD'S sacrifice, that I will punish the princes, and the king's children, and all such as are clothed with strange apparel.

9 In the same day also will I punish all those that leap on the threshold, which fill their masters' houses with violence and deceit.

10 And it shall come to pass in that day, saith the LORD, that there shall be the noise of a cry from the fish gate, and an howling from the second, and a great crashing from the hills.

11 Howl, ye inhabitants of Maktesh, (African gentile old folks) for all the merchant people are cut down; all they that bear silver are cut off.

12 And it shall come to pass at that time, that I will search Jerusalem (Africa) with candles, and punish the men that are settled on their lees: that say in their heart, The LORD will not do good, neither will he do evil.

13 Therefore their goods shall become a booty, and their houses a desolation: they shall also build houses, but not inhabit them; and they shall plant vineyards, but not drink the wine thereof.

14 The great day of the LORD is near, it is near, and hasteth greatly, even the voice of the day of the LORD: the mighty man shall cry there bitterly.

15 That day is a day of wrath, a day of trouble and distress, a day of wasteness and desolation, a day of darkness and gloominess, a day of clouds and thick darkness,

16 A day of the trumpet and alarm against the fenced cities, and against the high towers.

17 And I will bring distress upon men, that they shall walk like blind men, because they have sinned against the LORD: and their blood shall be poured out as dust, and their flesh as the dung.

18 Neither their silver nor their gold shall be able to deliver them in the day of the LORD'S wrath; but the whole land shall be devoured by the fire of his jealousy: for he shall make even a speedy riddance

of all them that dwell in the land.

(Zephaniah 1:1-18).

630/3592

Zephaniah 2:1-3 GOD tells the African nations to repent before they are destroyed.

1 Gather yourselves together, yea, gather together, O nation not desired;

2 Before the decree bring forth, before the day pass as the chaff, before the fierce anger of the LORD come upon you, before the day of the LORD'S anger come upon you.

3 Seek ye the LORD, all ye meek of the earth, which have wrought his judgment; seek righteousness, seek meekness: it may be ye shall be hid in the day of the LORD'S anger.

(Zephaniah 2:1-3).

630/3592

Zephaniah 2:4-6...GOD explains how HE will destroy the African Gentile Nations of Africa because of their evil. All locations such as Gaza, Ashkelon, Ashdod, etc, are 'Gentile Afican nations.

4 For Gaza shall be forsaken, and Ashkelon a desolation: they shall drive out Ashdod at the noon day, and Ekron shall be rooted up.

5 Woe unto the inhabitants of the sea coast, the nation of the Cherethites! the word of the LORD is against you; O Canaan, the land of the Philistines, I will even destroy thee, that there shall be no inhabitant.

6 And the sea coast shall be dwellings and cottages for shepherds, and folds for flocks.

(Zephaniah 2:4-6).

630/3592

Zephaniah 2:7...GOD explains how a portion of the land of Africa will be preserved for the return of the Children of Israel, when they leave America.

7 And the coast shall be for the remnant of the house of Judah; (African Hebrews) they shall feed thereupon: in the houses of Ashkelon (African gentile nation) shall they lie down in the evening: for the LORD their God shall visit them, and turn away their captivity.

(Zephaniah 2:7).

630/3592

Zephaniah 2:8-11....GOD tells the African Gentiles that they will be punished for making fun of the Children of Israel while in Africa. Moab and Ammon= African Gentiles.

8 I have heard the reproach of Moab, and the revilings of the children of Ammon, whereby they have reproached my people, (African Hewbrews) and magnified themselves against their border.

9 Therefore as I live, saith the LORD of hosts, the God of Israel, Surely Moab shall be as Sodom, and the children of Ammon as Gomorrah, even the breeding of nettles, and saltpits, and a perpetual desolation: the residue of my people shall spoil them, and the remnant of my people shall possess them.

10 This shall they have for their pride, because they have reproached and magnified themselves against the people of the LORD of hosts.

11 The LORD will be terrible unto them: for he will famish all the gods of the earth; and men shall worship him, every one from his place, even all the isles of the heathen.

(Zephaniah 2:8-11).

630/3592

Zephaniah 2:12...As we look at the land of Africa today, we see this verse being fulfilled. People of Africa (Ethiopians) today are being destroyed in alarming numbers.

12 Ye Ethiopians also, ye shall be slain by my sword.

(Zephaniah 2:12).

630/3592

Zephaniah 2:13-15....GOD explains what HE will do to America in the coming days.. Assyria & Ninevah are Anachronisms for 'America'.

13 And he will stretch out his hand against the north, (North America) and destroy Assyria; (America) and will make Nineveh (America) a desolation, and dry like a wilderness.

14 And flocks shall lie down in the midst of her, all the beasts of the nations: both the cormorant and the bittern shall lodge in the upper lintels of it; their voice shall sing in the windows; desolation shall be in the thresholds: for he shall uncover the cedar work.

15 This is the rejoicing city that dwelt carelessly, that said in her heart, I am, and there is none beside me: how is she become a desolation, a place for beasts to lie down in! every one that passeth by her shall hiss, and wag his hand.

(Zephaniah 2:13-15).

630/3592

Zephaniah 3:1-7...How GOD punished Africa.

1 Woe to her that is filthy and polluted, to the oppressing city!

2 She obeyed not the voice; she received not correction; she trusted not in the LORD; she drew not near to her God.

3 Her princes within her are roaring lions; her judges are evening wolves; they gnaw not the bones till the morrow.

4 Her prophets are light and treacherous persons: her priests have polluted the sanctuary, they have done violence to the law.

5 The just LORD is in the midst thereof; he will not do iniquity: every morning doth he bring his judgment to light, he faileth not; but the unjust knoweth no shame.

6 I have cut off the nations: their towers are desolate; I made their streets waste, that none passeth by: their cities are destroyed, so that there is no man, that there is none inhabitant.

7 I said, Surely thou wilt fear me, thou wilt receive instruction; so

their dwelling should not be cut off, howsoever I punished them: but they rose early, and corrupted all their doings.

(Zephaniah 3:1-7).

630/3592

Zephaniah 3:8...GOD promising HIS fierce anger upon the nations of the world.

8 Therefore wait ye upon me, saith the LORD, until the day that I rise up to the prey: for my determination is to gather the nations, that I may assemble the kingdoms, to pour upon them mine indignation, even all my fierce anger: for all the earth shall be devoured with the fire of my jealousy.

(Zephaniah 3:8).

Zephaniah 3:9-20...How GOD will deliver, redeem, and love the Children of Israel again. GOD will make the African Hebrew Israelites a 'praise' among all people.

9 For then will I turn to the people a pure language, that they may all call upon the name of the LORD, to serve him with one consent.

10 From beyond the rivers of Ethiopia (Africa) my suppliants, even the daughter of my dispersed, shall bring mine offering.

11 In that day shalt thou (African Hebrews) not be ashamed for all thy doings, wherein thou hast transgressed against me: for then I will take away out of the midst of thee them that rejoice in thy pride, and thou shalt no more be haughty because of my holy mountain.

12 I will also leave in the midst of thee an afflicted and poor people, and they shall trust in the name of the LORD.

13 The remnant of Israel (African Hebrews) shall not do iniquity, nor speak lies; neither shall a deceitful tongue be found in their mouth: for they shall feed and lie down, and none shall make them afraid.

14 Sing, O daughter of Zion; (African Hebrews) shout, O Israel; (African Hebrews) be glad and rejoice with all the heart, O daughter of Jerusalem. (African Hebrews)

15 The LORD hath taken away thy judgments, he hath cast out thine enemy: the king of Israel, even the LORD, is in the midst of thee: thou shalt not see evil any more.

16 In that day it shall be said to Jerusalem,(African Hebrews) Fear thou not: and to Zion,(African Hebrews) Let not thine hands be slack.

17 The LORD thy God in the midst of thee is mighty; he will save, he will rejoice over thee with joy; he will rest in his love, he will joy over thee with singing.

18 I will gather them that are sorrowful for the solemn assembly, who are of thee, to whom the reproach of it was a burden.

19 Behold, at that time I will undo all that afflict thee: and I will save her that halteth, and gather her that was driven out; and I will get them praise and fame in every land where they have been put to shame.

20 At that time will I bring you again, even in the time that I gather you: for I will make you a name and a praise among all people of the earth, when I turn back your captivity before your eyes, saith the LORD.

(Zephaniah 3:9-20).

629/3593

Jeremiah 1:14-16. GOD sent the Prophet Jeremiah to the Children of Israel, to tell them that HE was going to bring the 'new folks' from the 'north' (North America). People must understand that it was the 'will' and 'power' of GOD that caused 'new folks' to go to Africa and bring the 'old folks' to North America and oppress them for 400 years. Most black folks blame 'new folks' for enslaving them, but they must understand that it was the 'Almighty GOD' that caused this Historic calamity. (Read, Read, Read)

14 Then the LORD said unto me, Out of the north (North America) an evil shall break forth upon all the inhabitants of the land. (Africa)

15 For, lo, I will call all the families of the kingdoms of the north, (North America) saith the LORD; and they shall come, and

they shall set every one his throne at the entering of the gates of Jerusalem, (Africa) and against all the walls thereof round about, and against all the cities of Judah. (Africa)

16 And I will utter my judgments against them (African Hebrews) touching all their wickedness, who have forsaken me, and have burned incense unto other gods, and worshipped the works of their own hands.

(Jeremiah 1:14-16).

629/3593

Jeremiah Chapter 2. GOD rejecting the Children of Israel. GOD sent a message to the African Hebrews explaining why HE was rejecting them and preparing them for punishment. By reading this chapter, we can get an idea of how GOD really feels about HIS people, the 'African Hebrews'(African Americans), and how hurt GOD was. GOD's chosen people had turned their backs on HIM, and now GOD was preparing to turn HIS anger towards Israel. GOD said, the African Hebrews 400 years of punishment in America, is the result of GOD's anger.

1 Moreover the word of the LORD came to me, saying,

2 Go and cry in the ears of Jerusalem, (Africa) saying, Thus saith the LORD; I remember thee, the kindness of thy youth, the love of thine espousals, when thou wentest after me in the wilderness, in a land that was not sown.

3 Israel was holiness unto the LORD, and the firstfruits of his increase: all that devour him shall offend; evil shall come upon them, saith the LORD.

4 Hear ye the word of the LORD, O house of Jacob, (African Hebrews) and all the families of the house of Israel:(African Hebrews)

5 Thus saith the LORD, What iniquity have your fathers found in me, that they are gone far from me, and have walked after vanity, and are become vain?

6 Neither said they, Where is the LORD that brought us up out of the land of Egypt, that led us through the wilderness, through a land of deserts and of pits, through a land of drought, and of the

shadow of death, through a land that no man passed through, and where no man dwelt?

7 And I brought you into a plentiful country, to eat the fruit thereof and the goodness thereof; but when ye entered, ye defiled my land, and made mine heritage an abomination.

8 The priests said not, Where is the LORD? and they that handle the law knew me not: the pastors also transgressed against me, and the prophets prophesied by Baal, and walked after things that do not profit.

9 Wherefore I will yet plead with you, saith the LORD, and with your children's children will I plead.

10 For pass over the isles of Chittim, (African location) and see; and send unto Kedar, (African location) and consider diligently, and see if there be such a thing.

11 Hath a nation changed their gods, which are yet no gods? but my people have changed their glory for that which doth not profit.

12 Be astonished, O ye heavens, at this, and be horribly afraid, be ye very desolate, saith the LORD.

13 For my people have committed two evils; they have forsaken me the fountain of living waters, and hewed them out cisterns, broken cisterns, that can hold no water.

14 Is Israel a servant? is he a homeborn slave? why is he spoiled?

15 The young lions roared upon him, and yelled, and they made his land waste: his cities are burned without inhabitant.

16 Also the children of Noph (Gentile Africans) and Tahapanes (Gentile Africans) have broken the crown of thy head.

17 Hast thou not procured this unto thyself, in that thou hast forsaken the LORD thy God, when he led thee by the way?

18 And now what hast thou to do in the way of Egypt, (Gentiles) to drink the waters of Sihor? (Gentiles) or what hast thou to do in the way of Assyria, (Gentiles) to drink the waters of the river?

19 Thine (African Hebrews) own wickedness shall correct thee, and

thy backslidings shall reprove thee: know therefore and see that it is an evil thing and bitter, that thou hast forsaken the LORD thy God, and that my fear is not in thee, saith the Lord GOD of hosts.

20 For of old time I have broken thy yoke, and burst thy bands; and thou saidst, I will not transgress; when upon every high hill and under every green tree thou wanderest, playing the harlot.

21 Yet I had planted thee a noble vine, wholly a right seed: how then art thou turned into the degenerate plant of a strange vine unto me?

22 For though thou wash thee with nitre, and take thee much soap, yet thine iniquity is marked before me, saith the Lord GOD.

23 How canst thou say, I am not polluted, I have not gone after Baalim? (African gentile idol) see thy way in the valley, know what thou hast done: thou art a swift dromedary traversing her ways;

24 A wild ass used to the wilderness, that snuffeth up the wind at her pleasure; in her occasion who can turn her away? all they that seek her will not weary themselves; in her month they shall find her.

25 Withhold thy foot from being unshod, and thy throat from thirst: but thou saidst, There is no hope: no; for I have loved strangers, and after them will I go.

26 As the thief is ashamed when he is found, so is the house of Israel (African Hebrews) ashamed; they, their kings, their princes, and their priests, and their prophets,

27 Saying to a stock, Thou art my father; and to a stone, Thou hast brought me forth: for they have turned their back unto me, and not their face: but in the time of their trouble they will say, Arise, and save us.

28 But where are thy gods that thou hast made thee? let them arise, if they can save thee in the time of thy trouble: for according to the number of thy cities are thy gods, O Judah.(African Hebrews)

29 Wherefore will ye plead with me? ye all have transgressed against me, saith the LORD.

30 In vain have I smitten your children; they received no correction: your own sword hath devoured your prophets, like a destroying lion.

31 O generation, see ye the word of the LORD. Have I been a wilderness unto Israel? a land of darkness? wherefore say my people, We are lords; we will come no more unto thee?

32 Can a maid forget her ornaments, or a bride her attire? yet my people have forgotten me days without number.

33 Why trimmest thou thy way to seek love? therefore hast thou also taught the wicked ones thy ways.

34 Also in thy skirts is found the blood of the souls of the poor innocents: I have not found it by secret search, but upon all these.

35 Yet thou sayest, Because I am innocent, surely his anger shall turn from me. Behold, I will plead with thee, because thou sayest, I have not sinned.

36 Why gaddest thou about so much to change thy way? thou also shalt be ashamed of Egypt, as thou wast ashamed of Assyria.

37 Yea, thou shalt go forth from him, and thine hands upon thine head: for the LORD hath rejected thy confidences, and thou shalt not prosper in them.

(Jeremiah 2:1-37).

629/3593

Jeremiah Chapter 3. GOD telling The Children of Israel to 'return' unto HIM so HE can gather them, and take them back to Africa. Verse 12--GOD is telling the African American to 'return' to the Ten Commandments so that HE can remove HIS anger. (North in verse 12 = North America.)

12 Go and proclaim these words toward the north, (North America) and say, Return, thou backsliding Israel, saith the LORD; and I will not cause mine anger to fall upon you: for I am merciful, saith the LORD, and I will not keep anger for ever.

(Jeremiah 3:12).

vs. 15--GOD telling us that we will no longer have ignorant ministers teaching us lies and foolishness.

15 And I will give you pastors according to mine heart, which shall feed you with knowledge and understanding.

(Jeremiah 3:15).

In Vs 16, GOD is telling all present-day so-called Jews, whether 'black' or 'white', that using the "ARK OF THE COVENANT" (Torah) in their worship services, will become "NULL AND VOID

16 And it shall come to pass, when ye be multiplied and increased in the land, in those days, saith the LORD, they shall say no more, The ark of the covenant of the LORD: neither shall it come to mind: neither shall they remember it; neither shall they visit it; neither shall that be done any more.

(Jeremiah 3:16).

Vs. 17, All nations shall look to the African Hebrew Israelites for Spiritual guidance. 'Man-made' religions will cease to exist.

17 At that time they (Gentiles) shall call Jerusalem (African Hebrews) the throne of the LORD; and all the nations shall be gathered unto it, to the name of the LORD, to Jerusalem:(African Hebrews) neither shall they (Gentiles) walk any more after the imagination of their evil heart.

(Jeremiah 3:17).

Vs. 18, All African Hebrews that live in America will unite, and return to Africa together. (North = North America)

18 In those days the house of Judah (African Hebrews) shall walk with the house of Israel, (African Hebrews) and they shall come together out of the land of the north (North America) to the land (Africa) that I have given for an inheritance unto your fathers.

(Jeremiah 3:18).

vs. 21-25, The pain, sorrow, anguish, grief and disappointed among African Americans is so great because they are not keeping the Ten Commandments.

21 A voice was heard upon the high places, weeping and supplications of the children of Israel: for they have perverted their way, and they have forgotten the LORD their God.

22 Return, ye backsliding children, and I will heal your backslidings. Behold, we come unto thee; for thou art the LORD our God.

23 Truly in vain is salvation hoped for from the hills, and from the multitude of mountains: truly in the LORD our God is the salvation of Israel.

24 For shame hath devoured the labour of our fathers from our youth; their flocks and their herds, their sons and their daughters.

25 We lie down in our shame, and our confusion covereth us: for we have sinned against the LORD our God, we and our fathers, from our youth even unto this day, and have not obeyed the voice of the LORD our God.

(Jeremiah 3:21-25).

626/3596

Habakkuk Chapter 1:1-11 God speaks to the fearful vengeance that HE would afflict upon the African Hebrew Israelites for breaking the Ten Commandments. GOD almost scared the Prophet Habakkuk to death when HE shewed him how HE would create 'new folks' and what HE created them to do. In Chapter 1:6, the 'Chaldeans' is the Anachronism for 'newfolks., or Americans.

1 The burden which Habakkuk the prophet did see.

2 O LORD, how long shall I cry, and thou wilt not hear! even cry out unto thee of violence, and thou wilt not save!

3 Why dost thou shew me iniquity, and cause me to behold grievance? for spoiling and violence are before me: and there are that raise up strife and contention.

4 Therefore the law is slacked, and judgment doth never go forth: for the wicked doth compass about the righteous; therefore wrong judgment proceedeth.

5 Behold ye among the heathen, and regard, and wonder marvellously: for I will work a work in your days, which ye will not believe, though it be told you.

6 For, lo, I raise up the Chaldeans, (New folks) that bitter and hasty nation, which shall march through the breadth of the land, (Africa) to possess the dwellingplaces that are not theirs.

7 They are terrible and dreadful: their judgment and their dignity shall proceed of themselves.

8 Their horses also are swifter than the leopards, and are more fierce than the evening wolves: and their horsemen shall spread themselves, and their horsemen shall come from far; they shall fly as the eagle that hasteth to eat.

9 They shall come all for violence: their faces shall sup up as the east wind, and they shall gather the captivity as the sand.

10 And they shall scoff at the kings, (of Africa) and the princes shall be a scorn unto them: they shall deride every strong hold; for they shall heap dust, and take it.

11 Then shall his mind change, and he shall pass over, and offend, imputing this his power unto his god.

(Habakkuk 1:1-11).

612/3610

Jeremiah 4:6. The Prophet Jeremiah tells the African Children of Israel that GOD will bring the 'new folks' (White folks) from North America to destroy Africa. ('North'= America)

6 Set up the standard toward Zion:(Africa) retire, stay not: for I will bring evil from the north, (North America) and a great destruction.

(Jeremiah 4:6).

612/3610

Jeremiah Chapter 5. The Children of Israel provoked GOD. GOD bringing 'new folks' (White Folks) to destroy the African Hebrew Israelites from Africa.

1 Run ye to and fro through the streets of Jerusalem, (Africa) and see now, and know, and seek in the broad places thereof, if ye can find a man, if there be any that executeth judgment, that seeketh the TRUTH ; and I will pardon it.

2 And though they say, The LORD liveth; surely they swear falsely.

3 O LORD, are not thine eyes upon the TRUTH? thou hast stricken them, but they have not grieved; thou hast consumed them, but they have refused to receive correction: they have made their faces harder than a rock; they have refused to return.

4 Therefore I said, Surely these are poor; they are foolish: for they know not the way of the LORD, nor the judgment of their God.

5 I will get me unto the great men, and will speak unto them; for they have known the way of the LORD, and the judgment of their God: but these have altogether broken the yoke, and burst the bonds.

6 Wherefore a lion (new folks) out of the forest shall slay them, and a wolf (new folks) of the evenings shall spoil them, a leopard (new folks) shall watch over their cities: every one that goeth out thence shall be torn in pieces: because their transgressions are many, and their backslidings are increased.

7 How shall I pardon thee for this? thy children have forsaken me, and sworn by them that are no gods: when I had fed them to the full, they then committed adultery, and assembled themselves by troops in the harlots' houses.

8 They were as fed horses in the morning: every one neighed after his neighbour's wife.

9 Shall I not visit for these things? saith the LORD: and shall not my soul be avenged on such a nation as this? (Africa)

10 Go ye up upon her (Africa) walls, and destroy; but make not a full end: take away her battlements; for they are not the LORD'S.

11 For the house of Israel (African Hebrews) and the house of Judah (African Hebrews) have dealt very treacherously against me, saith the LORD.

12 They have belied the LORD, and said, It is not he; neither shall evil come upon us; neither shall we see sword nor famine:

13 And the prophets shall become wind, and the word is not in them: thus shall it be done unto them.

14 Wherefore thus saith the LORD God of hosts, Because ye speak

this word, behold, I will make my words in thy mouth fire, and this people wood, and it shall devour them.

15 Lo, I will bring a nation(new folks) upon you from far, O house of Israel, saith the LORD: it is a mighty nation, it is an ancient nation, (ancient because it was spoken of in Genesis 15:13-14) a nation whose language thou knowest not, neither understandest what they say.

16 Their quiver is as an open sepulchre, they are all mighty men.

17 And they (new folks) shall eat up thine harvest, and thy bread, which thy sons and thy daughters should eat: they shall eat up thy flocks and thine herds: they shall eat up thy vines and thy fig trees: they shall impoverish thy fenced cities, wherein thou trustedst, with the sword.

18 Nevertheless in those days, saith the LORD, I will not make a full end with you.

19 And it shall come to pass, when ye shall say, Wherefore doeth the LORD our God all these things unto us? then shalt thou answer them, Like as ye have forsaken me, and served strange gods in your land, (Africa) so shall ye serve strangers in a land ,that is not yours. (As promised in Genesis 15:13-14)

20 Declare this in the house of Jacob, (African Hebrews) and publish it in Judah, (African Hebrews) saying,

21 Hear now this, O foolish people, and without understanding; which have eyes, and see not; which have ears, and hear not:

22 Fear ye not me? saith the LORD: will ye not tremble at my presence, which have placed the sand for the bound of the sea by a perpetual decree, that it cannot pass it: and though the waves thereof toss themselves, yet can they not prevail; though they roar, yet can they not pass over it?

23 But this people (African Hebrews) hath a revolting and a rebellious heart; they are revolted and gone.

24 Neither say they in their heart, Let us now fear the LORD our God, that giveth rain, both the former and the latter, in his season: he reserveth unto us the appointed weeks of the harvest.

25 Your iniquities have turned away these things, and your sins have withholden good things from you.

26 For among my people are found wicked men: they lay wait, as he that setteth snares; they set a trap, they catch men.

27 As a cage is full of birds, so are their houses full of deceit: therefore they are become great, and waxen rich.

28 They are waxen fat, they shine: yea, they overpass the deeds of the wicked: they judge not the cause, the cause of the fatherless, yet they prosper; and the right of the needy do they not judge.

29 Shall I not visit for these things? saith the LORD: shall not my soul be avenged on such a nation as this?

30 A wonderful and horrible thing is committed in the land;

31 The prophets prophesy falsely, and the priests bear rule by their means; and my people love to have it so: and what will ye do in the end thereof?

(Jeremiah 5:1-31).

612/3610

Jeremiah 6:1. Again, GOD tells the Prophet Jeremiah that HE will send the 'new folks' from North America to destroy the land of Africa.

1 O ye children of Benjamin, (African Hebrews) gather yourselves to flee out of the midst of Jerusalem, (Africa) and blow the trumpet in Tekoa, (Africa) and set up a sign of fire in Bethhaccerem:(Africa) for evil appeareth out of the north, (North America) and great destruction.

(Jeremiah 6:1).

612/3610

Jeremiah 6:19-30. Here, again we see GOD announcing that HE will bring the 'new folks' (white folks) from North America to destroy HIS people in Africa. GOD is also explaining the 'vile' character that the 'new folks' will possess. The Prophet Jeremiah received this message from GOD many years before GOD created 'new folks' (white folks.)

19 Hear, O earth: behold, I will bring evil upon this people, (African Hebrews) even the fruit of their thoughts, because they have not hearkened unto my words, nor to my law, but rejected it.

20 To what purpose cometh there to me incense from Sheba, (Africa) and the sweet cane from a far country? your burnt offerings are not acceptable, nor your sacrifices sweet unto me.

21 Therefore thus saith the LORD, Behold, I will lay stumblingblocks before this people, (African Hebrews) and the fathers and the sons together shall fall upon them; the neighbour and his friend shall perish.

22 Thus saith the LORD, Behold, a people (new folks) cometh from the north country, (North America) and a great nation shall be raised from the sides of the earth.

23 They shall lay hold on bow and spear; they are cruel, and have no mercy; their voice roareth like the sea; and they ride upon horses, set in array as men for war against thee, O daughter of Zion. (African Hebrews)

24 We have heard the fame thereof: our hands wax feeble: anguish hath taken hold of us, and pain, as of a woman in travail.

25 Go not forth into the field, nor walk by the way; for the sword of the enemy and fear is on every side.

26 O daughter of my people, gird thee with sackcloth, and wallow thyself in ashes: make thee mourning, as for an only son, most bitter lamentation: for the spoiler (new folks) shall suddenly come upon us.

27 I have set thee (new folks) for a tower and a fortress among my people, that thou mayest know and try their way.

28 They are all grievous revolters, walking with slanders: they are brass and iron; they are all corrupters.

29 The bellows are burned, the lead is consumed of the fire; the founder melteth in vain: for the wicked are not plucked away.

30 Reprobate silver shall men call them, because the LORD hath rejected them.

(Jeremiah 6:19-30).

609/3613

Jeremiah Chapter 22:1-9. GOD told the Prophet Jeremiah to urge the African Children of Israel to 'repent' for their evil ways. As recorded in verse 7, the 'new folks' were prepared by GOD to destroy the African Hebrews and place them in America for 400 years according to Genesis 15:13-14.

1 Thus saith the LORD; Go down to the house of the king of Judah, (African Hebrews) and speak there this word,

2 And say, Hear the word of the LORD, O king of Judah, that sittest upon the throne of David, thou, and thy servants, and thy people that enter in by these gates:

3 Thus saith the LORD; Execute ye judgment and righteousness, and deliver the spoiled out of the hand of the oppressor: and do no wrong, do no violence to the stranger, the fatherless, nor the widow, neither shed innocent blood in this place.

4 For if ye do this thing indeed, then shall there enter in by the gates of this house kings sitting upon the throne of David, riding in chariots and on horses, he, and his servants, and his people.

5 But if ye will not hear these words, I swear by myself, saith the LORD, that this house shall become a desolation.

6 For thus saith the LORD unto the king's house of Judah; Thou art Gilead (land owned by the (African Hebrews) unto me, and the head of Lebanon: yet surely I will make thee a wilderness, and cities which are not inhabited.

7 And I will prepare destroyers (new folks) against thee, every one with his weapons: and they shall cut down thy choice cedars, and cast them into the fire.

8 And many nations shall pass by this city, (Africa) and they shall say every man to his neighbour, Wherefore hath the LORD done thus unto this great city?

9 Then they shall answer, Because they have forsaken the covenant of the LORD their God, and worshipped other gods, and served them.

(Jeremiah 22:1-9).

608/3614

Jeremiah 11:10-11. GOD pronounces evil and destruction upon the House of the Hebrew Israelites for breaking the Ten Commandments. If you look at the condition of the African American, you will find that it has not improved much. This is because the African Americans do not know WHO they 'really' are. Because they are unaware of 'WHAT' and 'WHO' they are, they cannot escape the constant destruction that is upon them on a daily basis. As recorded in verse 11, "I will bring evil upon them, (prison, drugs, aids, poverty, crime, hopelessness etc) which they shall not be able to escape; and though they shall cry unto me, I will not hearken unto them". The African American people cry everyday in America. This is because they have not been taught the TRUTH--GOD's TRUTH... and only GOD's TRUTH can set them free from their 'SORROW', 'GRIEF', and 'DISAPPOINTMENT'.

10 They (African Americans) are turned back to the iniquities of their forefathers (while in Africa), which refused to hear my words; and they went after other gods to serve them: the house of Israel and the house of Judah have broken my covenant which I made with their fathers.

11 Therefore thus saith the LORD, Behold, I will bring evil upon them, (African Hebrews) which they shall not be able to escape; and though they shall cry unto me, I will not hearken unto them.

(Jeremiah 11:10-11).

608/3614

Jeremiah 12:14-17. GOD will remove the African Americans from America after they serve their 400 years. will have compassion on them and take the African Americans back to their own land in Africa. If the 'new folks' will learn the ways of the African Hebrews and learn how to do that which is right, then they will be spared, but if they will not obey, they shall be plucked up and destroyed.

14 Thus saith the LORD against all mine evil neighbours, (new folks) that touch the inheritance which I have caused my people Israel (African Hebrews) to inherit; Behold, I will pluck them out of their land, (America) and pluck out the house of Judah (African Hebrews) from among them.

15 And it shall come to pass, after that I have plucked them (African Hebrews) out I will return, and have compassion on them, and will bring them again, every man to his heritage, and every man to his land. (Africa)

16 And it shall come to pass, if they (Gentiles) will diligently learn the ways of my people, (African Hebrews) to swear by my name, The LORD liveth; as they taught my people to swear by Baal; (Christianity) then shall they (new folks) be built in the midst of my people. (African Hebrews)

17 But if they will not obey, I will utterly pluck up and destroy that nation, (new folks) saith the LORD.

(Jeremiah 12:14-17).

608/3614

Jehoahaz was king over the African Hebrew Kingdom of Judah for only 3 months. He died a prisoner in Egypt. 2 Kings 23:30; 2 Chron. 36:1-3

608/3614

Jehoiakim (Eliakim) was the king of the African Hebrew Kingdom of Judah for 11 years. He was EVIL and died just before Jerusalem was captured by the African Gentile king Nebuchadnezzar. 2 Kings 23:34,24:6; 2 Chron. 36:5-8

606/3616

Jeremiah Chapter 25. While in Africa, the Children of Israel served a 70 year captivity in Babylon for breaking the Ten Commandments. This chapter also speaks to the many curses that GOD planned for the nations of Africa. GOD told Jeremiah in verse 9 that HE will bring the 'new folks' (white folks) from 'North America to destroy all of the nations of Africa.

606/3616

Jeremiah 26:11-15. The African Hebrew Israelites threatened to kill the Prophet Jeremiah because of his devastating prophecy from GOD. Jeremiah was arrested, tried and released.

11 Then spake the priests and the prophets unto the princes and

to all the people, saying, This man is worthy to die; for he hath prophesied against this city, as ye have heard with your ears.

12 Then spake Jeremiah unto all the princes and to all the people, saying, The LORD sent me to prophesy against this house and against this city all the words that ye have heard.

13 Therefore now amend your ways and your doings, and obey the voice of the LORD your God; and the LORD will repent him of the evil that he hath pronounced against you.

14 As for me, behold, I am in your hand: do with me as seemeth good and meet unto you.

15 But know ye for certain, that if ye put me to death, ye shall surely bring innocent blood upon yourselves, and upon this city, and upon the inhabitants thereof: for of a truth the LORD hath sent me unto you to speak all these words in your ears.

(Jeremiah 26:11-15).

606/3616

Jeremiah 30:1-8. GOD tells Jeremiah that the African Hebrew Israelites that are presently residing in North America, will be freed from their 400 year captivity and will return to their land in Africa.

1 The word that came to Jeremiah from the LORD, saying,

2 Thus speaketh the LORD God of Israel, saying, Write thee all the words that I have spoken unto thee in a book.

3 For, lo, the days come, saith the LORD, that I will bring again the captivity of my people Israel and Judah, (African Hebrews) saith the LORD: and I will cause them to return to the land (Africa) that I gave to their fathers, and they shall possess it.

4 And these are the words that the LORD spake concerning Israel and concerning Judah.

5 For thus saith the LORD; We have heard a voice of trembling, of fear, and not of peace. (black folks suffering in America)

6 Ask ye now, and see whether a man doth travail with child?

wherefore do I see every man with his hands on his loins, as a woman in travail, and all faces are turned into paleness?

7 Alas! for that day is great, so that none is like it: it is even the time of Jacob's trouble; but he shall be saved out of it.

8 For it shall come to pass in that day, saith the LORD of hosts, that I will break his (new folks) yoke from off thy neck, and will burst thy bonds, and strangers (new folks)shall no more serve themselves of him:

(Jeremiah 30:1-8).

606/3616

Jeremiah 30:10-24. Even though GOD scattered the African Hebrew Israelites all over the world, HE will save them, correct them, and return them to their land in Africa....but only if they harken and start keeping the Ten Commandments.

10 Therefore fear thou not, O my servant Jacob, (African Hebrews) saith the LORD; neither be dismayed, O Israel: (African Hebrews) for, lo, I will save thee from afar,(America) and thy seed from the land of their captivity; and Jacob (African Hebrews) shall return, and shall be in rest, and be quiet, and none shall make him afraid.

11 For I am with thee, saith the LORD, to save thee: though I make a full end of all nations whither I have scattered thee, yet will I not make a full end of thee: but I will correct thee in measure, and will not leave thee altogether unpunished.

12 For thus saith the LORD, Thy bruise is incurable, and thy wound is grievous.

13 There is none to plead thy cause, that thou mayest be bound up: thou hast no healing medicines.

14 All thy lovers have forgotten thee; they seek thee not; for I have wounded thee with the wound of an enemy, with the chastisement of a cruel one, for the multitude of thine iniquity; because thy sins were increased.

15 Why criest thou for thine affliction? thy sorrow is incurable for

the multitude of thine iniquity: because thy sins were increased, I have done these things unto thee.

16 Therefore all they that devour thee shall be devoured; and all thine adversaries, every one of them, shall go into captivity; and they that spoil thee shall be a spoil, and all that prey upon thee will I give for a prey.

17 For I will restore health unto thee, and I will heal thee of thy wounds, saith the LORD; because they called thee an Outcast, saying, This is Zion, whom no man seeketh after.

18 Thus saith the LORD; Behold, I will bring again the captivity of Jacob's tents, and have mercy on his dwellingplaces; and the city shall be builded upon her own heap, and the palace shall remain after the manner thereof.

19 And out of them shall proceed thanksgiving and the voice of them that make merry: and I will multiply them, and they shall not be few; I will also glorify them, and they shall not be small.

20 Their children also shall be as aforetime, and their congregation shall be established before me, and I will punish all that oppress them.

21 And their nobles shall be of themselves, and their governor shall proceed from the midst of them; and I will cause him to draw near, and he shall approach unto me: for who is this that engaged his heart to approach unto me? saith the LORD.

22 And ye shall be my people, and I will be your God.

23 Behold, the whirlwind of the LORD goeth forth with fury, a continuing whirlwind: it shall fall with pain upon the head of the wicked.

24 The fierce anger of the LORD shall not return, until he have done it, and until he have performed the intents of his heart: in the latter days ye shall consider it.

(Jeremiah 30:10-24).

606/3616

Jeremiah 31:1-24. The 400 year affliction in America is almost over for the African Hebrew Israelites. As indicated in verse 8, the African Americans that return to GOD's Ten Commandments will be released from North America and will enjoy a peaceful life in Africa.

1 At the same time, saith the LORD, will I be the God of all the families of Israel, (African Hebrews) and they shall be my people.

2 Thus saith the LORD, The people which were left of the sword found grace in the wilderness; even Israel, when I went to cause him to rest.

3 The LORD hath appeared of old unto me, saying, Yea, I have loved thee with an everlasting love: therefore with lovingkindness have I drawn thee.

4 Again I will build thee, and thou shalt be built, O virgin of Israel: (African Hebrews) thou shalt again be adorned with thy tabrets, and shalt go forth in the dances of them that make merry.

5 Thou shalt yet plant vines upon the mountains of Samaria:(Africa) the planters shall plant, and shall eat them as common things.

6 For there shall be a day, that the watchmen upon the mount Ephraim (Africa) shall cry, Arise ye, and let us go up to Zion (Africa) unto the LORD our God.

7 For thus saith the LORD; Sing with gladness for Jacob,(African Hebrews) and shout among the chief of the nations: publish ye, praise ye, and say, O LORD, save thy people, the remnant of Israel. (African Hebrews)

8 Behold, I will bring them (African Hebrews) from the north country, (North America) and gather them from the coasts of the earth, and with them the blind and the lame, the woman with child and her that travaileth with child together: a great company shall return thither.

9 They shall come with weeping, and with supplications will I lead them: I will cause them to walk by the rivers of waters in a straight way, wherein they shall not stumble: for I am a father to

Israel, (African Hebrews) and Ephraim (African Hebrews) is my firstborn.

10 Hear the word of the LORD, O ye nations, and declare it in the isles afar off, and say, He that scattered Israel (African Hebrews) will gather him, and keep him, as a shepherd doth his flock.

11 For the LORD hath redeemed Jacob, (African Hebrews) and ransomed him from the hand of him (New folks) that was stronger than he.

12 Therefore they shall come and sing in the height of Zion, (Africa) and shall flow together to the goodness of the LORD, for wheat, and for wine, and for oil, and for the young of the flock and of the herd: and their soul shall be as a watered garden; and they shall not sorrow any more at all.

13 Then shall the virgin rejoice in the dance, both young men and old together: for I will turn their mourning into joy, and will comfort them, and make them rejoice from their sorrow.

14 And I will satiate the soul of the priests with fatness, and my people shall be satisfied with my goodness, saith the LORD.

15 Thus saith the LORD; A voice was heard in Ramah, (A city owned by the African Hebrews while in Africa) lamentation, and bitter weeping; Rahel (Rachel, wife of Jacob) weeping for her children refused to be comforted for her children, because they were not.

16 Thus saith the LORD; Refrain thy voice from weeping, and thine eyes from tears: for thy work shall be rewarded, saith the LORD; and they shall come again from the land of the enemy.

17 And there is hope in thine end, saith the LORD, that thy children shall come again to their own border.

18 I have surely heard Ephraim (African Hebrews) bemoaning himself thus; Thou hast chastised me, and I was chastised, as a bullock unaccustomed to the yoke: turn thou me, and I shall be turned; for thou art the LORD my God.

19 Surely after that I was turned, I repented; and after that I was instructed, I smote upon my thigh: I was ashamed, yea, even confounded, because I did bear the reproach of my youth.

20 Is Ephraim my dear son? is he a pleasant child? for since I spake against him, I do earnestly remember him still: therefore my bowels are troubled for him; I will surely have mercy upon him, saith the LORD.

21 Set thee up waymarks, make thee high heaps: set thine heart toward the highway, even the way which thou wentest: turn again, O virgin of Israel, turn again to these thy cities.

22 How long wilt thou go about, O thou backsliding daughter? for the LORD hath created a new thing in the earth, A woman shall compass a man.

23 Thus saith the LORD of hosts, the God of Israel; As yet they shall use this speech in the land of Judah (Africa) and in the cities thereof, when I shall bring again their captivity; The LORD bless thee, O habitation of justice, and mountain of holiness.

24 And there shall dwell in Judah (Africa) itself, and in all the cities thereof together, husbandmen, and they that go forth with flocks.

(Jeremiah 31:1-24).

606/3616

Jeremiah 31:27..HOW GOD CREATED "WHITE FOLKS'.(NEW FOLKS) As mentioned earlier, the Old Testament is a Historical report between the relationship between GOD and the Children of Israel who are black folks (old folks). We have also proved thus far, that the Old Testament gives no report or account of the existence of 'white folks' (new folks). We have travelled 3616 years since the actual creation of the black man, and GOD is just now telling the prophet Jeremiah how HE will create 'new folks' (white folks). We have for many years read lies and heard false stories about the creation of man, according to man. Now let us hear what GOD says concerning the matter. Black folks were created (or evolved) from the 109 universal elements. In this verse GOD said HE created 'new folks' (white folks) from "black folks' and the 'beast'. "Behold, the days come, saith the LORD, that I will "SOW' the house of Israel and the house of Judah with the "SEED" of "MAN", and the "SEED" of "BEAST".

27 Behold, the days come, saith the LORD, that I will sow the house

of Israel (African Hebrews) and the house of Judah (African Hebrews) with the seed of man, and with the seed of beast.

(Jeremiah 31:27).

Because the CREATION OF 'NEW FOLKS' (WHITE FOLKS) is so important, the writer broke the 'CHRONOLOGY' in order to keep all Scripture references to the 'creation of 'new folks', together.

785/3437

Hosea Chapter 1. The Children of Israel (African Hebrews) committed so much adultery and whoredom, that GOD told the African Prophet Hosea to go and marry a whore. This was done to illustrate and expose the African Hebrews' level of adultery and iniquity. The African Hebrews were having so much sex, that GOD used the transaction of 'SEX', to create the 'new folks' (white folks)

VITAL

Once again it is proven that 'white folks' (new folks") did not exist during the time of the Old Testament. Here we are 3,437 years after the creation of the first man Adam (the African), and GOD is telling the African Prophet Hosea how HE will create 'new folks' (white folks)

785 b.c.e.---3437 actual year

THE CREATION OF 'NEW FOLKS' (WHITE FOLKS) HOSEA 2:18

We explained how 'old folks' (black folks) were created when we began this writing. The so-called black man was created from the 109 elements of the universe. African people can be regarded as the grand symbol of the universe, or the 'crown of creation', because everything that is contained in the universe is contained in African people, who were the 'first' people. For years we have been taught that man is the descendant of apelike beast that lived millions of years ago. Well, the African did not come from beast. But who did? Let us look again at Jeremiah 31:27. God said, He would sow the African Hebrews with the seed of man (Africans), and with the seed of beast. From this we know that someone came from the beast, but it was not 'black folks' (old folks). This verse suggest that God made the African Hebrews go into beast to bring forth a new kind of people (new folks). Let us prove this fact. In the first two chapters of the book of Hosea, we find God continuing to reject the African Hebrews for their iniquity. The African Hebrews committed so much adultery and whoredom, that God told the Prophet Hosea to go and marry a whore. All thru the Old Testament God promised that He would bring a different, strange people to destroy the African Hebrews for breaking the Ten Commandments. Excerpts from Deuteronomy Chapter 28. "The Lord shall bring a nation against thee from far, from the end of the earth, a nation whose tongue thou shalt not understand; The Lord shall bring thee unto a nation which neither thou nor thy fathers have known; and there shalt thou serve other gods, wood and stone. The stranger that is within thee shall get up above thee very high; and thou shalt come down very low; he shall lend to thee, and thou shalt not lend to him, he shall be the head, and thou shalt be the tail.... Again this proves that new folks (white folks) did not exist during the time of the Old Testament ; God spoke only of their 'coming'. Well how did 'new folks' get here if they did not exist during the time of the Old Testament. In the year

606/3616 God told the Prophet Jeremiah how new folks would be created (Jere. 31:27). In the year 785/3437, God told the Prophet Hosea how He would create 'new folks' (white folks). We will now explain Hosea 2:18

18 And in that day will I make a covenant for them with the beasts of the field, and with the fowls of heaven, and with the creeping things of the ground: and I will break the bow and the sword and the battle out of the earth, and will make them to lie down safely.

(Hosea 2:18).

"And in that day will I make a COVENANT for the African Hebrews with the beasts of the field, and with the fowls of heaven, and with the creeping things of the ground: (The covenant means; the beast of the field shall be at peace with thee.) "And I will break the bow and the sword and the battle out of the earth, and will make them to lie down safely. It is a natural fact that when man and beast meet, especially in Africa, a fight begins using the 'bow and sword'. But God made a covenant with the beast so that they would lie down and allow the African Hebrews to go in unto them and impregnate them. That's right folks, believe it or not, it is the TRUTH. But guess what,,-this did not happen in Africa. At this time in World history, Africa/Asia were the only inhabited locations existing. It was not until God stretched forth His hand to cause the "Continental Divide" or the "Continental Drift" that other Continents and Countries came into existence.. When God stretched forth His hand and separated the African land mass into other Continents and Countries, the African Hebrews were 'scattered' to every land in the world.

THE 'SCATTERING'

Let us take a brief trip thru the Bible and prove this 'scattering' fact. Lev. 26:33,

33 And I will scatter you among the heathen, and will draw out a sword after you: and your land shall be desolate, and your cities waste.

(Leviticus 26:33).

27 And the LORD shall scatter you among the nations, and ye shall be left few in number among the heathen, whither the LORD shall lead you.

(Deuteronomy 4:27).

64 And the LORD shall scatter thee among all people, from the one end of the earth even unto the other; and there thou shalt serve other gods, which neither thou nor thy fathers have known, even wood and stone.

(Deuteronomy 28:64).

26 I said, I would scatter them into corners, I would make the remembrance of them to cease from among men:

(Deuteronomy 32:26).

8 Remember, I beseech thee, the word that thou commandedst thy servant Moses, saying, If ye transgress, I will scatter you abroad among the nations:

(Nehemiah 1:8).

16 I will scatter them also among the heathen, whom neither they nor their fathers have known: and I will send a sword after them, till I have consumed them.

(Jeremiah 9:16).

24 Therefore will I scatter them as the stubble that passeth away by the wind of the wilderness.

(Jeremiah 13:24).

17 I will scatter them as with an east wind before the enemy; I will shew them the back, and not the face, in the day of their calamity.

(Jeremiah 18:17).

32 And their camels shall be a booty, and the multitude of their cattle a spoil: and I will scatter into all winds them that are in the utmost corners; and I will bring their calamity from all sides thereof, saith the LORD.

(Jeremiah 49:32).

The 'SCATTERING' continues in the following references: Ezekiel 5:2, 5:10, 12:14-15, 20:23-24, 22:15, 29:12,(Egypt and Egyptians = Africa and Africans). 30:23.

After GOD split the African land mass into other Countries and Continents, and the African Hebrews were scattered throughout the world, God implemented Jeremiah 31:27 and Hosea 2:18. God made the African Hebrews go into the 'beast', 'fowl', and the creeping things in each land to bring forth the 'new folks' (white folks).

Therefore, the 'new folks' (white folks) are the TRUE descendant of the beast, the fowl, and the creeping things. It is interesting to point out that it took a very long time for 'new folks' to develop to the human level and become completely human. Why? Because the first offspring came out, 90% animal, 10% human, (80%-20%, 70%-30%, etc.) The African Hebrews had to continue this impregnation process over and over again until the 'new folks' (white folks) developed to the human level. The period of time when 'new folks' were developing to the 'human level' was called, the **'DARK AGES', OR 'MIDDLE AGES**, which brought forth, **'MYTHOLOGY'**, which was the period of time that graphically depicts 'half man-half beast',etc. Some research into 'Mythology' will prove that Jeremiah 31:27 and Hosea 2:18 are true as the Rocks of Ages. Therefore, when we see pictures representing the evolution of man coming from the monkeys and apes, it is in TRUTH; the 'new folks' (white folks) ancestry, not the 'black man'. Some misinformed people have likened African people to the monkey and the ape because of color. Consider this: the beast, fowl, and creeping things have at least seven characteristics that relate directly and specifically to 'new folks' (white folks), not black folks (old folks). **(1)** The **HAIR** is identical to 'new folks' hair; in color, texture and smell, especially when the hair is wet. **(2)** If you move or 'part' the hair , you will find that the **SKIN** is identical to 'new folks' skin. **(3)** The **LIPS** of all beast, fowl and creeping things are thin like the 'new folks'. **(4)** New folks **SMELL/ODOR** is identical to the beast, fowl and creeping thing. **(5)** The color of the **EYES** of 'new folks' are identical to the BFC's (beast, fowl, creeping things). **(6)** When you look at animals walking around on all fours, you notice that they have no **HIPS.** If most new folks got down on all fours, they would be hip-less or 'flat' like animals. **(7)** The **NOSE** is pointed and slim like the BFC's, and cannot endure a hot climax like Africa, because it would be hard for them to breath. A cool, clammy (air conditioned) cave-like environment is more conducive to them for breathing, because of their narrow nose. New folks seemingly have an infinity and a natural relationship with the BFC's (beast, fowl, creeping things) . This relationship causes them to be more compassionate toward animals then they are with humans in many cases. It seems as though there are more laws to protect the animals (BFC's) then there are to protect humans against homelessness, child abuse, famine and lawlessness. Anyway, the 'Old Testament' proves that 'new folks' (white folks) were created from the African and the beast, fowl and creeping things. If 'new folks' want to know which BFC they came from, they must look to the country where they originated from. Each country has a dominant beast, fowl, or creeping thing, and the characteristic, symbol, spirit, emblem and behavior of that 'BFC', is reflected in the people from that specific land or region. For example, if you researched to find what "BFC" the Russians came from, you would note that their 'stature, clothing and emblems would reflect the characteristics of a 'BEAR'. If you moved to the Far East , you would note that the 'stature' and emblems of the Orient are small. (Creeping Things). If you researched the original American, you would find that the African Hebrew Israelite went into the 'Eagle' and brought forth the 'Indian'. Have you ever noticied the emblems of the Indians? Feathers, etc. Eagles were always reflected in the Indian's culture. When the Europeans massacred the Indians and stole their land (America), they also stole the symbol of the 'eagle', and still use it as their national symbol.today...the noted 'American Eagle'. So in TRUTH, 'old folks' (black folks) were the first people that set foot in every land in the whole wide world. God scattered them to every land in the world, and used the African Hebrew to create 'new folks' (white folks). So without 'old folks' (black folks) and the beast, fowl, and creeping things, no other people would exist, 'anywhere'. New folks were created during the timeframe between the Old and New Testaments...a timeframe of 462 years.

IS IT "R A C I S M",, OR IS IT "E N M I T Y"

Now that we understand how 'new folks' (white folks) were created, we can now explain the origin of what is called 'racism'.

RACISM--is a belief that race is the primary determinant of human traits and capacities, and that racial differences produces an inherent superiority of a particular race.

ENMITY--is a positive, active, and typically mutual hatred or ill-will---a deep-seated, dislike.

Racism is a 'belief'. Enmity is 'an active expression'. A belief cannot hurt you. An active expression can. Please note the following composites of 'enmity':

Hostility:	Hositle action, overt acts of warfare.
Antipathy:	Opposition in feeling.
Antagonism:	Actively expressed opposition.
Rancor:	Bitter deep-seated ill will.
Animosity:	Ill will or resentment tending toward active hostility.
Animus:	Basic attitude or governing spirit--prejudiced and often spiteful.

If we look closely at the definitions of 'racism' and 'enmity', we must conclude that the relationship between 'old folks' and 'new folks' (black folks and white folks) is more '**ENMITY**' than '**RACISM**'. Enmity prevails between the races because 'new folks' (white folks) were created from the beast, fowl, and creeping things. There is a natural 'enmity' between most animals and humans when face to face. Enmity evolved from the beast into the 'new folks' (white folks) when GOD created them from the beast (BFC) and black folks. Enmity is what we see expressed through the behavior of 'new folks' as they relate and transact with 'old folks',not 'racism'. Here are a few references that prove that GOD used 'enmity' through 'new folks' to oppress and afflict African people throughout the world:

Isaiah 19:4

4 And the Egyptians (Africans)will I give over into the hand of a cruel lord; (new folks) and a fierce king (New folks-White folks) shall rule over them, saith the Lord, the LORD of hosts.

(Isaiah 19:4).

Isaiah 10:5-6

5 O Assyrian, (Americans)the rod of mine anger, and the staff in their hand is mine indignation.

6 I will send him (New Folks) against an hypocritical nation, (African Hebrews) and against the people of my wrath (old folks) will I

give him (New Folks) a charge, to take the spoil, and to take the prey, and to tread them down like the mire of the streets.

(Isaiah 10:5-6).

Isaiah 22:17-19

17 Behold, the LORD will carry thee (African Hebrews) away with a mighty captivity, and will surely cover thee.

18 He (New Folks) will surely violently turn and toss thee like a ball into a large country: (North America) there shalt thou die, and there the chariots of thy glory shall be the shame of thy lord's house.

19 And I will drive thee from thy station (Africa), and from thy state shall he (New Folks) pull thee down.

(Isaiah 22:17-19).

Isaiah 47:6

6 I was wroth with my people, (African people) I have polluted mine inheritance, (African Hebrews) and given them into thine hand: (New folks hands), thou didst shew them no mercy; upon the ancient (old folks-black folks) hast thou very heavily laid thy yoke.

(Isaiah 47:6).

<u>THE 'NORTH COUNTRY'==NORTH AMERICA</u>

Jeremiah 1:14-16

14 Then the LORD said unto me, Out of the north (North America) an evil shall break forth upon all the inhabitants of the land. (Africa)

15 For, lo, I will call all the families of the kingdoms of the north, (North America)saith the LORD; and they shall come, and they shall set every one his throne at the entering of the gates of Jerusalem, (Africa) and against all the walls thereof round about, and against all the cities of Judah.(African Hebrews)

16 And I will utter my judgments against them touching all their wickedness, who have forsaken me, and have burned incense unto other gods, and worshipped the works of their own hands.

(Jeremiah 1:14-16).

Jeremiah 4:6

6 Set up the standard toward Zion: (Africa) retire, stay not: for I will bring evil from the north, (North America) and a great destruction.

(Jeremiah 4:6).

Jeremiah 5:15-17

15 Lo, I will bring a nation (America) upon you from far, O house of Israel, saith the LORD: it is a mighty nation, it is an ancient nation, (spoken of in Gen. 15:13-14) a nation whose language thou knowest not, neither understandest what they say.

16 Their quiver is as an open sepulchre, they are all mighty men.

17 And they shall eat up thine harvest, and thy bread, which thy sons and thy daughters should eat: they shall eat up thy flocks and thine herds: they shall eat up thy vines and thy fig trees: they shall impoverish thy fenced cities, wherein thou trustedst, with the sword.

(Jeremiah 5:15-17).

Jeremiah 6:1

1 O ye children of Benjamin, (African Hebrews) gather yourselves to flee out of the midst of Jerusalem, (Africa) and blow the trumpet in Tekoa, (Africa) and set up a sign of fire in Bethhaccerem:(Africa) for evil appeareth out of the north, (North America) and great destruction.

(Jeremiah 6:1).

Jeremiah 6:19

19 Hear, O earth: behold, I will bring evil upon this people, (African

Hebrews) even the fruit of their thoughts, because they have not hearkened unto my words, nor to my law, but rejected it.

(Jeremiah 6:19).

Jeremiah 6:21-23

21 Therefore thus saith the LORD, Behold, I will lay stumblingblocks before this people, (African Hebrews) and the fathers and the sons together shall fall upon them; the neighbour and his friend shall perish.

22 Thus saith the LORD, Behold, a people cometh from the north country, (North America) and a great nation shall be raised from the sides of the earth.

23 They shall lay hold on bow and spear; they are cruel, and have no mercy; their voice roareth like the sea; and they ride upon horses, set in array as men for war against thee, O daughter of Zion.(African Hebrews).

(Jeremiah 6:21-23).

Jeremiah 11:10-11

10 They are turned back to the iniquities of their forefathers, which refused to hear my words; and they went after other gods to serve them: the house of Israel (African Hebrews) and the house of Judah (African Hebrews) have broken my covenant which I made with their fathers.

11 Therefore thus saith the LORD, Behold, I will bring evil upon them, which they shall not be able to escape; and though they shall cry unto me, I will not hearken unto them.

(Jeremiah 11:10-11).

Jeremiah 46:24

24 The daughter of Egypt (Africa) shall be confounded; she shall be delivered into the hand of the people of the north. (North America).

(Jeremiah 46:24).

The question may arise, why did GOD use the beast, fowl, and creeping things BFC's) to create 'new folks' (white folks)? For two reasons:

1. This was necessary because a specific, destructive charateristic was needed to punish the African Hebrews for breaking GOD's 10 Commandments. A characteristic that was 'void' of 'mercy' was needed to afflict the African Hebrews, and animals possess the savage instinct to attack and destroy without any sense of consciousness.

2. GOD always uses that which already exists, to create something else...for example; before the first black man was created, the universal elements existed,,,,,,GOD used the universal elements to create Adam, the first man. (African)....Africans and animals existed and GOD used them to create something else,,,,,,'new folks/white folks...............you got it??????????

606/3616

Jeremiah 31:31-37 GOD'S NEW COVENANT . The 'New Covenant' is simply, understanding and applying the natural unchanging "LAWS" that governs the lives of all human beings. Mankind will never be able to live in peace with one another until mankind understands the 'universal laws', and apply these laws to their daily lives. vs. 33.

33 But this shall be the covenant that I will make with the house of Israel; (African Hebrews) After those days, saith the LORD, I will put my **law** in their inward parts, and write it in their hearts; and will be their God, and they shall be my people.

(Jeremiah 31:33).

.."I will put my LAW in their inward parts, and write it in their hearts." Once again, we must realize that everything in the Universe is governed by 'unfailing LAW', and only by properly applying these LAWS can mankind expect positive change. The African Hebrew Israelites were given the wisdom to understand and apply this 'universal law'. GOD made a covenant with them. This covenant was to apply this law, and teach it to all mankind. The African Hebrew Israelites failed while in Africa, and were punished because they forsook the law of GOD. As a result of their failure, the whole world is living contrary to GOD's natural law.

In other words, 'the world is upside down.'. There can never be a permanent solution to the many problems of the world without understanding and applying GOD's Commandments. This is the only way mankind can live in harmony with each other. GOD's law must be in our 'inward parts', in our hearts. There is no such thing as 'LUCK',only "LAW". Everything that happens in life is a result of a series of causes, and "LAW" is the cause of it all. LAW is the instrument that GOD used to establish 'order' in the universe. All natural elements obey Universal LAW, if they did not, there would be a tremendous conflict between the Sun and Moon, the Night and Day, etc,...everything and everyone must obey the LAW of their being. Without 'LAW', the process of 'decay' becomes active and we experience a breakdown in the natural order of things. So, GOD will put HIS law in the inward parts of the African Hebrew Israelites, and all mankind, and they will have one more chance to get it right.

31 Behold, the days come, saith the LORD, that I will make a new covenant with the house of Israel, (African Hebrews) and with the house of Judah:(African Hebrews)

32 Not according to the covenant that I made with their fathers in the day that I took them by the hand to bring them out of the land of Egypt; which my covenant they brake, although I was an husband unto them, saith the LORD:

33 But this shall be the covenant that I will make with the house of Israel; (African Hebrews) After those days, saith the LORD, I will put my law in their inward parts, and write it in their hearts; and will be their God, and they shall be my people.

34 And they shall teach no more every man his neighbour, and every man his brother, saying, Know the LORD: for they shall all know me, from the least of them unto the greatest of them, saith the LORD: for I will forgive their iniquity, and I will remember their sin no more.

35 Thus saith the LORD, which giveth the sun for a light by day, and the ordinances of the moon and of the stars for a light by night, which divideth the sea when the waves thereof roar; The LORD of hosts is his name:

36 If those ordinances depart from before me, saith the LORD, then

the seed of Israel (African Hebrews) also shall cease from being a nation before me for ever.

37 Thus saith the LORD; If heaven above can be measured, and the foundations of the earth searched out beneath, I will also cast off all the seed of Israel (African Hebrews) for all that they have done, saith the LORD.

(Jeremiah 31:31-37).

Vs. 34...'And they shall teach no more every man his neighbour and every man his brother saying, Know the Lord: for they shall all know me, from the least of them unto the greatest of them, saith the Lord:'.

This means, no more will people try to force you into "Religion". No more will people try to teach you 'False Doctrine'. No more will people try to brainwash you into believing something that is not 'true'. No more will people knock on your door trying to sell you a religious concept that is equal to the belief in Santa Claus. No more will people judge you based on their own personal 'value system'. Everyone will know "LAW"..... Everyone will forget "Religion"... GOD made LAW.. Man made Religion.....GOD's LAW prevails... Man's Religions fail.....Man's Religion is full of fault ...GOD's LAW is PERFECT......PSALMS 19:7 The LAW of the LORD is Perfect, converting the soul.....Religion, Churches and Ministers cannot convert a person....only GOD's LAW can convert.

PSALMS 119:165

Great peace have they which love thy LAW: and nothing shall offend them...

Guns can't always protect you....but GOD's LAW will always save you.

Vs. 36..The NEW COVENANT will give the African Hebrew Israelites one more chance to become the nation of people that will rule the world. This was GOD's plan for them over 3,000 years ago, and they will be cut off, if they do not become a source of blessing for all mankind. The NEW COVENANT will be established fully by the time the African Americans (African Hebrews) complete their 400 year punishment in America.

597/3625

Jehoiachin (Jeconiah, Coniah) was the king of the African Hebrew Kingdom of Judah for 2 months. He was EVIL, taken captive to Babylon; and released. 2 Kings 24:8, 25:27-30; 2 Chron. 36:9-10

597/3625

Zedekiah (Mattaniah) was the son of Josiah. He was king over the African Hebrew Kingdom of Judah for 11 years. He was EVIL. He was blinded and taken prisoner to Babylon, where he died. 2 Kings 24:17, 25:7; 2 Chron. 36:10-21

THE FOLLOWING IS A SUMMARY OF ALL OF THE AFRICAN HEBREW KINGS.

The African Kingdom of Judah TOTAL = 23

22 KINGS 1 QUEEN

8 WERE GOOD

11 WERE EVIL

4 (NO REPORT)

The African Kingdom of Israel TOTAL = 19

19 KINGS

ALL WERE EVIL

GRAND TOTAL = 42

607/3615

Jeremiah Chapters 46 thru 52. GOD could not punish the African Hebrew Israelites sufficiently, unless HE punished the African Gentiles as well. GOD had to punish 'all' Africans. WHY? Because the 'new folks' (white folks) that GOD created to punish the Children of Israel, would not be able to tell the difference between the African Hebrew, and the African Gentile when GOD sent them to destroy Africa, because they were both 'BLACK'. GOD had to punish all 'old folks' (Africans); that way HE would be certain that the Children of Israel would be punished for breaking the TEN COMMANDMENTS.

Ch. 46:6 No matter how valiantly the African people fought, they would fall and be placed in North America (NORTH), by way of the Atlantic Ocean (Euphrates).

6 Let not the swift flee away, nor the mighty man escape; they shall stumble, and fall toward the north (North America) by the river Euphrates. (Atlantic Ocean)

(Jeremiah 46:6).

Ch. 46:10 The destruction of the African people from Africa is an expression of GOD's anger upon HIS chosen people for breaking the Ten Commandments. Conforming to GOD's Ten Commandments is living according to 'natural law'. Living according to GOD's natural law brings 'PEACE', 'JOY' AND 'LOVE'. This is what the world needs more of, but will never have, until the world keeps GOD's Ten Commandments. Everything in the universe is governed by absolute, unfailing LAW. GOD made a covenant with the Children of Israel to 'keep the LAW' but Israel failed. As a result, GOD created a 'new people' to punish them for 400 years. According to verse 10, the African American is GOD's sacrifice in North America. (Euphrates= Anachronism for Atlantic Ocean)

10 For this is the day of the Lord GOD of hosts, a day of vengeance, that he may avenge him of his adversaries: and the sword shall devour, and it shall be satiate and made drunk with their blood: for the Lord GOD of hosts hath a sacrifice in the north country (North America) by the river Euphrates. (Atlantic Ocean)

(Jeremiah 46:10).

20 Egypt (Africa) is like a very fair heifer, but destruction cometh; it cometh out of the north. (North America)

(Jeremiah 46:20).

Ch. 46:24 The African Hebrew Israelites shall be delivered into the hands of the 'new folks' of North America. (Egypt=Africa) (North=North America)

24 The daughter of Egypt (Africa) shall be confounded; she shall be delivered into the hand of the people of the north. (North America)

(Jeremiah 46:24).

Ch. 47:2 The 'new folks' would come from the north country (North America) and take over the land of Africa.

2 Thus saith the LORD; Behold, waters rise up out of the north, (North America) and shall be an overflowing flood, and shall overflow the land, (Africa) and all that is therein; the city, and them that dwell therein: then the men shall cry, and all the inhabitants of the land shall howl.

(Jeremiah 47:2).

Ch. 48: This whole chapter speaks to the destruction of the African Gentile Nations. Moab, Nebo, Kiriathaim, Misgab, Heshbon, Chemosh, etc,., are all Anachronisms for AFRICAN Nations that 'new folks' presently control.

605/3617

Jeremiah 18:15-17... The Children of Israel and the Gentile old folks were punished because they turned their backs on God's laws.

15 Because my people (African Hebrews) hath forgotten me, they have burned incense to vanity, and they have caused them to stumble in their ways from the ancient paths, to walk in paths, in a way not cast up;

16 To make their land (Africa) desolate, and a perpetual hissing; every one that passeth thereby shall be astonished, and wag his head.

17 I will scatter them as with an east wind before the enemy; I will shew them the back, and not the face, in the day of their calamity.

(Jeremiah 18:15-17).

605/3617

Jeremiah Chapter 19 explains how God would bring evil upon the African Hebrews and punish them for forsaking Him.

1 Thus saith the LORD, Go and get a potter's earthen bottle, and take of the ancients of the people, and of the ancients of the priests;

2 And go forth unto the valley of the son of Hinnom, (Africa) which is by the entry of the east gate, and proclaim there the words that I shall tell thee,

3 And say, Hear ye the word of the LORD, O kings of Judah, (African Hebrews)and inhabitants of Jerusalem; (Africa) Thus saith the LORD of hosts, the God of Israel; Behold, I will bring evil upon this place, the which whosoever heareth, his ears shall tingle.

4 Because they have forsaken me, and have estranged this place, and have burned incense in it unto other gods, whom neither they nor their fathers have known, nor the kings of Judah, and have filled this place with the blood of innocents;

5 They have built also the high places of Baal, (Gentile idol) to burn their sons with fire for burnt offerings unto Baal, which I commanded not, nor spake it, neither came it into my mind:

6 Therefore, behold, the days come, saith the LORD, that this place shall no more be called Tophet, (An African valley where human sacrifices were made by Gentile Africans) or The valley of the son of Hinnom, (A dumping ground for human sacrifices) but The valley of slaughter.

7 And I will make void the counsel of Judah (African Hebrews) and Jerusalem (Africa) in this place; and I will cause them to fall by the sword before their enemies, and by the hands of them that seek their lives: and their carcases will I give to be meat for the fowls of the heaven, and for the beasts of the earth.

8 And I will make this city (African) desolate, and an hissing; every one that passeth thereby shall be astonished and hiss because of all the plagues thereof.

9 And I will cause them to eat the flesh of their sons and the flesh of their daughters, and they shall eat every one the flesh of his friend in the siege and straitness, wherewith their enemies, and they that seek their lives, shall straiten them.

10 Then shalt thou break the bottle in the sight of the men that go with thee,

11 And shalt say unto them, Thus saith the LORD of hosts; Even so will I break this people and this city, as one breaketh a potter's

vessel, that cannot be made whole again: and they shall bury them in Tophet, till there be no place to bury.

12 Thus will I do unto this place, saith the LORD, and to the inhabitants thereof, and even make this city as Tophet:

13 And the houses of Jerusalem, (Africa) and the houses of the kings of Judah,(African Hebrews) shall be defiled as the place of Tophet, because of all the houses upon whose roofs they have burned incense unto all the host of heaven, and have poured out drink offerings unto other gods.

14 Then came Jeremiah from Tophet, whither the LORD had sent him to prophesy; and he stood in the court of the LORD'S house; and said to all the people,

15 Thus saith the LORD of hosts, the God of Israel; Behold, I will bring upon this city and upon all her towns all the evil that I have pronounced against it, because they have hardened their necks, that they might not hear my words.

(Jeremiah 19:1-15).

602/3620

Jeremiah Chapter 13--God sending 'new folks' to strip the African Hebrews and the Gentile old folks from Africa.

1 Thus saith the LORD unto me, Go and get thee a linen girdle, and put it upon thy loins, and put it not in water.

2 So I got a girdle according to the word of the LORD, and put it on my loins.

3 And the word of the LORD came unto me the second time, saying,

4 Take the girdle that thou hast got, which is upon thy loins, and arise, go to Euphrates, (Longest river in Africa/Asia during the time of Jeremiah) and hide it there in a hole of the rock.

5 So I went, and hid it by Euphrates, as the LORD commanded me.

6 And it came to pass after many days, that the LORD said unto me, Arise, go to Euphrates, and take the girdle from thence, which I commanded thee to hide there.

7 Then I went to Euphrates, and digged, and took the girdle from the place where I had hid it: and, behold, the girdle was marred, it was profitable for nothing.

8 Then the word of the LORD came unto me, saying,

9 Thus saith the LORD, After this manner will I mar the pride of Judah, (African Hebrews) and the great pride of Jerusalem. (Africa)

10 This evil people, which refuse to hear my words, which walk in the imagination of their heart, and walk after other gods, to serve them, and to worship them, shall even be as this girdle, which is good for nothing.

11 For as the girdle cleaveth to the loins of a man, so have I caused to cleave unto me the whole house of Israel (African Hebrews) and the whole house of Judah, (African Hebrews) saith the LORD; that they might be unto me for a people, and for a name, and for a praise, and for a glory: but they would not hear.

12 Therefore thou shalt speak unto them this word; Thus saith the LORD God of Israel, Every bottle shall be filled with wine: and they shall say unto thee, Do we not certainly know that every bottle shall be filled with wine?

13 Then shalt thou say unto them, Thus saith the LORD, Behold, I will fill all the inhabitants of this land, even the kings that sit upon David's throne, and the priests, and the prophets, and all the inhabitants of Jerusalem, with drunkenness.

14 And I will dash them one against another, even the fathers and the sons together, saith the LORD: I will not pity, nor spare, nor have mercy, but destroy them.

15 Hear ye, and give ear; be not proud: for the LORD hath spoken.

16 Give glory to the LORD your God, before he cause darkness, and before your feet stumble upon the dark mountains, and, while ye look for light, he turn it into the shadow of death, and make it gross darkness.

17 But if ye will not hear it, my soul shall weep in secret places for your pride; and mine eye shall weep sore, and run down with tears, because the LORD'S flock is carried away captive.

18 Say unto the king and to the queen, Humble yourselves, sit down: for your principalities shall come down, even the crown of your glory.

19 The cities of the south shall be shut up, and none shall open them: Judah (African Hebrews) shall be carried away captive all of it, it shall be wholly carried away captive.

20 Lift up your eyes, and behold them that come from the north: (New folks from North America) where is the flock that was given thee, thy beautiful flock?

21 What wilt thou say when he shall punish thee? for thou hast taught them to be captains, and as chief over thee: shall not sorrows take thee, as a woman in travail?

22 And if thou say in thine heart, Wherefore come these things upon me? For the greatness of thine iniquity are thy skirts discovered, and thy heels made bare.

23 Can the Ethiopian (African) change his skin, or the leopard his spots? then may ye also do good, that are accustomed to do evil.

24 Therefore will I scatter them as the stubble that passeth away by the wind of the wilderness.

25 This is thy lot, the portion of thy measures from me, saith the LORD; because thou hast forgotten me, and trusted in falsehood.

26 Therefore will I discover thy skirts upon thy face, that thy shame may appear.

27 I have seen thine adulteries, and thy neighings, the lewdness of thy whoredom, and thine abominations on the hills in the fields. Woe unto thee, O Jerusalem! (African) wilt thou not be made clean? when shall it once be?

(Jeremiah 13:1-27).

601/3621

Jeremiah Chapter 14. In this chapter, Jeremiah pleaded for the Children of Israel, but he was too late. God had rejected the African Hebrews for sure.

1 The word of the LORD that came to Jeremiah concerning the dearth.

2 Judah (African Hebrews) mourneth, and the gates thereof languish; they are black unto the ground; and the cry of Jerusalem (Africa) is gone up.

3 And their nobles have sent their little ones to the waters: they came to the pits, and found no water; they returned with their vessels empty; they were ashamed and confounded, and covered their heads.

4 Because the ground is chapt, for there was no rain in the earth, the plowmen were ashamed, they covered their heads.

5 Yea, the hind also calved in the field, and forsook it, because there was no grass.

6 And the wild asses did stand in the high places, they snuffed up the wind like dragons; their eyes did fail, because there was no grass.

7 O LORD, though our iniquities testify against us, do thou it for thy name's sake: for our backslidings are many; we have sinned against thee.

8 O the hope of Israel, the saviour thereof in time of trouble, why shouldest thou be as a stranger in the land, and as a wayfaring man that turneth aside to tarry for a night?

9 Why shouldest thou be as a man astonied, as a mighty man that cannot save? yet thou, O LORD, art in the midst of us, and we are called by thy name; leave us not.

10 Thus saith the LORD unto this people, Thus have they loved to wander, they have not refrained their feet, therefore the LORD doth not accept them; he will now remember their iniquity, and visit their sins.

11 Then said the LORD unto me, Pray not for this people for their good.

12 When they fast, I will not hear their cry; and when they offer burnt offering and an oblation, I will not accept them: but I will consume them by the sword, and by the famine, and by the pestilence.

13 Then said I, Ah, Lord GOD! behold, the prophets say unto them, Ye shall not see the sword, neither shall ye have famine; but I will give you assured peace in this place.

14 Then the LORD said unto me, The prophets prophesy lies in my name: I sent them not, neither have I commanded them, neither spake unto them: they prophesy unto you a false vision and divination, and a thing of nought, and the deceit of their heart.

15 Therefore thus saith the LORD concerning the prophets that prophesy in my name, and I sent them not, yet they say, Sword and famine shall not be in this land; By sword and famine shall those prophets be consumed.

16 And the people to whom they prophesy shall be cast out in the streets of Jerusalem (Africa) because of the famine and the sword; and they shall have none to bury them, them, their wives, nor their sons, nor their daughters: for I will pour their wickedness upon them.

17 Therefore thou shalt say this word unto them; Let mine eyes run down with tears night and day, and let them not cease: for the virgin daughter of my people is broken with a great breach, with a very grievous blow.

18 If I go forth into the field, then behold the slain with the sword! and if I enter into the city, then behold them that are sick with famine! yea, both the prophet and the priest go about into a land that they know not.

19 Hast thou utterly rejected Judah? (African Hebrews) hath thy soul lothed Zion? (Africa) why hast thou smitten us, and there is no healing for us? we looked for peace, and there is no good; and for the time of healing, and behold trouble!

20 We acknowledge, O LORD, our wickedness, and the iniquity of our fathers: for we have sinned against thee.

21 Do not abhor us, for thy name's sake, do not disgrace the throne of thy glory: remember, break not thy covenant with us.

22 Are there any among the vanities of the Gentiles that can cause rain? or can the heavens give showers? art not thou he, O LORD our God? therefore we will wait upon thee: for thou hast made all these things.

(Jeremiah 14:1-22).

601/3621

Jeremiah 15:1-9. God explaining how He will destroy and punish the Children of Israel (Black Folks) for their sins.

1 Then said the LORD unto me, Though Moses and Samuel stood before me, yet my mind could not be toward this people: cast them out of my sight, and let them go forth.

2 And it shall come to pass, if they say unto thee, Whither shall we go forth? then thou shalt tell them, Thus saith the LORD; Such as are for death, to death; and such as are for the sword, to the sword; and such as are for the famine, to the famine; and such as are for the captivity, to the captivity.

3 And I will appoint over them four kinds, saith the LORD: the sword to slay, and the dogs to tear, and the fowls of the heaven, and the beasts of the earth, to devour and destroy.

4 And I will cause them to be removed into all kingdoms of the earth, because of Manasseh (African Hebrews) the son of Hezekiah king of Judah, for that which he did in Jerusalem.

5 For who shall have pity upon thee, O Jerusalem? (Africa) or who shall bemoan thee? or who shall go aside to ask how thou doest?

6 Thou hast forsaken me, saith the LORD, thou art gone backward: therefore will I stretch out my hand against thee, and destroy thee; I am weary with repenting.

7 And I will fan them with a fan in the gates of the land; I will bereave them of children, I will destroy my people, since they return not from their ways.

8 Their widows are increased to me above the sand of the seas: I have brought upon them against the mother of the young men a spoiler at noonday: I have caused him to fall upon it suddenly, and terrors upon the city.

9 She that hath borne seven languisheth: she hath given up the ghost; her sun is gone down while it was yet day: she hath been ashamed and confounded: and the residue of them will I deliver to the sword before their enemies, saith the LORD.

(Jeremiah 15:1-9).

601/3621

Jeremiah 15:11-14. God gave 'new folks' everything that the African Hebrews had when HE punished them. God put Israel on slave ships, and placed them in America for 400 years.

11 The LORD said, Verily it shall be well with thy remnant; verily I will cause the enemy to entreat thee well in the time of evil and in the time of affliction.

12 Shall iron break the northern iron and the steel?

13 Thy substance and thy treasures will I give to the spoil (new folks) without price, and that for all thy sins, even in all thy borders.

14 And I will make thee to pass with thine enemies into a land which thou knowest not:(America) for a fire is kindled in mine anger, which shall burn upon you.

(Jeremiah 15:11-14).

601/3621

Jeremiah 15:19-21. The African Hebrews will be delivered from America. Going back to Africa is un-thinkable to most black folks.(old folks) Since being in America, some feel that they have 'made it', and would not think of leaving their material possessions behind. But God is preparing to do a 'terrible' thing to America, and the 'old folks' that do not turn to God's Commandments, will perish in America and will not be able to return to Africa. We must remember that God did not place black folks (old folks) in America to be Americans. They were placed there for violating the Ten Commandments of GOD. God placed them there to be 'oppressed', and afflicted for 400 years. After that time, GOD will 'try them', 'test them', ';prove them', deliver them and place them in their own land, in Africa. The "American Way" is not the way for God's Chosen People, the Children of Israel, the African Hebrew Israelites, the African American.

19 Therefore thus saith the LORD, If thou return, then will I bring thee (African Hebrews) again, and thou shalt stand before me: and if thou take forth the precious from the vile, thou shalt be as my mouth: let them return unto thee; but return not thou unto them.

20 And I will make thee unto this people a fenced brasen wall: and they (Gentiles) shall fight against thee, but they shall not prevail against thee: for I am with thee to save thee and to deliver thee, saith the LORD.

21 And I will deliver thee out of the hand of the wicked, (new folks) and I will redeem thee out of the hand of the terrible. (new folks)

(Jeremiah 15:19-21).

601/3621

Jeremiah 16:1-9. Israel's life in America. After reading these verses, we should be able to clearly see that the Children of Israel are 'black folks' (old folks). Black Folks ('old folks') are the only people on earth that fit this description, and are the only people that have experienced the horrible things that are recorded in these verses.

1 The word of the LORD came also unto me, saying,

2 Thou shalt not take thee a wife, neither shalt thou have sons or daughters in this place. (American slavery)

3 For thus saith the LORD concerning the sons and concerning the daughters that are born in this place, (America) and concerning their mothers that bare them, and concerning their fathers that begat them in this land; (America)

4 They shall die of grievous deaths; they shall not be lamented; neither shall they be buried; but they shall be as dung upon the face of the earth: and they shall be consumed by the sword, and by famine; and their carcases shall be meat for the fowls of heaven, and for the beasts of the earth.

5 For thus saith the LORD, Enter not into the house of mourning, neither go to lament nor bemoan them: for I have taken away my peace from this people, (African Hebrews) saith the LORD, even lovingkindness and mercies.

6 Both the great and the small shall die in this land: (America) they shall not be buried, neither shall men lament for them, nor cut themselves, nor make themselves bald for them:

7 Neither shall men tear themselves for them in mourning, to comfort them for the dead; neither shall men give them the cup of

consolation to drink for their father or for their mother.

8 Thou shalt not also go into the house of feasting, to sit with them to eat and to drink.

9 For thus saith the LORD of hosts, the God of Israel; Behold, I will cause to cease out of this place in your eyes, and in your days, the voice of mirth, and the voice of gladness, the voice of the bridegroom, and the voice of the bride.

(Jeremiah 16:1-9).

601/3621

Jeremiah 16:10-13. God explains why HE placed the African Hebrews and the Gentile old folks in America.

10 And it shall come to pass, when thou shalt shew this people (black folks)all these words, and they shall say unto thee, Wherefore hath the LORD pronounced all this great evil against us? or what is our iniquity? or what is our sin that we have committed against the LORD our God?

11 Then shalt thou say unto them, Because your fathers have forsaken me, saith the LORD, and have walked after other gods, and have served them, and have worshipped them, and have forsaken me, and have not kept my law;

12 And ye have done worse than your fathers; for, behold, ye walk every one after the imagination of his evil heart, that they may not hearken unto me:

13 Therefore will I cast you out of this land (Africa) into a land that ye know not, (America) neither ye nor your fathers; and there shall ye serve other gods day and night; where I will not shew you favour.

(Jeremiah 16:10-13).

601/3621

Jeremiah 16:14-15. Israel going back to Africa. God's chosen people are scattered all over the world, but they will be gathered and returned to the mother-land of Africa. Emphasis are placed on the chosen people that reside in North America.

14 Therefore, behold, the days come, saith the LORD, that it shall no more be said, The LORD liveth, that brought up the children of Israel out of the land of Egypt; (The 1st Exodus)

15 But, The LORD liveth, that brought up the children of Israel from the land of the north, (North America) and from all the lands whither he had driven them: and I will bring them again into their land that I gave unto their fathers. (Africa) (The 2nd Exodus)

(Jeremiah 16:14-15).

601/3621

Jeremiah 16:19-21. What 'new folks' and 'gentile old folks will say when they see that the Children of Israel are GOd's true chosen people, and that 'GOD" is everyone's (only) saviour, not 'Jesus'.

19 O LORD, my strength, and my fortress, and my refuge in the day of affliction, the Gentiles shall come unto thee from the ends of the earth, and shall say, Surely our fathers have inherited LIES, vanity, and things wherein there is no profit.

20 Shall a man make gods unto himself, and they are no gods?

21 Therefore, behold, I will this once cause them to know, I will cause them to know mine hand and my might; and they shall know that my name is The LORD.

(Jeremiah 16:19-21).

601/3621

Jeremiah 17:1-4. God took everything from black folks (old folks), punished them and placed them in America to serve 'new folks' (white folks) for 400 years.

1 The sin of Judah (African Hebrews) is written with a pen of iron, and with the point of a diamond: it is graven upon the table of their heart, and upon the horns of your altars;

2 Whilst their children remember their altars and their groves by the green trees upon the high hills.

3 O my mountain in the field, I will give thy substance and all thy treasures to the spoil, (new folks) and thy high places for sin, throughout all thy borders.

4 And thou, even thyself, shalt discontinue from thine heritage that I gave thee; and I will cause thee to serve thine enemies in the land which thou knowest not:(America) for ye have kindled a fire in mine anger, which shall burn for ever.

(Jeremiah 17:1-4).

601/3621

Jeremiah 17:19-27. Hard-headed Israel kept breaking God's Sabbath Day, God's warning of revenge.

19 Thus said the LORD unto me; Go and stand in the gate of the children of the people, whereby the kings of Judah (African Hebrews) come in, and by the which they go out, and in all the gates of Jerusalem; (Africa)

20 And say unto them, Hear ye the word of the LORD, ye kings of Judah, and all Judah, and all the inhabitants of Jerusalem, (Africa) that enter in by these gates:

21 Thus saith the LORD; Take heed to yourselves, and bear no burden on the sabbath day, nor bring it in by the gates of Jerusalem;

22 Neither carry forth a burden out of your houses on the sabbath day, neither do ye any work, but hallow ye the sabbath day, as I commanded your fathers.

23 But they obeyed not, neither inclined their ear, but made their neck stiff, that they might not hear, nor receive instruction.

24 And it shall come to pass, if ye diligently hearken unto me, saith the LORD, to bring in no burden through the gates of this city on the sabbath day, but hallow the sabbath day, to do no work therein;

25 Then shall there enter into the gates of this city kings and princes sitting upon the throne of David, (African Hebrews) riding in chariots and on horses, they, and their princes, the men of Judah, (African Hebrews) and the inhabitants of Jerusalem: (Africa) and

this city shall remain for ever.

26 And they shall come from the cities of Judah, and from the places about Jerusalem, and from the land of Benjamin, and from the plain, and from the mountains, and from the south, bringing burnt offerings, and sacrifices, and meat offerings, and incense, and bringing sacrifices of praise, unto the house of the LORD.

27 But if ye will not hearken unto me to hallow the sabbath day, and not to bear a burden, even entering in at the gates of Jerusalem on the sabbath day; then will I kindle a fire in the gates thereof, and it shall devour the palaces of Jerusalem, and it shall not be quenched.

(Jeremiah 17:19-27).

600/3622

Jeremiah Chapter 7. In this whole chapter, God warned the Children of Israel to mend their ways, so HE wouldn't strip them from their land in Africa.

1 The word that came to Jeremiah from the LORD, saying,

2 Stand in the gate of the LORD'S house, and proclaim there this word, and say, Hear the word of the LORD, all ye of Judah, (African Hebrews) that enter in at these gates to worship the LORD.

3 Thus saith the LORD of hosts, the God of Israel, Amend your ways and your doings, and I will cause you to dwell in this place.

4 Trust ye not in lying words, saying, The temple of the LORD, The temple of the LORD, The temple of the LORD, are these.

5 For if ye throughly amend your ways and your doings; if ye throughly execute judgment between a man and his neighbour;

6 If ye oppress not the stranger, the fatherless, and the widow, and shed not innocent blood in this place, neither walk after other gods to your hurt:

7 Then will I cause you to dwell in this place, (Africa) in the land that I gave to your fathers, for ever and ever.

8 Behold, ye trust in lying words, that cannot profit.

9 Will ye steal, murder, and commit adultery, and swear falsely, and burn incense unto Baal, (Gentile idol) and walk after other gods whom ye know not;

10 And come and stand before me in this house, which is called by my name, and say, We are delivered to do all these abominations?

11 Is this house, which is called by my name, become a den of robbers in your eyes? Behold, even I have seen it, saith the LORD.

12 But go ye now unto my place which was in Shiloh, (A city in Africa where the tabernacle remained from the time of Joshua to the days of Samuel) where I set my name at the first, and see what I did to it for the wickedness of my people Israel.

13 And now, because ye have done all these works, saith the LORD, and I spake unto you, rising up early and speaking, but ye heard not; and I called you, but ye answered not;

14 Therefore will I do unto this house, which is called by my name, wherein ye trust, and unto the place which I gave to you and to your fathers, as I have done to Shiloh.

15 And I will cast you out of my sight, as I have cast out all your brethren, even the whole seed of Ephraim. (African Hebrews)

16 Therefore pray not thou for this people, neither lift up cry nor prayer for them, neither make intercession to me: for I will not hear thee.

17 Seest thou not what they do in the cities of Judah and in the streets of Jerusalem?

18 The children gather wood, and the fathers kindle the fire, and the women knead their dough, to make cakes to the queen of heaven, and to pour out drink offerings unto other gods, that they may provoke me to anger.

19 Do they provoke me to anger? saith the LORD: do they not provoke themselves to the confusion of their own faces?

20 Therefore thus saith the Lord GOD; Behold, mine anger and my fury shall be poured out upon this place, upon man, and upon

beast, and upon the trees of the field, and upon the fruit of the ground; and it shall burn, and shall not be quenched.

21 Thus saith the LORD of hosts, the God of Israel; Put your burnt offerings unto your sacrifices, and eat flesh.

22 For I spake not unto your fathers, nor commanded them in the day that I brought them out of the land of Egypt, concerning burnt offerings or sacrifices:

23 But this thing commanded I them, saying, Obey my voice, and I will be your God, and ye shall be my people: and walk ye in all the ways that I have commanded you, that it may be well unto you.

24 But they hearkened not, nor inclined their ear, but walked in the counsels and in the imagination of their evil heart, and went backward, and not forward.

25 Since the day that your fathers came forth out of the land of Egypt unto this day I have even sent unto you all my servants the prophets, daily rising up early and sending them:

26 Yet they hearkened not unto me, nor inclined their ear, but hardened their neck: they did worse than their fathers.

27 Therefore thou shalt speak all these words unto them; but they will not hearken to thee: thou shalt also call unto them; but they will not answer thee.

28 But thou shalt say unto them, This is a nation that obeyeth not the voice of the LORD their God, nor receiveth correction: TRUTH is perished, and is cut off from their mouth.

29 Cut off thine hair, O Jerusalem, (Africa) and cast it away, and take up a lamentation on high places; for the LORD hath rejected and forsaken the generation of his wrath.

30 For the children of Judah (African Hebrews) have done evil in my sight, saith the LORD: they have set their abominations in the house which is called by my name, to pollute it.

31 And they have built the high places of Tophet, which is in the valley of the son of Hinnom, to burn their sons and their daughters in the fire; which I commanded them not, neither came it into my heart.

32 Therefore, behold, the days come, saith the LORD, that it shall no more be called Tophet, nor the valley of the son of Hinnom, but the valley of slaughter: for they shall bury in Tophet, till there be no place.

33 And the carcases of this people shall be meat for the fowls of the heaven, and for the beasts of the earth; and none shall fray them away.

34 Then will I cause to cease from the cities of Judah, and from the streets of Jerusalem, the voice of mirth, and the voice of gladness, the voice of the bridegroom, and the voice of the bride: for the land shall be desolate.

(Jeremiah 7:1-34).

600/3622

Jeremiah 9:13-16. God preparing to punish the African Hebrews for forsaking HIS law, and scatter them among the 'new folks'. (white folks)

13 And the LORD saith, Because they (African Hebrews) \have forsaken my law which I set before them, and have not obeyed my voice, neither walked therein;

14 But have walked after the imagination of their own heart, and after Baalim, (Gentile false god/idol) which their fathers taught them:

15 Therefore thus saith the LORD of hosts, the God of Israel; Behold, I will feed them, (African Hebrews) even this people, with wormwood, and give them water of gall to drink.

16 I will scatter them also among the heathen, (new folks) whom neither they nor their fathers have known: (because 'new folks' had not been created yet) and I will send a sword after them, till I have consumed them.

(Jeremiah 9:13-16).

600/3622

Jeremiah 10:21-22. Pastors caused the people to fall because they did not teach the people to keep the Ten Commandments. The

African Hebrews and the African Gentile old folks, ended up in North America for breaking God's Ten Commandments.

21 For the pastors are become brutish, and have not sought the LORD: therefore they shall not prosper, and all their flocks shall be scattered.

22 Behold, the noise of the bruit (new folks) is come, and a great commotion out of the north country, (North America) to make the cities of Judah (Africa) desolate, and a den of dragons.

(Jeremiah 10:21-22).

600/3622

Chapter 47. God tells the Gentile old folks (Philistines) that they also will be punished and placed in North America for 400 years. Tyrus, Zidon, Caphtor, Gaza, Ashkelon are anachronisims for 'Gentile old folks' and their dwelling places.

1 The word of the LORD that came to Jeremiah the prophet against the Philistines, before that Pharaoh smote Gaza.

2 Thus saith the LORD; Behold, waters rise up out of the north, (North America) and shall be an overflowing flood, and shall overflow the land, (Africa) and all that is therein; the city, and them that dwell therein: then the men shall cry, and all the inhabitants of the land shall howl.

3 At the noise of the stamping of the hoofs of his (new folks) strong horses, at the rushing of his chariots, and at the rumbling of his wheels, the fathers shall not look back to their children for feebleness of hands;

4 Because of the day that cometh to spoil all the Philistines, (Gentile Africans) and to cut off from Tyrus (African Gentiles) and Zidon (Gentile Africans) every helper that remaineth: for the LORD will spoil the Philistines, the remnant of the country of Caphtor. (Gentile Africans)

5 Baldness is come upon Gaza; Ashkelon is cut off with the remnant of their valley: how long wilt thou cut thyself?

6 O thou sword of the LORD, how long will it be ere thou be quiet? put up thyself into thy scabbard, rest, and be still.

7 How can it be quiet, seeing the LORD hath given it a charge against Ashkelon, and against the sea shore? there hath he appointed it.

(Jeremiah 47:1-7).

600/3622

Chapter 48. God speaks to the same punishment for the Gentile old folks residing in Moab, Nebo, Kiriathaim, Misgab, Heshbon,Horonam, etc,. This chapter is full of African locations that are anachronisims for the 'gentile old folks'.

600/3622

Jeremiah Chapter 49. This chapter outlines God's judgements upon many African Gentile nations. The African Hebrews could not be punished without punishing the gentile old folks, because the 'new folks' (white folks) would not be able to distinguish one from another, because both were 'old folks' (black folks). All African locations in this chapter are 'anachronisims' for 'gentile old folks'. (Ammonites, Rabbah, Heshbon, Ai, Edom, Dedan, Esau, Bozrah, Damascus, Hamath, Hazor, Elam, etc,)

1 Concerning the Ammonites, thus saith the LORD; Hath Israel no sons? hath he no heir? why then doth their king inherit Gad, and his people dwell in his cities?

2 Therefore, behold, the days come, saith the LORD, that I will cause an alarm of war to be heard in Rabbah of the Ammonites; and it shall be a desolate heap, and her daughters shall be burned with fire: then shall Israel be heir unto them that were his heirs, saith the LORD.

3 Howl, O Heshbon, for Ai is spoiled: cry, ye daughters of Rabbah, gird you with sackcloth; lament, and run to and fro by the hedges; for their king shall go into captivity, and his priests and his princes together.

4 Wherefore gloriest thou in the valleys, thy flowing valley, O backsliding daughter? that trusted in her treasures, saying, Who shall come unto me?

5 Behold, I will bring a fear upon thee, saith the Lord GOD of hosts, from all those that be about thee; and ye shall be driven out every man right forth; and none shall gather up him that wandereth.

6 And afterward I will bring again the captivity of the children of Ammon, saith the LORD.

7 Concerning Edom, thus saith the LORD of hosts; Is wisdom no more in Teman? is counsel perished from the prudent? is their wisdom vanished?

8 Flee ye, turn back, dwell deep, O inhabitants of Dedan; for I will bring the calamity of Esau upon him, the time that I will visit him.

9 If grapegatherers come to thee, would they not leave some gleaning grapes? if thieves by night, they will destroy till they have enough.

10 But I have made Esau bare, I have uncovered his secret places, and he shall not be able to hide himself: his seed is spoiled, and his brethren, and his neighbours, and he is not.

11 Leave thy fatherless children, I will preserve them alive; and let thy widows trust in me.

12 For thus saith the LORD; Behold, they whose judgment was not to drink of the cup have assuredly drunken; and art thou he that shall altogether go unpunished? thou shalt not go unpunished, but thou shalt surely drink of it.

13 For I have sworn by myself, saith the LORD, that Bozrah shall become a desolation, a reproach, a waste, and a curse; and all the cities thereof shall be perpetual wastes.

14 I have heard a rumour from the LORD, and an ambassador is sent unto the heathen, saying, Gather ye together, and come against her, and rise up to the battle.

15 For, lo, I will make thee small among the heathen, and despised among men.

16 Thy terribleness hath deceived thee, and the pride of thine heart, O thou that dwellest in the clefts of the rock, that holdest the height of the hill: though thou shouldest make thy nest as high as the eagle, I will bring thee down from thence, saith the LORD.

17 Also Edom shall be a desolation: every one that goeth by it shall be astonished, and shall hiss at all the plagues thereof.

18 As in the overthrow of Sodom and Gomorrah and the neighbour

cities thereof, saith the LORD, no man shall abide there, neither shall a son of man dwell in it.

19 Behold, he shall come up like a lion from the swelling of Jordan against the habitation of the strong: but I will suddenly make him run away from her: and who is a chosen man, that I may appoint over her? for who is like me? and who will appoint me the time? and who is that shepherd that will stand before me?

20 Therefore hear the counsel of the LORD, that he hath taken against Edom; and his purposes, that he hath purposed against the inhabitants of Teman: Surely the least of the flock shall draw them out: surely he shall make their habitations desolate with them.

21 The earth is moved at the noise of their fall, at the cry the noise thereof was heard in the Red sea.

22 Behold, he shall come up and fly as the eagle, and spread his wings over Bozrah: and at that day shall the heart of the mighty men of Edom be as the heart of a woman in her pangs.

23 Concerning Damascus. Hamath is confounded, and Arpad: for they have heard evil tidings: they are fainthearted; there is sorrow on the sea; it cannot be quiet.

24 Damascus is waxed feeble, and turneth herself to flee, and fear hath seized on her: anguish and sorrows have taken her, as a woman in travail.

25 How is the city of praise not left, the city of my joy!

26 Therefore her young men shall fall in her streets, and all the men of war shall be cut off in that day, saith the LORD of hosts.

27 And I will kindle a fire in the wall of Damascus, and it shall consume the palaces of Benhadad.

28 Concerning Kedar, and concerning the kingdoms of Hazor, which Nebuchadrezzar king of Babylon shall smite, thus saith the LORD; Arise ye, go up to Kedar, and spoil the men of the east.

29 Their tents and their flocks shall they take away: they shall take to themselves their curtains, and all their vessels, and their camels; and they shall cry unto them, Fear is on every side.

30 Flee, get you far off, dwell deep, O ye inhabitants of Hazor, saith the LORD; for Nebuchadrezzar king of Babylon hath taken counsel against you, and hath conceived a purpose against you.

31 Arise, get you up unto the wealthy nation, that dwelleth without care, saith the LORD, which have neither gates nor bars, which dwell alone.

32 And their camels shall be a booty, and the multitude of their cattle a spoil: and I will scatter into all winds them that are in the utmost corners; and I will bring their calamity from all sides thereof, saith the LORD.

33 And Hazor shall be a dwelling for dragons, and a desolation for ever: there shall no man abide there, nor any son of man dwell in it.

34 The word of the LORD that came to Jeremiah the prophet against Elam in the beginning of the reign of Zedekiah king of Judah, saying,

35 Thus saith the LORD of hosts; Behold, I will break the bow of Elam, the chief of their might.

36 And upon Elam will I bring the four winds from the four quarters of heaven, and will scatter them toward all those winds; and there shall be no nation whither the outcasts of Elam shall not come.

37 For I will cause Elam to be dismayed before their enemies, and before them that seek their life: and I will bring evil upon them, even my fierce anger, saith the LORD; and I will send the sword after them, till I have consumed them:

38 And I will set my throne in Elam, and will destroy from thence the king and the princes, saith the LORD.

39 But it shall come to pass in the latter days, that I will bring again the captivity of Elam, saith the LORD.

(Jeremiah 49:1-39).

599/3623

Jeremiah 23:1-2. God is talking to the Pastors that caused God's people to go astray from the Ten Commandments while in Africa. Pastors today will also be punished for turning the people away from God's law.

1 Woe be unto the pastors that destroy and scatter the sheep of my pasture! saith the LORD.

2 Therefore thus saith the LORD God of Israel against the pastors that feed my people; Ye have scattered my flock, and driven them away, and have not visited them: behold, I will visit upon you the evil of your doings, saith the LORD.

(Jeremiah 23:1-2).

599/3623

Jeremiah 23:3-4. God will gather the African Hebrews from all countries, bless them, comfort them and unite them into one nation of people again.

3 And I will gather the remnant of my flock (African Hebrews) out of all countries whither I have driven them, and will bring them again to their folds; and they shall be fruitful and increase.

4 And I will set up shepherds over them which shall feed them: and they shall fear no more, nor be dismayed, neither shall they be lacking, saith the LORD.

(Jeremiah 23:3-4).

599/3623

Jeremiah 23:7-8. Most people are familiar with the story in the book of Exodus where the African Hebrew escaped from the land of Egypt. Well these two verses tell how the Children of Israel (old folks) will be brought out of North America and other countries where they were driven, and how they will live in Africa again.

7 Therefore, behold, the days come, saith the LORD, that they (African Hebrews) shall no more say, The LORD liveth, which brought up the children of Israel out of the land of Egypt;

8 But, The LORD liveth, which brought up and which led the seed

of the house of Israel (African Hebrews) out of the north country, (North America) and from all countries whither I had driven them; and they shall dwell in their own land.

(Jeremiah 23:7-8).

599/3623

Jeremiah 23:9-40. God explaining how the Prophets and the Priest caused His chosen people to err, and why He had to make 'black folks' (old folks) a perpetual shame.

9 Mine heart within me is broken because of the prophets; all my bones shake; I am like a drunken man, and like a man whom wine hath overcome, because of the LORD, and because of the words of his holiness.

10 For the land (Africa) is full of adulterers; for because of swearing the land mourneth; the pleasant places of the wilderness are dried up, and their course is evil, and their force is not right.

11 For both prophet and priest are profane; yea, in my house have I found their wickedness, saith the LORD.

12 Wherefore their way shall be unto them as slippery ways in the darkness: they shall be driven on, and fall therein: for I will bring evil upon them, even the year of their visitation, saith the LORD.

13 And I have seen folly in the prophets of Samaria; (Another name for the Northern Kingdom of the Children of Israel/African Hebrews) they prophesied in Baal, and caused my people Israel to err.

14 I have seen also in the prophets of Jerusalem an horrible thing: they commit adultery, and walk in lies: they strengthen also the hands of evildoers, that none doth return from his wickedness: they are all of them unto me as Sodom, and the inhabitants thereof as Gomorrah.

15 Therefore thus saith the LORD of hosts concerning the prophets; Behold, I will feed them with wormwood, and make them drink the water of gall: for from the prophets of Jerusalem is profaneness gone forth into all the land.

16 Thus saith the LORD of hosts, Hearken not unto the words of the

prophets that prophesy unto you: they make you vain: they speak a vision of their own heart, and not out of the mouth of the LORD.

17 They say still unto them that despise me, The LORD hath said, Ye shall have peace; and they say unto every one that walketh after the imagination of his own heart, No evil shall come upon you.

18 For who hath stood in the counsel of the LORD, and hath perceived and heard his word? who hath marked his word, and heard it?

19 Behold, a whirlwind of the LORD is gone forth in fury, even a grievous whirlwind: it shall fall grievously upon the head of the wicked.

20 The anger of the LORD shall not return, until he have executed, and till he have performed the thoughts of his heart: in the latter days ye shall consider it perfectly.

21 I have not sent these prophets, yet they ran: I have not spoken to them, yet they prophesied.

22 But if they had stood in my counsel, and had caused my people to hear my words, then they should have turned them from their evil way, and from the evil of their doings.

23 Am I a God at hand, saith the LORD, and not a God afar off?

24 Can any hide himself in secret places that I shall not see him? saith the LORD. Do not I fill heaven and earth? saith the LORD.

25 I have heard what the prophets said, that prophesy lies in my name, saying, I have dreamed, I have dreamed.

26 How long shall this be in the heart of the prophets that prophesy lies? yea, they are prophets of the deceit of their own heart;

27 Which think to cause my people to forget my name by their dreams which they tell every man to his neighbour, as their fathers have forgotten my name for Baal. (Gentile false idol)

28 The prophet that hath a dream, let him tell a dream; and he that hath my word, let him speak my word faithfully. What is the chaff to the wheat? saith the LORD.

29 Is not my word like as a fire? saith the LORD; and like a hammer that breaketh the rock in pieces?

30 Therefore, behold, I am against the prophets, saith the LORD, that steal my words every one from his neighbour.

31 Behold, I am against the prophets, saith the LORD, that use their tongues, and say, He saith.

32 Behold, I am against them that prophesy false dreams, saith the LORD, and do tell them, and cause my people to err by their lies, and by their lightness; yet I sent them not, nor commanded them: therefore they shall not profit this people at all, saith the LORD.

33 And when this people, or the prophet, or a priest, shall ask thee, saying, What is the burden of the LORD? thou shalt then say unto them, What burden? I will even forsake you, saith the LORD.

34 And as for the prophet, and the priest, and the people, that shall say, The burden of the LORD, I will even punish that man and his house.

35 Thus shall ye say every one to his neighbour, and every one to his brother, What hath the LORD answered? and, What hath the LORD spoken?

36 And the burden of the LORD shall ye mention no more: for every man's word shall be his burden; for ye have perverted the words of the living God, of the LORD of hosts our God.

37 Thus shalt thou say to the prophet, What hath the LORD answered thee? and, What hath the LORD spoken?

38 But since ye say, The burden of the LORD; therefore thus saith the LORD; Because ye say this word, The burden of the LORD, and I have sent unto you, saying, Ye shall not say, The burden of the LORD;

39 Therefore, behold, I, even I, will utterly forget you, and I will forsake you, and the city that I gave you and your fathers, and cast you out of my presence:

40 And I will bring an everlasting reproach upon you, and a perpetual shame, which shall not be forgotten.

(Jeremiah 23:9-40).

598/3624

Jeremiah 24:5-7. The African Hebrews are likened unto 'good figs'. In other words they were placed in America to be purified for 'good'. After the 400 year captivity they will turn to God with their whole heart, and God will take them back to Africa. (Chaldeans = Anachronism for America)

5 Thus saith the LORD, the God of Israel; Like these good figs, so will I acknowledge them that are carried away captive of Judah, (African Hebrews) whom I have sent out of this place into the land of the Chaldeans (Americans) for their good.

6 For I will set mine eyes upon them for good, and I will bring them again to this land: (Africa) and I will build them, and not pull them down; and I will plant them, and not pluck them up.

7 And I will give them an heart to know me, that I am the LORD: and they shall be my people, and I will be their God: for they shall return unto me with their whole heart.

(Jeremiah 24:5-7).

598/3624

Jeremiah 24:9-10. The African Hebrews are likened unto 'bad figs'. In other words they broke the Ten Commandments so much that their sins destroyed them from Africa. They lost everything; their name, their land, their heritage, their nativity, their language, their GOD. They became a reproach, a byword, a taunt, a curse, and called 'nigger' everywhere they went. Millions were killed by the sword when God sent the new folks to Africa. Millions were killed and buried in the Atlantic Ocean, and many are still dying by famine and pestilence. All this and more happened to 'old folks' (black folks) because they violated God's universal laws, and refused to keep the Ten Commandments.

9 And I will deliver them (African Hebrews) to be removed into all the kingdoms of the earth for their hurt, to be a reproach and a proverb, a taunt and a curse, in all places whither I shall drive them.

10 And I will send the sword, the famine, and the pestilence, among them, till they be consumed from off the land (Africa) that I gave unto them and to their fathers.

(Jeremiah 24:9-10).

597/3625

The first Babylonian captivity of the African Hebrews.

595/3627

Jeremiah 50:1-3. God told the Prophet Jeremiah to tell the people of Babylon and other African gentile nations that HE will send the 'new folks' (white folks) from North America to destroy them for their Idolatry. Babylon, Chaldeans, Bel, and Merodach are 'anachronisms' for African Gentile locations.

1 The word that the LORD spake against Babylon and against the land of the Chaldeans by Jeremiah the prophet.

2 Declare ye among the nations, and publish, and set up a standard; publish, and conceal not: say, Babylon is taken, Bel is confounded, Merodach is broken in pieces; her idols are confounded, her images are broken in pieces.

3 For out of the north (North America) there cometh up a nation against her, (Africa) which shall make her land desolate, and none shall dwell therein: they shall remove, they shall depart, both man and beast.

(Jeremiah 50:1-3).

595/3627

Jeremiah 50:4-8. The day is coming when 'old folks' (black folks) will recognize that they are a 'lost, confused, confounded and troubled people'. They will unite together and seek the 'one true GOD', and turn from the Ministers, Pastors and shepherds that have led them astray.

4 In those days, and in that time, saith the LORD, the children of Israel (African Hebrews)shall come, they and the children of Judah (African Hebrews) together, going and weeping: they shall go, and seek the LORD their God.

5 They shall ask the way to Zion (Africa) with their faces thitherward, saying, Come, and let us join ourselves to the LORD in a perpetual covenant that shall not be forgotten.

6 My people hath been lost sheep: their shepherds (False Ministers,

Pastors etc) have caused them to go astray, they have turned them away on the mountains: they have gone from mountain to hill, they have forgotten their restingplace.

7 All that found them have devoured them: and their adversaries (new folks) said, We offend not, because they have sinned against the LORD, the habitation of justice, even the LORD, the hope of their fathers.

8 Remove out of the midst of Babylon, (America in this case) and go forth out of the land of the Chaldeans, (new folks) and be as the he goats before the flocks.

(Jeremiah 50:4-8).

595/3627

Jeremiah 50:9-16. God telling the African gentiles that they will be destroyed by the people from North America for rejoicing when the African Hebrews were punished. (Chaldea and Babylon are anachronisms for the African Gentiles) The balance of Chapter 50 repeats the prophecy of destruction for the African gentile old folks. Verses 41 repeats that the new folks will come from North America, and verse 42 speaks to their 'spirit', 'attitude', character and their personality. In Chapter 51, the judgement prophecy against the gentile old folks continues. North America is mentioned again in verse 48.

9 For, lo, I will raise and cause to come up against Babylon (African Gentiles) an assembly of great nations from the north country:(North America) and they shall set themselves in array against her; from thence she shall be taken: their arrows shall be as of a mighty expert man; none shall return in vain.

10 And Chaldea (African Gentile location) shall be a spoil: all that spoil her shall be satisfied, saith the LORD.

11 Because ye were glad, because ye rejoiced, O ye destroyers of mine heritage, because ye are grown fat as the heifer at grass, and bellow as bulls;

12 Your mother shall be sore confounded; she that bare you shall be ashamed: behold, the hindermost of the nations shall be a wilderness, a dry land, and a desert.

13 Because of the wrath of the LORD it shall not be inhabited, but it shall be wholly desolate: every one that goeth by Babylon (Gentile Africans) shall be astonished, and hiss at all her plagues.

14 Put yourselves in array against Babylon (Gentile African)round about: all ye that bend the bow, shoot at her, spare no arrows: for she hath sinned against the LORD.

15 Shout against her round about: she hath given her hand: her foundations are fallen, her walls are thrown down: for it is the vengeance of the LORD: take vengeance upon her; as she hath done, do unto her.

16 Cut off the sower from Babylon, (African Gentiles) and him that handleth the sickle in the time of harvest: for fear of the oppressing sword they shall turn every one to his people, and they shall flee every one to his own land.

(Jeremiah 50:9-16).

595/3627

Ezekiel Chapters 1-4. God preparing the Prophet Ezekiel for his work.

594/3628

Ezekiel 5:5-11. God explaining why HE destroyed the African Hebrews and the African Gentiles from Africa.

5 Thus saith the Lord GOD; This is Jerusalem: (The royal city of the African Hebrews) I have set it in the midst of the nations and countries that are round about her.

6 And she hath changed my judgments into wickedness more than the nations, and my statutes more than the countries that are round about her: for they have refused my judgments and my statutes, they have not walked in them.

7 Therefore thus saith the Lord GOD; Because ye multiplied more than the nations that are round about you, and have not walked in my statutes, neither have kept my judgments, neither have done according to the judgments of the nations that are round about you;

8 Therefore thus saith the Lord GOD; Behold, I, even I, am against thee, and will execute judgments in the midst of thee in the sight of the nations.

9 And I will do in thee that which I have not done, and whereunto I will not do any more the like, because of all thine abominations.

10 Therefore the fathers shall eat the sons in the midst of thee, and the sons shall eat their fathers; and I will execute judgments in thee, and the whole remnant of thee will I scatter into all the winds.

11 Wherefore, as I live, saith the Lord GOD; Surely, because thou hast defiled my sanctuary with all thy detestable things, and with all thine abominations, therefore will I also diminish thee; neither shall mine eye spare, neither will I have any pity.

(Ezekiel 5:5-11).

594/3628

Ezekiel 5:12. God explaining 'how' HE destroyed 'old folks' in Africa. This is very important, so we will break it down into three parts. READ THE FIRST PART:

12 A third part of thee shall die with the pestilence, and with famine shall they be consumed in the midst of thee:

(Ezekiel 5:12).

One third of all black folks in Africa were scattered into the vast jungles. God stripped them of everything, including their 'natural mentality'. This why they put bones in their noses, carved and burned their own bodies with symbols and experienced cannibalism. They were a lost, destroyed people. So lost, that many had to communicate thru drums. Even unto this very day, famine and pestilence are still destroying the 'old folks' (black folks) in Africa, and no one can do anything to eliminate this condition. Only God can bring an end to the curse of famine and pestilence that is destroying the 'old folks' in Africa. READ THE SECOND PART.:

12 and a third part shall fall by the sword round about thee;

(Ezekiel 5:12).

When God sent the 'new folks' to Africa to bring the Children of Israel out for slaves, 'one third' of all the 'old folks' in Africa died in their battles with the 'new folks' (white folks). The old folks fought hard to retain their kingdoms, but GOD had other plans for Israel because they broke the Ten Commandments. It took over 400 years to drain Africa of it's natural civilization. During that period, one third of all the 'old folks' in Africa were murdered by the 'new folks', due to the hand and retribution of the Almighty God. <u>READ THE THIRD PART:</u>

12 and I will scatter a third part into all the winds, and I will draw out a sword after them.

(Ezekiel 5:12).

Scattered, confounded and confused. That's what God did to the other third. And here they are in North America and throughout the world, a lost confused African people.

12 A third part of thee (African Hebrews) shall die with the pestilence, and with famine shall they be consumed in the midst of thee: and a third part shall fall by the sword round about thee; and I will scatter a third part into all the winds, and I will draw out a sword after them.

(Ezekiel 5:12).

594/3628

Ezekiel 5:13-17. God explaining how hard HE would be on 'old folks' for violating the Ten Commandments.

13 Thus shall mine anger be accomplished, and I will cause my fury to rest upon them, (African people)and I will be comforted: and they shall know that I the LORD have spoken it in my zeal, when I have accomplished my fury in them.

14 Moreover I will make thee waste, and a reproach among the nations that are round about thee, in the sight of all that pass by.

15 So it shall be a reproach (embarrassment) and a taunt, (niggers)an instruction (violators of GOD's law) and an astonishment (hopelessness) unto the nations that are round about thee, when I shall execute judgments in thee in anger and in fury and in furious

rebukes. I the LORD have spoken it.

16 When I shall send upon them the evil arrows of famine, (African starvation)which shall be for their destruction, and which I will send to destroy you: and I will increase the famine upon you, and will break your staff of bread:

17 So will I send upon you famine and evil beasts, and they shall bereave thee; and pestilence and blood shall pass through thee; and I will bring the sword upon thee. I the LORD have spoken it.

(Ezekiel 5:13-17).

594/3628

Ezekiel Chapter 6. This whole chapter speaks to the destruction of the Children of Israel, and how they would be driven from Africa because their high rate of 'IDOLATRY'.

1 And the word of the LORD came unto me, saying,

2 Son of man, set thy face toward the mountains of Israel, (African Hebrews) and prophesy against them,

3 And say, Ye mountains of Israel, hear the word of the Lord GOD; Thus saith the Lord GOD to the mountains, and to the hills, to the rivers, and to the valleys; Behold, I, even I, will bring a sword upon you, (new folks) and I will destroy your high places.

4 And your altars shall be desolate, and your images shall be broken: and I will cast down your slain men before your idols.

5 And I will lay the dead carcases of the children of Israel (African Hebrews) before their idols; and I will scatter your bones round about your altars.

6 In all your dwellingplaces the cities shall be laid waste, and the high places shall be desolate; that your altars may be laid waste and made desolate, and your idols may be broken and cease, and your images may be cut down, and your works may be abolished.

7 And the slain shall fall in the midst of you, and ye shall know that I am the LORD.

8 Yet will I leave a remnant, that ye may have some that shall escape

the sword among the nations, when ye shall be scattered through the countries.

9 And they that escape of you shall remember me among the nations whither they shall be carried captives, because I am broken with their whorish heart, which hath departed from me, and with their eyes, which go a whoring after their idols: and they shall lothe themselves for the evils which they have committed in all their abominations.

10 And they shall know that I am the LORD, and that I have not said in vain that I would do this evil unto them.

11 Thus saith the Lord GOD; Smite with thine hand, and stamp with thy foot, and say, Alas for all the evil abominations of the house of Israel! for they shall fall by the sword, by the famine, and by the pestilence.

12 He that is far off shall die of the pestilence; and he that is near shall fall by the sword; and he that remaineth and is besieged shall die by the famine: thus will I accomplish my fury upon them.

13 Then shall ye know that I am the LORD, when their slain men shall be among their idols round about their altars, upon every high hill, in all the tops of the mountains, and under every green tree, and under every thick oak, the place where they did offer sweet savour to all their idols.

14 So will I stretch out my hand upon them, and make the land (Africa) desolate, yea, more desolate than the wilderness toward Diblath, in all their habitations: and they shall know that I am the LORD.

(Ezekiel 6:1-14).

594/3628

Ezekiel Chapter 7. This whole chapter describes the desolation and doom that God prepared to destroy the African Hebrews for violating God's laws.

1 Moreover the word of the LORD came unto me, saying,

2 Also, thou son of man, thus saith the Lord GOD unto the land of

Israel; (African Hebrews) An end, the end is come upon the four corners of the land. (Africa)

3 Now is the end come upon thee, and I will send mine anger upon thee, and will judge thee according to thy ways, and will recompense upon thee all thine abominations.

4 And mine eye shall not spare thee, neither will I have pity: but I will recompense thy ways upon thee, and thine abominations shall be in the midst of thee: and ye shall know that I am the LORD.

5 Thus saith the Lord GOD; An evil, an only evil, behold, is come. (new folks)

6 An end is come, the end is come: (the end of African freedom) it watcheth for thee; behold, it is come.

7 The morning is come unto thee, O thou that dwellest in the land: (Africa) the time is come, the day of trouble is near, and not the sounding again of the mountains.

8 Now will I shortly pour out my fury upon thee, and accomplish mine anger upon thee: and I will judge thee according to thy ways, and will recompense thee for all thine abominations.

9 And mine eye shall not spare, neither will I have pity: I will recompense thee according to thy ways and thine abominations that are in the midst of thee; and ye shall know that I am the LORD that smiteth.

10 Behold the day, behold, it is come: the morning is gone forth; the rod hath blossomed, pride hath budded.

11 Violence is risen up into a rod of wickedness: none of them shall remain, nor of their multitude, nor of any of theirs: neither shall there be wailing for them.

12 The time is come, the day draweth near: let not the buyer rejoice, nor the seller mourn: for wrath is upon all the multitude thereof.

13 For the seller shall not return to that which is sold, although they were yet alive: for the vision is touching the whole multitude thereof, which shall not return; neither shall any strengthen himself in the iniquity of his life.

14 They have blown the trumpet, even to make all ready; but none goeth to the battle: for my wrath is upon all the multitude thereof.

15 The sword is without, and the pestilence and the famine within: he that is in the field shall die with the sword; and he that is in the city, famine and pestilence shall devour him.

16 But they that escape of them shall escape, and shall be on the mountains like doves of the valleys, all of them mourning, every one for his iniquity.

17 All hands shall be feeble, and all knees shall be weak as water.

18 They shall also gird themselves with sackcloth, and horror shall cover them; and shame shall be upon all faces, and baldness upon all their heads.

19 They shall cast their silver in the streets, and their gold shall be removed: their silver and their gold shall not be able to deliver them in the day of the wrath of the LORD: they shall not satisfy their souls, neither fill their bowels: because it is the stumblingblock of their iniquity.

20 As for the beauty of his ornament, he set it in majesty: but they made the images of their abominations and of their detestable things therein: therefore have I set it far from them.

21 And I will give it into the hands of the strangers (new folks) for a prey, and to the wicked of the earth for a spoil; and they shall pollute it.

22 My face will I turn also from them, and they (new folks)shall pollute my secret place: (the Holy of Holies, Sacred scrolls, Torah, Ark of the Covenant, etc.,) for the robbers shall enter into it, and defile it.

23 Make a chain: for the land is full of bloody crimes, and the city is full of violence.

24 Wherefore I will bring the worst of the heathen, (new folks) and they shall possess their houses: I will also make the pomp of the strong to cease; and their holy places shall be defiled.

25 Destruction cometh; and they shall seek peace, and there shall be none.

26 Mischief shall come upon mischief, and rumour shall be upon rumour; then shall they seek a vision of the prophet; but the law shall perish from the priest, and counsel from the ancients.

27 The king shall mourn, and the prince shall be clothed with desolation, and the hands of the people of the land shall be troubled: I will do unto them after their way, and according to their deserts will I judge them; and they shall know that I am the LORD.

(Ezekiel 7:1-27).

594/3628

Ezekiel Chapter 8. God shews the Prophet Ezekiel the many sins of the African Hebrew Israelites.

1 And it came to pass in the sixth year, in the sixth month, in the fifth day of the month, as I sat in mine house, and the elders of Judah (African Hebrews) sat before me, that the hand of the Lord GOD fell there upon me.

2 Then I beheld, and lo a likeness as the appearance of fire: from the appearance of his loins even downward, fire; and from his loins even upward, as the appearance of brightness, as the colour of amber.

3 And he put forth the form of an hand, and took me by a lock of mine head; and the spirit lifted me up between the earth and the heaven, and brought me in the visions of God to Jerusalem, to the door of the inner gate that looketh toward the north; where was the seat of the image of jealousy, which provoketh to jealousy.

4 And, behold, the glory of the God of Israel was there, according to the vision that I saw in the plain.

5 Then said he unto me, Son of man, lift up thine eyes now the way toward the north. So I lifted up mine eyes the way toward the north, and behold northward at the gate of the altar this image of jealousy in the entry.

6 He said furthermore unto me, Son of man, seest thou what they do? even the great abominations that the house of Israel committeth here, that I should go far off from my sanctuary? but turn thee yet again, and thou shalt see greater abominations.

7 And he brought me to the door of the court; and when I looked, behold a hole in the wall.

8 Then said he unto me, Son of man, dig now in the wall: and when I had digged in the wall, behold a door.

9 And he said unto me, Go in, and behold the wicked abominations that they do here.

10 So I went in and saw; and behold every form of creeping things, and abominable beasts, and all the idols of the house of Israel, (African Hebrews) pourtrayed upon the wall round about.

11 And there stood before them seventy men of the ancients of the house of Israel, (African Hebrews) and in the midst of them stood Jaazaniah (Gentile leader in idolatrous worship) the son of Shaphan, with every man his censer in his hand; and a thick cloud of incense went up.

12 Then said he unto me, Son of man, hast thou seen what the ancients of the house of Israel do in the dark, every man in the chambers of his imagery? for they say, The LORD seeth us not; the LORD hath forsaken the earth.

13 He said also unto me, Turn thee yet again, and thou shalt see greater abominations that they do.

14 Then he brought me to the door of the gate of the LORD'S house which was toward the north; and, behold, there sat women weeping for Tammuz. (Gentile Africans worshipped him as a fertility god)

15 Then said he unto me, Hast thou seen this, O son of man? turn thee yet again, and thou shalt see greater abominations than these.

16 And he brought me into the inner court of the LORD'S house, and, behold, at the door of the temple of the LORD, between the porch and the altar, were about five and twenty men, with their backs toward the temple of the LORD, and their faces toward the east; and they worshipped the sun toward the east.

17 Then he said unto me, Hast thou seen this, O son of man? Is it a light thing to the house of Judah (African Hebrews) that they commit the abominations which they commit here? for they have

filled the land with violence, and have returned to provoke me to anger: and, lo, they put the branch to their nose.

18 Therefore will I also deal in fury: mine eye shall not spare, neither will I have pity: and though they cry in mine ears with a loud voice, yet will I not hear them.

(Ezekiel 8:1-18).

594/3628

Ezekiel Chapter 9. God shews Ezekiel that HE will not 'spare' when HE destroys the Children of Israel.

1 He cried also in mine ears with a loud voice, saying, Cause them that have charge over the city to draw near, even every man with his destroying weapon in his hand.

2 And, behold, six men came from the way of the higher gate, which lieth toward the north, and every man a slaughter weapon in his hand; and one man among them was clothed with linen, with a writer's inkhorn by his side: and they went in, and stood beside the brasen altar.

3 And the glory of the God of Israel was gone up from the cherub, whereupon he was, to the threshold of the house. And he called to the man clothed with linen, which had the writer's inkhorn by his side;

4 And the LORD said unto him, Go through the midst of the city, through the midst of Jerusalem, (Africa) and set a mark upon the foreheads of the men that sigh and that cry for all the abominations that be done in the midst thereof.

5 And to the others he said in mine hearing, Go ye after him through the city, and smite: let not your eye spare, neither have ye pity:

6 Slay utterly old and young, both maids, and little children, and women: but come not near any man upon whom is the mark; and begin at my sanctuary. Then they began at the ancient men which were before the house.

7 And he said unto them, Defile the house, and fill the courts with the slain: go ye forth. And they went forth, and slew in the city.

8 And it came to pass, while they were slaying them, and I was left, that I fell upon my face, and cried, and said, Ah Lord GOD! wilt thou destroy all the residue of Israel (African Hebrews) in thy pouring out of thy fury upon Jerusalem? (Africa)

9 Then said he unto me, The iniquity of the house of Israel and Judah (African Hebrews) is exceeding great, and the land is full of blood, and the city full of perverseness: for they say, The LORD hath forsaken the earth, and the LORD seeth not.

10 And as for me also, mine eye shall not spare, neither will I have pity, but I will recompense their way upon their head.

11 And, behold, the man clothed with linen, which had the inkhorn by his side, reported the matter, saying, I have done as thou hast commanded me.

(Ezekiel 9:1-11).

594/3628

Ezekiel 11:1-12. Another 'cause' for the destruction of the African Children of Israel, was because of the Princes that ruled over God's people. God said, they devised mischief and gave wicked counsel to the people and caused them to err in their way.

1 Moreover the spirit lifted me up, and brought me unto the east gate of the LORD'S house, which looketh eastward: and behold at the door of the gate five and twenty men; among whom I saw Jaazaniah (Leader in Idolatrous worship) the son of Azur, and Pelatiah the son of Benaiah, princes of the people.

2 Then said he unto me, Son of man, these are the men that devise mischief, and give wicked counsel in this city:

3 Which say, It is not near; let us build houses: this city is the caldron, and we be the flesh.

4 Therefore prophesy against them, prophesy, O son of man.

5 And the Spirit of the LORD fell upon me, and said unto me, Speak; Thus saith the LORD; Thus have ye said, O house of Israel: for I know the things that come into your mind, every one of them.

6 Ye have multiplied your slain in this city, and ye have filled the

streets thereof with the slain.

7 Therefore thus saith the Lord GOD; Your slain whom ye have laid in the midst of it, they are the flesh, and this city is the caldron: but I will bring you forth out of the midst of it.

8 Ye have feared the sword; and I will bring a sword upon you, saith the Lord GOD.

9 And I will bring you out of the midst thereof, and deliver you into the hands of strangers, and will execute judgments among you.

10 Ye shall fall by the sword; I will judge you in the border of Israel; and ye shall know that I am the LORD.

11 This city shall not be your caldron, neither shall ye be the flesh in the midst thereof; but I will judge you in the border of Israel:

12 And ye shall know that I am the LORD: for ye have not walked in my statutes, neither executed my judgments, but have done after the manners of the heathen that are round about you.

(Ezekiel 11:1-12).

594/3628

Ezekiel 11:16-21. Although GOD stripped the Children of Israel and the Gentile old folks from Africa, HE will gather those who keep HIS laws, and return them to Africa.

16 Therefore say, Thus saith the Lord GOD; Although I have cast them (African Americans) far off among the heathen, (American/new folks) and although I have scattered them among the countries, yet will I be to them as a little sanctuary in the countries where they shall come.

17 Therefore say, Thus saith the Lord GOD; I will even gather you from the people, and assemble you out of the countries where ye have been scattered, and I will give you the land of Israel. (Africa)

18 And they shall come thither, and they shall take away all the detestable things thereof and all the abominations thereof from thence.

19 And I will give them one heart, and I will put a new spirit within you; and I will take the stony heart out of their flesh, and will give them an heart of flesh:

20 That they may walk in my statutes, and keep mine ordinances, and do them: and they shall be my people, and I will be their God.

21 But as for them whose heart walketh after the heart of their detestable things and their abominations, I will recompense their way upon their own heads, saith the Lord GOD.

(Ezekiel 11:16-21).

594/3628

Ezekiel 13:19-23. God will deliver the Children of Israel from the hands of their oppressors, and no more will they have to live by the 'lies' of the wicked.

19 And will ye (new folks) pollute me among my people (African people all over the world) for handfuls of barley and for pieces of bread, to slay the souls that should not die, and to save the souls alive that should not live, by your lying to my people that hear your lies?

20 Wherefore thus saith the Lord GOD; Behold, I am against your pillows, wherewith ye there hunt the souls to make them fly, and I will tear them from your arms, and will let the souls go, even the souls that ye hunt to make them fly.

21 Your kerchiefs also will I tear, and deliver my people out of your hand, and they shall be no more in your hand to be hunted; and ye shall know that I am the LORD.

22 Because with lies ye have made the heart of the righteous sad, whom I have not made sad; and strengthened the hands of the wicked, that he should not return from his wicked way, by promising him life:

23 Therefore ye shall see no more vanity, nor divine divinations: for I will deliver my people out of your hand: and ye shall know that I am the LORD.

(Ezekiel 13:19-23).

594/3628

Ezekiel 14:9-11. False prophets, ministers and pastors have been preaching and teaching lies for a very long time. GOD will destroy them for their iniquity and the House of Israel (African Hebrews) will go astray no more.

9 And if the prophet be deceived when he hath spoken a thing, I the LORD have deceived that prophet, and I will stretch out my hand upon him, and will destroy him from the midst of my people Israel.

10 And they shall bear the punishment of their iniquity: the punishment of the prophet shall be even as the punishment of him that seeketh unto him;

11 That the house of Israel (African Hebrews) may go no more astray from me, neither be polluted any more with all their transgressions; but that they may be my people, and I may be their God, saith the Lord GOD.

(Ezekiel 14:9-11).

594/3628

Ezekiel Chapter 16. In this chapter, God is talking to the Children of Israel (African Hebrews) the same way a parent would talk to a child before punishing it. Be sure to read the whole chapter so that you can understand the 'attitude' of GOD the Creator..

593/3629

Ezekiel 20:34-44. How the African Hebrew Israelites will be purged, purified and brought into the 'bond' of God's New Covenant. God's New Covenant is recorded in Jeremiah 31:31-37.

34 And I will bring you (African Hebrews) out from the people, and will gather you out of the countries wherein ye are scattered, with a mighty hand, and with a stretched out arm, and with fury poured out.

35 And I will bring you into the wilderness of the people, and there will I plead with you face to face.

36 Like as I pleaded with your fathers in the wilderness of the land of

Egypt, so will I plead with you, saith the Lord GOD.

37 And I will cause you to pass under the rod, (The 'rod' is the resistance from 'new folks" when 'old folks' return unto GOD's 10 Commandments, and start keeping GOD's Sabbath like it should be done on Saturday, and stop praising a dead, white picture called Jesus as their saviour.) and I will bring you into the bond of the covenant:

38 And I will purge out from among you the rebels, and them that transgress against me: I will bring them forth out of the country where they sojourn, and they shall not enter into the land of Israel: (Africa) and ye shall know that I am the LORD.

39 As for you, O house of Israel, (African Hebrews) thus saith the Lord GOD; Go ye, serve ye every one his idols, and hereafter also, if ye will not hearken unto me: but pollute ye my holy name no more with your gifts, and with your idols.

40 For in mine holy mountain, in the mountain of the height of Israel, saith the Lord GOD, there shall all the house of Israel, (African Hebrews) all of them in the land, serve me: there will I accept them, and there will I require your offerings, and the firstfruits of your oblations, with all your holy things.

41 I will accept you with your sweet savour, when I bring you out from the people, and gather you out of the countries wherein ye have been scattered; and I will be sanctified in you before the heathen. (new folks)

42 And ye shall know that I am the LORD, when I shall bring you into the land of Israel, (Africa) into the country for the which I lifted up mine hand to give it to your fathers.

43 And there shall ye remember your ways, and all your doings, wherein ye have been defiled; and ye shall lothe yourselves in your own sight for all your evils that ye have committed.

44 And ye shall know that I am the LORD, when I have wrought with you for my name's sake, not according to your wicked ways, nor according to your corrupt doings, O ye house of Israel, saith the Lord GOD.

(Ezekiel 20:34-44).

593/3629

Ezekiel Chapter 21. This whole chapter tells of the downfall of the Children of Israel, and how GOD will bring the sword upon <u>all</u> African people.

1 And the word of the LORD came unto me, saying,

2 Son of man, set thy face toward Jerusalem, (Africa) and drop thy word toward the holy places, and prophesy against the land of Israel, (Africa)

3 And say to the land of Israel, Thus saith the LORD; Behold, I am against thee, and will draw forth my sword out of his sheath, and will cut off from thee the righteous and the wicked.

4 Seeing then that I will cut off from thee the righteous and the wicked, therefore shall my sword go forth out of his sheath against all flesh from the south to the north:

5 That all flesh may know that I the LORD have drawn forth my sword out of his sheath: it shall not return any more.

6 Sigh therefore, thou son of man, with the breaking of thy loins; and with bitterness sigh before their eyes.

7 And it shall be, when they say unto thee, Wherefore sighest thou? that thou shalt answer, For the tidings; because it cometh: and every heart shall melt, and all hands shall be feeble, and every spirit shall faint, and all knees shall be weak as water: behold, it cometh, and shall be brought to pass, saith the Lord GOD.

8 Again the word of the LORD came unto me, saying,

9 Son of man, prophesy, and say, Thus saith the LORD; Say, A sword, a sword is sharpened, and also furbished:

10 It is sharpened to make a sore slaughter; it is furbished that it may glitter: should we then make mirth? it contemneth the rod of my son, as every tree.

11 And he hath given it to be furbished, that it may be handled: this sword is sharpened, and it is furbished, to give it into the hand of the slayer.

12 Cry and howl, son of man: for it shall be upon my people, it shall be upon all the princes of Israel: (African Hebrews) terrors by reason of the sword shall be upon my people: smite therefore upon thy thigh.

13 Because it is a trial, and what if the sword contemn even the rod? it shall be no more, saith the Lord GOD.

14 Thou therefore, son of man, prophesy, and smite thine hands together, and let the sword be doubled the third time, the sword of the slain: it is the sword of the great men that are slain, which entereth into their privy chambers.

15 I have set the point of the sword against all their gates, that their heart may faint, and their ruins be multiplied: ah! it is made bright, it is wrapped up for the slaughter.

16 Go thee one way or other, either on the right hand, or on the left, whithersoever thy face is set.

17 I will also smite mine hands together, and I will cause my fury to rest: I the LORD have said it.

18 The word of the LORD came unto me again, saying,

19 Also, thou son of man, appoint thee two ways, that the sword of the king of Babylon (Gentiles) may come: both twain shall come forth out of one land: and choose thou a place, choose it at the head of the way to the city.

20 Appoint a way, that the sword may come to Rabbath of the Ammonites, (Gentiles Africans))- and to Judah in Jerusalem the defenced. (African Hebrews in Africa)

21 For the king of Babylon stood at the parting of the way, at the head of the two ways, to use divination: he made his arrows bright, he consulted with images, he looked in the liver.

22 At his right hand was the divination for Jerusalem, to appoint captains, to open the mouth in the slaughter, to lift up the voice with shouting, to appoint battering rams against the gates, to cast a mount, and to build a fort.

23 And it shall be unto them as a false divination in their sight, to

them that have sworn oaths: but he will call to remembrance the iniquity, that they may be taken.

24 Therefore thus saith the Lord GOD; Because ye have made your iniquity to be remembered, in that your transgressions are discovered, so that in all your doings your sins do appear; because, I say, that ye are come to remembrance, ye shall be taken with the hand.

25 And thou, profane wicked prince of Israel, whose day is come, when iniquity shall have an end,

26 Thus saith the Lord GOD; Remove the diadem, and take off the crown: this shall not be the same: exalt him that is low, and abase him that is high.

27 I will overturn, overturn, overturn, it: and it shall be no more, until he come whose right it is; and I will give it him.

28 And thou, son of man, prophesy and say, Thus saith the Lord GOD concerning the Ammonites, (African Gentiles) and concerning their reproach; even say thou, The sword, the sword is drawn: for the slaughter it is furbished, to consume because of the glittering:

29 Whiles they see vanity unto thee, whiles they divine a lie unto thee, to bring thee upon the necks of them that are slain, of the wicked, whose day is come, when their iniquity shall have an end.

30 Shall I cause it to return into his sheath? I will judge thee in the place where thou wast created, in the land of thy nativity.

31 And I will pour out mine indignation upon thee, I will blow against thee in the fire of my wrath, and deliver thee into the hand of brutish men, and skilful to destroy.

32 Thou shalt be for fuel to the fire; thy blood shall be in the midst of the land; thou shalt be no more remembered: for I the LORD have spoken it.

(Ezekiel 21:1-32).

593/3629

Ezekiel Chapter 22. This whole chapter shews the sins and abominations of the Children of Israel. The sins of the prophets, priests, princes and the people are catalogued.

1 Moreover the word of the LORD came unto me, saying,

2 Now, thou son of man, wilt thou judge, wilt thou judge the bloody city? (Africa) yea, thou shalt shew her all her abominations.

3 Then say thou, Thus saith the Lord GOD, The city sheddeth blood in the midst of it, that her time may come, and maketh idols against herself to defile herself.

4 Thou art become guilty in thy blood that thou hast shed; and hast defiled thyself in thine idols which thou hast made; and thou hast caused thy days to draw near, and art come even unto thy years: therefore have I made thee a reproach unto the heathen, (new folks) and a mocking to all countries.

5 Those that be near, and those that be far from thee, shall mock (nigger, sambo, buckwheat, snowflake, etc.,) thee, which art infamous and much vexed.

6 Behold, the princes of Israel, every one were in thee to their power to shed blood.

7 In thee have they set light by father and mother: in the midst of thee have they dealt by oppression with the stranger: in thee have they vexed the fatherless and the widow.

8 Thou hast despised mine holy things, (Improper worship) and hast profaned my sabbaths. (Wrong day)

9 In thee are men that carry tales to shed blood: and in thee they eat upon the mountains: in the midst of thee they commit lewdness.

10 In thee have they discovered their fathers' nakedness: in thee have they humbled her that was set apart for pollution.

11 And one hath committed abomination with his neighbour's wife; and another hath lewdly defiled his daughter in law; and another in thee hath humbled his sister, his father's daughter.

12 In thee have they taken gifts to shed blood; thou hast taken usury and increase, and thou hast greedily gained of thy neighbours by extortion, and hast forgotten me, saith the Lord GOD.

13 Behold, therefore I have smitten mine hand at thy dishonest gain which thou hast made, and at thy blood which hath been in the midst of thee.

14 Can thine heart endure, or can thine hands be strong, in the days that I shall deal with thee? I the LORD have spoken it, and will do it.

15 And I will scatter thee among the heathen, (new folks) and disperse thee in the countries, and will consume thy filthiness out of thee.

16 And thou shalt take thine inheritance in thyself in the sight of the heathen, and thou shalt know that I am the LORD.

17 And the word of the LORD came unto me, saying,

18 Son of man, the house of Israel (African Hebrews) is to me become dross: all they are brass, and tin, and iron, and lead, in the midst of the furnace; they are even the dross of silver.

19 Therefore thus saith the Lord GOD; Because ye are all become dross, behold, therefore I will gather you into the midst of Jerusalem. (Africa)

20 As they gather silver, and brass, and iron, and lead, and tin, into the midst of the furnace, to blow the fire upon it, to melt it; so will I gather you in mine anger and in my fury, and I will leave you there, and melt you.

21 Yea, I will gather you, and blow upon you in the fire of my wrath, and ye shall be melted in the midst thereof.

22 As silver is melted in the midst of the furnace, so shall ye be melted in the midst thereof; and ye shall know that I the LORD have poured out my fury upon you.

23 And the word of the LORD came unto me, saying,

24 Son of man, say unto her, Thou art the land that is not cleansed, nor rained upon in the day of indignation.

25 There is a conspiracy of her prophets in the midst thereof, like a roaring lion ravening the prey; they have devoured souls; they have taken the treasure and precious things; they have made her many widows in the midst thereof.

26 Her priests have violated my law, and have profaned mine holy things: they have put no difference between the holy and profane, neither have they shewed difference between the unclean and the clean, and have hid their eyes from my sabbaths, and I am profaned among them.

27 Her princes in the midst thereof are like wolves ravening the prey, to shed blood, and to destroy souls, to get dishonest gain.

28 And her prophets have daubed them with untempered morter, seeing vanity, and divining lies unto them, saying, Thus saith the Lord GOD, when the LORD hath not spoken.

29 The people of the land (Africa) have used oppression, and exercised robbery, and have vexed the poor and needy: yea, they have oppressed the stranger wrongfully.

30 And I sought for a man among them, that should make up the hedge, and stand in the gap before me for the land, that I should not destroy it: but I found none.

31 Therefore have I poured out mine indignation upon them; I have consumed them with the fire of my wrath: their own way have I recompensed upon their heads, saith the Lord GOD.

(Ezekiel 22:1-31).

593/3629

Ezekiel Chapter 23. Thou shalt not commit adultery, is the seventh Commandment. This whole chapter reveals the level of adultery, whoredom and lewdness of the African Hebrews and Gentile Africans while in Africa. Their punishment for this wickedness is expressed in the whole chapter. (Notice how **ENMITY IS EXPRESSED THROUGHOUT THIS CHAPTER.)**

1 The word of the LORD came again unto me, saying,

2 Son of man, there were two women, the daughters of one mother:

3 And they committed whoredoms in Egypt; they committed whoredoms in their youth: there were their breasts pressed, and there they bruised the teats of their virginity.

4 And the names of them were Aholah the elder, and Aholibah her sister: and they were mine, and they bare sons and daughters. Thus were their names; Samaria is Aholah, (Samaria was the capital of the African Hebrews Northern Kingdom--Aholah means 'tent-woman', who was spiritually adulterous) and Jerusalem Aholibah.

5 And Aholah played the harlot when she was mine; and she doted on her lovers, on the Assyrians her neighbours,

6 Which were clothed with blue, captains and rulers, all of them desirable young men, horsemen riding upon horses.

7 Thus she committed her whoredoms with them, with all them that were the chosen men of Assyria, (African Gentiles) and with all on whom she doted: with all their idols she defiled herself.

8 Neither left she her whoredoms brought from Egypt: for in her youth they lay with her, and they bruised the breasts of her virginity, and poured their whoredom upon her.

9 Wherefore I have delivered her into the hand of her lovers, into the hand of the Assyrians, upon whom she doted.

10 These discovered her nakedness: they took her sons and her daughters, and slew her with the sword: and she became famous among women; for they had executed judgment upon her.

11 And when her sister Aholibah saw this, she was more corrupt in her inordinate love than she, and in her whoredoms more than her sister in her whoredoms.

12 She doted upon the Assyrians her neighbours, captains and rulers clothed most gorgeously, horsemen riding upon horses, all of them desirable young men.

13 Then I saw that she was defiled, that they took both one way,

14 And that she increased her whoredoms: for when she saw men pourtrayed upon the wall, the images of the Chaldeans pourtrayed with vermilion,

15 Girded with girdles upon their loins, exceeding in dyed attire upon their heads, all of them princes to look to, after the manner of the Babylonians of Chaldea, (Gentiles) the land of their nativity:

16 And as soon as she saw them with her eyes, she doted upon them, and sent messengers unto them into Chaldea.

17 And the Babylonians came to her into the bed of love, and they defiled her with their whoredom, and she was polluted with them, and her mind was alienated from them.

18 So she discovered her whoredoms, and discovered her nakedness: then my mind was alienated from her, like as my mind was alienated from her sister.

19 Yet she multiplied her whoredoms, in calling to remembrance the days of her youth, wherein she had played the harlot in the land of Egypt.

20 For she doted upon their paramours, whose flesh is as the flesh of asses, and whose issue is like the issue of horses.

21 Thus thou calledst to remembrance the lewdness of thy youth, in bruising thy teats by the Egyptians for the paps of thy youth.

22 Therefore, O Aholibah, thus saith the Lord GOD; Behold, I will raise up thy lovers against thee, from whom thy mind is alienated, and I will bring them against thee on every side;

23 The Babylonians, and all the Chaldeans, Pekod, and Shoa, and Koa, and all the Assyrians (all African Gentiles) with them: all of them desirable young men, captains and rulers, great lords and renowned, all of them riding upon horses.

24 And they shall come against thee with chariots, wagons, and wheels, and with an assembly of people, which shall set against thee buckler and shield and helmet round about: and I will set judgment before them, and they shall judge thee according to their judgments.

25 And I will set my jealousy against thee, and they shall deal furiously with thee: they shall take away thy nose and thine ears; and thy remnant shall fall by the sword: they shall take thy sons and thy daughters; and thy residue shall be devoured by the fire.

26 They shall also strip thee out of thy clothes, and take away thy fair jewels.

27 Thus will I make thy lewdness to cease from thee, and thy whoredom brought from the land of Egypt: Africa) so that thou shalt not lift up thine eyes unto them, nor remember Egypt (Africa) any more.

28 For thus saith the Lord GOD; Behold, I will deliver thee (African people everywhere) into the hand of them whom thou hatest, into the hand of them from whom thy mind is alienated: (new folks)

29 And they shall deal with thee hatefully, and shall take away all thy labour, and shall leave thee naked and bare: and the nakedness of thy whoredoms shall be discovered, both thy lewdness and thy whoredoms.

30 I will do these things unto thee, because thou hast gone a whoring after the heathen, and because thou art polluted with their idols.

31 Thou hast walked in the way of thy sister; therefore will I give her cup into thine hand.

32 Thus saith the Lord GOD; Thou shalt drink of thy sister's cup deep and large: thou shalt be laughed to scorn and had in derision; it containeth much.

33 Thou shalt be filled with drunkenness and sorrow, with the cup of astonishment and desolation, with the cup of thy sister Samaria.

34 Thou shalt even drink it and suck it out, and thou shalt break the sherds thereof, and pluck off thine own breasts: for I have spoken it, saith the Lord GOD.

35 Therefore thus saith the Lord GOD; Because thou hast forgotten me, and cast me behind thy back, therefore bear thou also thy lewdness and thy whoredoms.

36 The LORD said moreover unto me; Son of man, wilt thou judge Aholah and Aholibah? yea, declare unto them their abominations;

37 That they have committed adultery, and blood is in their hands, and with their idols have they committed adultery, and have also

caused their sons, whom they bare unto me, to pass for them through the fire, to devour them.

38 Moreover this they have done unto me: they have defiled my sanctuary in the same day, and have profaned my sabbaths.

39 For when they had slain their children to their idols, then they came the same day into my sanctuary to profane it; and, lo, thus have they done in the midst of mine house.

40 And furthermore, that ye have sent for men to come from far, unto whom a messenger was sent; and, lo, they came: for whom thou didst wash thyself, paintedst thy eyes, and deckedst thyself with ornaments,

41 And satest upon a stately bed, and a table prepared before it, whereupon thou hast set mine incense and mine oil.

42 And a voice of a multitude being at ease was with her: and with the men of the common sort were brought Sabeans from the wilderness, which put bracelets upon their hands, and beautiful crowns upon their heads.

43 Then said I unto her that was old in adulteries, Will they now commit whoredoms with her, and she with them?

44 Yet they went in unto her, as they go in unto a woman that playeth the harlot: so went they in unto Aholah and unto Aholibah, the lewd women.

45 And the righteous men, they shall judge them after the manner of adulteresses, and after the manner of women that shed blood; because they are adulteresses, and blood is in their hands.

46 For thus saith the Lord GOD; I will bring up a company upon them, and will give them to be removed and spoiled.

47 And the company shall stone them with stones, and dispatch them with their swords; they shall slay their sons and their daughters, and burn up their houses with fire.

48 Thus will I cause lewdness to cease out of the land, that all women may be taught not to do after your lewdness.

49 And they shall recompense your lewdness upon you, and ye shall

bear the sins of your idols: and ye shall know that I am the Lord GOD.

(Ezekiel 23:1-49).

590/3632

Ezekiel 24:1-14. The Children of Israel were taken into Babylon on two different occasions. This chapter describes the destruction of Jerusalem in the form of a 'boiling pot.

1 Again in the ninth year, in the tenth month, in the tenth day of the month, the word of the LORD came unto me, saying,

2 Son of man, write thee the name of the day, even of this same day: the king of Babylon set himself against Jerusalem this same day.

3 And utter a parable unto the rebellious house, and say unto them, Thus saith the Lord GOD; Set on a pot, set it on, and also pour water into it:

4 Gather the pieces thereof into it, even every good piece, the thigh, and the shoulder; fill it with the choice bones.

5 Take the choice of the flock, and burn also the bones under it, and make it boil well, and let them seethe the bones of it therein.

6 Wherefore thus saith the Lord GOD; Woe to the bloody city, to the pot whose scum is therein, and whose scum is not gone out of it! bring it out piece by piece; let no lot fall upon it.

7 For her blood is in the midst of her; she set it upon the top of a rock; she poured it not upon the ground, to cover it with dust;

8 That it might cause fury to come up to take vengeance; I have set her blood upon the top of a rock, that it should not be covered.

9 Therefore thus saith the Lord GOD; Woe to the bloody city! I will even make the pile for fire great.

10 Heap on wood, kindle the fire, consume the flesh, and spice it well, and let the bones be burned.

11 Then set it empty upon the coals thereof, that the brass of it may be hot, and may burn, and that the filthiness of it may be molten

in it, that the scum of it may be consumed.

12 She hath wearied herself with lies, and her great scum went not forth out of her: her scum shall be in the fire.

13 In thy filthiness is lewdness: because I have purged thee, and thou wast not purged, thou shalt not be purged from thy filthiness any more, till I have caused my fury to rest upon thee.

14 I the LORD have spoken it: it shall come to pass, and I will do it; I will not go back, neither will I spare, neither will I repent; according to thy ways, and according to thy doings, shall they judge thee, saith the Lord GOD.

(Ezekiel 24:1-14).

590/3632

Ezekiel Chapters 25 - 26 - and 27. These three chapters shews God's vengeance and judgement on many of the African Gentile Nations. Ammonites, Moab, Seir, Edom, Philistines, Cherethims, Tyrus, Rabbah are all Gentile locations.

590/3632

Jeremiah 32:37-44. The African Hebrew Israelites will possess Africa again. Many people today feel that because of the present condition of Africa today, it could never be inhabited in an acceptable way. But in verse 43, GOD shews what will happen. Chaldeans = 'new folks'.

37 Behold, I will gather them (African people) out of all countries, whither I have driven them in mine anger, and in my fury, and in great wrath; and I will bring them again unto this place, (Africa) and I will cause them to dwell safely:

38 And they shall be my people, and I will be their God:

39 And I will give them one heart, and one way, that they may fear me for ever, for the good of them, and of their children after them:

40 And I will make an everlasting covenant with them, that I will not turn away from them, to do them good; but I will put my fear in their hearts, that they shall not depart from me.

41 Yea, I will rejoice over them to do them good, and I will plant them in this land (Africa) assuredly with my whole heart and with my whole soul.

42 For thus saith the LORD; Like as I have brought all this great evil upon this people, so will I bring upon them all the good that I have promised them.

43 And fields shall be bought in this land, (Africa) whereof ye say, It is desolate without man or beast; it is given into the hand of the Chaldeans. (new folks)

44 Men shall buy fields for money, and subscribe evidences, and seal them, and take witnesses in the land of Benjamin, (African Hebrews) and in the places about Jerusalem, (Africa)and in the cities of Judah, and in the cities of the mountains, and in the cities of the valley, and in the cities of the south: for I will cause their captivity to return, saith the LORD.

(Jeremiah 32:37-44).

590/3632

Jeremiah 33:24-26. the African Hebrew Israelites are GOD's 'chosen people', no matter what people say or think.

24 Considerest thou not what this people have spoken, saying, The two families which the LORD hath chosen, he hath even cast them off? thus they have despised my people, that they should be no more a nation before them.

25 Thus saith the LORD; If my covenant be not with day and night, and if I have not appointed the ordinances of heaven and earth;

26 Then will I cast away the seed of Jacob, (African Hebrews) and David my servant, (African Hebrews) so that I will not take any of his seed to be rulers over the seed of Abraham, Isaac, and Jacob: for I will cause their captivity to return, and have mercy on them.

(Jeremiah 33:24-26).

589/3633

Ezekiel 29:1-12. God tells Ezekiel that Africa (Egypt) will be maimed, and destroyed and African people will be scattered all over the world.

1 In the tenth year, in the tenth month, in the twelfth day of the month, the word of the LORD came unto me, saying,

2 Son of man, set thy face against Pharaoh king of Egypt, (African king)and prophesy against him, and against all Egypt: (Africa)

3 Speak, and say, Thus saith the Lord GOD; Behold, I am against thee, Pharaoh king of Egypt, the great dragon that lieth in the midst of his rivers, which hath said, My river is mine own, and I have made it for myself.

4 But I will put hooks in thy jaws, and I will cause the fish of thy rivers to stick unto thy scales, and I will bring thee up out of the midst of thy rivers, and all the fish of thy rivers shall stick unto thy scales.

5 And I will leave thee thrown into the wilderness, thee and all the fish of thy rivers: thou shalt fall upon the open fields; thou shalt not be brought together, nor gathered: I have given thee for meat to the beasts of the field and to the fowls of the heaven.

6 And all the inhabitants of Egypt (Africa) shall know that I am the LORD, because they have been a staff of reed to the house of Israel.\ (African Hebrews)

7 When they took hold of thee by thy hand, thou didst break, and rend all their shoulder: and when they leaned upon thee, thou brakest, and madest all their loins to be at a stand.

8 Therefore thus saith the Lord GOD; Behold, I will bring a sword upon thee, and cut off man and beast out of thee.

9 And the land of Egypt (Africa) shall be desolate and waste; and they shall know that I am the LORD: because he hath said, The river is mine, and I have made it.

10 Behold, therefore I am against thee, and against thy rivers, and I will make the land of Egypt utterly waste and desolate, from the tower of Syene even unto the border of Ethiopia. (Africa)

11 No foot of man shall pass through it, nor foot of beast shall pass through it, neither shall it be inhabited forty years.

12 And I will make the land of Egypt (Africa) desolate in the midst of the countries that are desolate, and her cities among the cities that are laid waste shall be desolate forty years: and I will scatter the Egyptians (Africans) among the nations, and will disperse them through the countries.

(Ezekiel 29:1-12).

589/3633

Ezekiel 29:13-16. God will gather the African people from all of the lands where they were scattered, and return them to their land in Africa. (Egypt and Egyptians are anachronisms for Africa and Africans.)

13 Yet thus saith the Lord GOD; At the end of forty years will I gather the Egyptians (Africans) from the people whither they were scattered:

14 And I will bring again the captivity of Egypt, (Africa) and will cause them to return into the land of Pathros, (Africa) into the land of their habitation; and they shall be there a base kingdom.

15 It shall be the basest of the kingdoms; neither shall it exalt itself any more above the nations: for I will diminish them, that they shall no more rule over the nations.

16 And it shall be no more the confidence of the house of Israel, (African Hebrews) which bringeth their iniquity to remembrance, when they shall look after them: but they shall know that I am the Lord GOD.

(Ezekiel 29:13-16).

588/3634

The year of LAMENTATIONS. After God shewed the Prophet Jeremiah all of the terrible things that would happen to the Children of Israel for their sins, Jeremiah went and cried about it. These five chapters of Lamentations, express the 'woe' that Jeremiah felt when God shewed him the affliction that the African Hebrews and the African Gentiles would suffer.

588/3634

Ezekiel 28:6-23. God bringing the 'new folks' to destroy African Gentiles. (Tyrus, Zidon and Egypt are African nations.)

6 Therefore thus saith the Lord GOD; Because thou hast set thine heart as the heart of God;

7 Behold, therefore I will bring strangers (new folks) upon thee, the terrible of the nations: and they shall draw their swords against the beauty of thy wisdom, and they shall defile thy brightness.

8 They shall bring thee down to the pit, and thou shalt die the deaths of them that are slain in the midst of the seas.

9 Wilt thou yet say before him that slayeth thee, I am God? but thou shalt be a man, and no God, in the hand of him that slayeth thee.

10 Thou shalt die the deaths of the uncircumcised by the hand of strangers: for I have spoken it, saith the Lord GOD.

11 Moreover the word of the LORD came unto me, saying,

12 Son of man, take up a lamentation upon the king of Tyrus, and say unto him, Thus saith the Lord GOD; Thou sealest up the sum, full of wisdom, and perfect in beauty.

13 Thou hast been in Eden the garden of God; every precious stone was thy covering, the sardius, topaz, and the diamond, the beryl, the onyx, and the jasper, the sapphire, the emerald, and the carbuncle, and gold: the workmanship of thy tabrets and of thy pipes was prepared in thee in the day that thou wast created.

14 Thou art the anointed cherub that covereth; and I have set thee so: thou wast upon the holy mountain of God; thou hast walked up and down in the midst of the stones of fire.

15 Thou wast perfect in thy ways from the day that thou wast created, till iniquity was found in thee.

16 By the multitude of thy merchandise they have filled the midst of thee with violence, and thou hast sinned: therefore I will cast thee as profane out of the mountain of God: and I will destroy thee, O covering cherub, from the midst of the stones of fire.

17 Thine heart was lifted up because of thy beauty, thou hast corrupted thy wisdom by reason of thy brightness: I will cast thee to the ground, I will lay thee before kings, that they may behold thee.

18 Thou hast defiled thy sanctuaries by the multitude of thine iniquities, by the iniquity of thy traffick; therefore will I bring forth a fire from the midst of thee, it shall devour thee, and I will bring thee to ashes upon the earth in the sight of all them that behold thee.

19 All they that know thee among the people shall be astonished at thee: thou shalt be a terror, and never shalt thou be any more.

20 Again the word of the LORD came unto me, saying,

21 Son of man, set thy face against Zidon, and prophesy against it,

22 And say, Thus saith the Lord GOD; Behold, I am against thee, O Zidon; (Gentiles) and I will be glorified in the midst of thee: and they shall know that I am the LORD, when I shall have executed judgments in her, and shall be sanctified in her.

23 For I will send into her pestilence, and blood into her streets; and the wounded shall be judged in the midst of her by the sword upon her on every side; and they shall know that I am the LORD.

(Ezekiel 28:6-23).

588/3634

Ezekiel 28:24-26. God will gather the African Hebrews from 'new folks'. The House of Israel will be exalted and returned to their African homeland.

24 And there shall be no more a pricking brier unto the house of Israel, (African Hebrews) nor any grieving thorn of all that are round about them, that despised them; and they shall know that I am the Lord GOD.

25 Thus saith the Lord GOD; When I shall have gathered the house of Israel (African Hebrews) from the people among whom they are scattered, (new folks) and shall be sanctified in them in the sight of the heathen, then shall they dwell in their land (Africa) that I have given to my servant Jacob.

26 And they shall dwell safely therein, and shall build houses, and plant vineyards; yea, they shall dwell with confidence, when I have executed judgments upon all those that despise them round about them; and they shall know that I am the LORD their God.

(Ezekiel 28:24-26).

588/3634

Ezekiel 30:20-26. God shewing us how HE will use 'new folks' to destroy the African Gentiles. (The 'king of Babylon' in these verses is the anachronism for 'new folks'.)

20 And it came to pass in the eleventh year, in the first month, in the seventh day of the month, that the word of the LORD came unto me, saying,

21 Son of man, I have broken the arm of Pharaoh king of Egypt; (Africa) and, lo, it shall not be bound up to be healed, to put a roller to bind it, to make it strong to hold the sword.

22 Therefore thus saith the Lord GOD; Behold, I am against Pharaoh king of Egypt, and will break his arms, the strong, and that which was broken; and I will cause the sword to fall out of his hand.

23 And I will scatter the Egyptians (Africans) among the nations, and will disperse them through the countries.

24 And I will strengthen the arms of the king of Babylon, (new folks) and put my sword in his hand: but I will break Pharaoh's arms, (Africans)and he shall groan before him with the groanings of a deadly wounded man.

25 But I will strengthen the arms of the king of Babylon,(new folks) and the arms of Pharaoh (Africans) shall fall down; and they shall know that I am the LORD, when I shall put my sword into the hand of the king of Babylon,(new folks) and he shall stretch it out upon the land of Egypt. (Africa)

26 And I will scatter the Egyptians (Africans) among the nations, and disperse them among the countries; and they shall know that I am the LORD.

(Ezekiel 30:20-26).

588/3634

Ezekiel Chapters 31 and 32. These two chapters find the Prophet Ezekiel lamenting because God shewed him the great destruction that was coming to destroy the land of Africa.

587/3635

Ezekiel Chapter 33. The Prophet Ezekiel is admonished in this chapter to be sure that he does a good job warning the Children of Israel. All through the Old Testament, God sent judges, prophets and priests, to warn the African Hebrews of the danger of breaking the Ten Commandments.

587/3635

Ezekiel 34:11-22. God will deliver HIS chosen people from America and all places where they have been scattered, and bring them to their own land in Africa.

11 For thus saith the Lord GOD; Behold, I, even I, will both search my sheep, (African Hebrews) and seek them out.

12 As a shepherd seeketh out his flock in the day that he is among his sheep that are scattered; so will I seek out my sheep, and will deliver them out of all places where they have been scattered in the cloudy and dark day.

13 And I will bring them out from the people, and gather them from the countries, and will bring them to their own land, (Africa) and feed them upon the mountains of Israel by the rivers, and in all the inhabited places of the country.

14 I will feed them in a good pasture, and upon the high mountains of Israel shall their fold be: there shall they lie in a good fold, and in a fat pasture shall they feed upon the mountains of Israel.

15 I will feed my flock, and I will cause them to lie down, saith the Lord GOD.

16 I will seek that which was lost, and bring again that which was driven away, and will bind up that which was broken, and will strengthen that which was sick: but I will destroy the fat and the strong; I will feed them with judgment.

17 And as for you, O my flock, thus saith the Lord GOD; Behold, I judge between cattle and cattle, between the rams and the he goats.

18 Seemeth it a small thing unto you to have eaten up the good pasture, but ye must tread down with your feet the residue of your pastures? and to have drunk of the deep waters, but ye must foul the residue with your feet?

19 And as for my flock, they eat that which ye have trodden with your feet; and they drink that which ye have fouled with your feet.

20 Therefore thus saith the Lord GOD unto them; Behold, I, even I, will judge between the fat cattle and between the lean cattle.

21 Because ye have thrust with side and with shoulder, and pushed all the diseased with your horns, till ye have scattered them abroad;

22 Therefore will I save my flock, and they shall no more be a prey; and I will judge between cattle and cattle.

(Ezekiel 34:11-22).

587/3635

Ezekiel 34:25-31. After GOD's 'New Covenant' is implemented (Jeremiah 31:31-37), the African Hebrews will return and dwell safely in Africa.

25 And I will make with them (African Hebrews) a covenant of peace, and will cause the evil beasts to cease out of the land: and they shall dwell safely in the wilderness, and sleep in the woods.

26 And I will make them and the places round about my hill a blessing; and I will cause the shower to come down in his season; there shall be showers of blessing.

27 And the tree of the field shall yield her fruit, and the earth shall yield her increase, and they shall be safe in their land, (Africa) and

shall know that I am the LORD, when I have broken the bands of their yoke, and delivered them out of the hand of those that served themselves of them.

28 And they shall no more be a prey to the heathen, (new folks) neither shall the beast of the land devour them; but they shall dwell safely, and none shall make them afraid.

29 And I will raise up for them a plant of renown, and they shall be no more consumed with hunger in the land, neither bear the shame of the heathen any more.

30 Thus shall they know that I the LORD their God am with them, and that they, even the house of Israel, (African Hebrews) are my people, saith the Lord GOD.

31 And ye my flock, the flock of my pasture, are men, and I am your God, saith the Lord GOD.

(Ezekiel 34:25-31).

587/3635

Ezekiel Chapter 35. This chapter explains how GOD will punish America for their wickedness. (Mt. Seir is the anachronism for America.)

1 Moreover the word of the LORD came unto me, saying,

2 Son of man, set thy face against mount Seir, (America) and prophesy against it,

3 And say unto it, Thus saith the Lord GOD; Behold, O mount Seir, I am against thee, and I will stretch out mine hand against thee, and I will make thee most desolate.

4 I will lay thy cities waste, and thou shalt be desolate, and thou shalt know that I am the LORD.

5 Because thou hast had a perpetual hatred, and hast shed the blood of the children of Israel (African Hebrews) by the force of the sword in the time of their calamity, in the time that their iniquity had an end:

6 Therefore, as I live, saith the Lord GOD, I will prepare thee unto

blood, and blood shall pursue thee: sith thou hast not hated blood, even blood shall pursue thee.

7 Thus will I make mount Seir most desolate, and cut off from it him that passeth out and him that returneth.

8 And I will fill his mountains with his slain men: in thy hills, and in thy valleys, and in all thy rivers, shall they fall that are slain with the sword.

9 I will make thee perpetual desolations, and thy cities shall not return: and ye shall know that I am the LORD.

10 Because thou hast said, These two nations and these two countries shall be mine, and we will possess it; whereas the LORD was there:

11 Therefore, as I live, saith the Lord GOD, I will even do according to thine anger, and according to thine envy which thou hast used out of thy hatred against them; and I will make myself known among them, when I have judged thee.

12 And thou shalt know that I am the LORD, and that I have heard all thy blasphemies which thou hast spoken against the mountains of Israel, saying, They are laid desolate, they are given us to consume.

13 Thus with your mouth ye have boasted against me, and have multiplied your words against me: I have heard them.

14 Thus saith the Lord GOD; When the whole earth rejoiceth, I will make thee desolate.

15 As thou didst rejoice at the inheritance of the house of Israel, because it was desolate, so will I do unto thee: thou shalt be desolate, O mount Seir, and all Idumea, even all of it: and they shall know that I am the LORD.

(Ezekiel 35:1-15).

587/3635

Ezekiel 36:1-15. God speaking to the <u>'LAND'</u> of Africa, and how the Children of Israel will possess it again.

1 Also, thou son of man, prophesy unto the mountains of Israel, and say, Ye mountains of Israel, hear the word of the LORD:

2 Thus saith the Lord GOD; Because the enemy hath said against you, Aha, even the ancient high places are ours in possession:

3 Therefore prophesy and say, Thus saith the Lord GOD; Because they have made you desolate, and swallowed you up on every side, that ye might be a possession unto the residue of the heathen, and ye are taken up in the lips of talkers, and are an infamy of the people:

4 Therefore, ye mountains of Israel, hear the word of the Lord GOD; Thus saith the Lord GOD to the mountains, and to the hills, to the rivers, and to the valleys, to the desolate wastes, and to the cities that are forsaken, which became a prey and derision to the residue of the heathen that are round about;

5 Therefore thus saith the Lord GOD; Surely in the fire of my jealousy have I spoken against the residue of the heathen, and against all Idumea, (another name for Edom-African gentiles) which have appointed my land into their possession with the joy of all their heart, with despiteful minds, to cast it out for a prey.

6 Prophesy therefore concerning the land of Israel, and say unto the mountains, and to the hills, to the rivers, and to the valleys, Thus saith the Lord GOD; Behold, I have spoken in my jealousy and in my fury, because ye have borne the shame of the heathen:

7 Therefore thus saith the Lord GOD; I have lifted up mine hand, Surely the heathen that are about you, they shall bear their shame.

8 But ye, O mountains of Israel, ye shall shoot forth your branches, and yield your fruit to my people of Israel; for they are at hand to come.

9 For, behold, I am for you, and I will turn unto you, and ye shall be tilled and sown:

10 And I will multiply men upon you, all the house of Israel, even all of it: and the cities shall be inhabited, and the wastes shall be builded:

11 And I will multiply upon you man and beast; and they shall increase and bring fruit: and I will settle you after your old estates, and will do better unto you than at your beginnings: and ye shall know that I am the LORD.

12 Yea, I will cause men to walk upon you, even my people Israel; and they shall possess thee, and thou shalt be their inheritance, and thou shalt no more henceforth bereave them of men.

13 Thus saith the Lord GOD; Because they say unto you, Thou land devourest up men, and hast bereaved thy nations;

14 Therefore thou shalt devour men no more, neither bereave thy nations any more, saith the Lord GOD.

15 Neither will I cause men to hear in thee the shame of the heathen any more, neither shalt thou bear the reproach of the people any more, neither shalt thou cause thy nations to fall any more, saith the Lord GOD.

(Ezekiel 36:1-15).

587/3635

Ezekiel 36:16-24. God explaining why the African Hebrews and African Gentile were driven from Africa, and how HE will take the Children of Israel back to their land in Africa.

16 Moreover the word of the LORD came unto me, saying,

17 Son of man, when the house of Israel (African Hebrews) dwelt in their own land, (Africa) they defiled it by their own way and by their doings: their way was before me as the uncleanness of a removed woman.

18 Wherefore I poured my fury upon them for the blood that they had shed upon the land, and for their idols wherewith they had polluted it:

19 And I scattered them among the heathen, (Gentile Africans and Gentile New Folks) and they were dispersed through the countries: according to their way and according to their doings I judged them.

20 And when they entered unto the heathen, whither they went, they

profaned my holy name, when they said to them, These are the people of the LORD, and are gone forth out of his land.

21 But I had pity for mine holy name, which the house of Israel had profaned among the heathen, whither they went.

22 Therefore say unto the house of Israel, Thus saith the Lord GOD; I do not this for your sakes, O house of Israel, but for mine holy name's sake, which ye have profaned among the heathen, whither ye went.

23 And I will sanctify my great name, which was profaned among the heathen, which ye have profaned in the midst of them; and the heathen shall know that I am the LORD, saith the Lord GOD, when I shall be sanctified in you before their eyes.

24 For I will take you from among the heathen, (new folks) and gather you out of all countries, and will bring you into your own land. (Africa)

(Ezekiel 36:16-24).

587/3635

Ezekiel 36:25-38. GOD will cleanse Israel, and they will dwell in the land that HE gave their forefathers in Africa.

25 Then will I sprinkle clean water upon you, (African Hebrews) and ye shall be clean: from all your filthiness, and from all your idols, will I cleanse you.

26 A new heart also will I give you, and a new spirit will I put within you: and I will take away the stony heart out of your flesh, and I will give you an heart of flesh.

27 And I will put my spirit within you, and cause you to walk in my statutes, and ye shall keep my judgments, and do them.

28 And ye shall dwell in the land that I gave to your fathers; (Africa) and ye shall be my people, and I will be your God.

29 I will also save you from all your uncleannesses: and I will call for the corn, and will increase it, and lay no famine upon you.

30 And I will multiply the fruit of the tree, and the increase of the field, that ye shall receive no more reproach of famine among the heathen.

31 Then shall ye remember your own evil ways, and your doings that were not good, and shall lothe yourselves in your own sight for your iniquities and for your abominations.

32 Not for your sakes do I this, saith the Lord GOD, be it known unto you: be ashamed and confounded for your own ways, O house of Israel. (African Hebrews)

33 Thus saith the Lord GOD; In the day that I shall have cleansed you from all your iniquities I will also cause you to dwell in the cities, and the wastes shall be builded.

34 And the desolate land shall be tilled, whereas it lay desolate in the sight of all that passed by.

35 And they shall say, This land that was desolate is become like the garden of Eden; and the waste and desolate and ruined cities are become fenced, and are inhabited.

36 Then the heathen that are left round about you shall know that I the LORD build the ruined places, and plant that that was desolate: I the LORD have spoken it, and I will do it.

37 Thus saith the Lord GOD; I will yet for this be enquired of by the house of Israel, to do it for them; I will increase them with men like a flock.

38 As the holy flock, as the flock of Jerusalem in her solemn feasts; so shall the waste cities be filled with flocks of men: and they shall know that I am the LORD.

(Ezekiel 36:25-38).

587/3635

Ezekiel 37:1-14. The 'true' Children of Israel are black, poor and very confused about their true identity. Spirits are low, hopelessness prevails and the weight of America is heavy upon them. But God will open Israel's grave, put a new spirit in their 'dry bones', and take them back to Africa, where they will live in peace.

1 The hand of the LORD was upon me, and carried me out in the spirit of the LORD, and set me down in the midst of the valley which was full of bones,

2 And caused me to pass by them round about: and, behold, there were very many in the open valley; and, lo, they were very dry.

3 And he said unto me, Son of man, can these bones live? And I answered, O Lord GOD, thou knowest.

4 Again he said unto me, Prophesy upon these bones, and say unto them, O ye dry bones, hear the word of the LORD.

5 Thus saith the Lord GOD unto these bones; Behold, I will cause breath to enter into you, and ye shall live:

6 And I will lay sinews upon you, and will bring up flesh upon you, and cover you with skin, and put breath in you, and ye shall live; and ye shall know that I am the LORD.

7 So I prophesied as I was commanded: and as I prophesied, there was a noise, and behold a shaking, and the bones came together, bone to his bone.

8 And when I beheld, lo, the sinews and the flesh came up upon them, and the skin covered them above: but there was no breath in them.

9 Then said he unto me, Prophesy unto the wind, prophesy, son of man, and say to the wind, Thus saith the Lord GOD; Come from the four winds, O breath, and breathe upon these slain, that they may live.

10 So I prophesied as he commanded me, and the breath came into them, and they lived, and stood up upon their feet, an exceeding great army.

11 Then he said unto me, Son of man, these bones are the whole house of Israel: (African Hebrews) behold, they say, Our bones are dried, and our hope is lost: we are cut off for our parts.

12 Therefore prophesy and say unto them, Thus saith the Lord GOD; Behold, O my people, (African Hebrews) I will open your graves, and cause you to come up out of your graves, and bring you into the land of Israel. (Africa)

13 And ye shall know that I am the LORD, when I have opened your graves, O my people, and brought you up out of your graves,

14 And shall put my spirit in you, and ye shall live, and I shall place you in your own land: (Africa) then shall ye know that I the LORD have spoken it, and performed it, saith the LORD.

(Ezekiel 37:1-14).

587/3635

Ezekiel 37:16-23. The Children of Israel that reside in Africa (Judah), and the Children of Israel that reside in America (Ephraim), will be joined together and dwell together as one nation again in Africa. (All references in these verses are to the African Hebrews).

16 Moreover, thou son of man, take thee one stick, and write upon it, For Judah, and for the children of Israel his companions: then take another stick, and write upon it, For Joseph, the stick of Ephraim, and for all the house of Israel his companions:

17 And join them one to another into one stick; and they shall become one in thine hand.

18 And when the children of thy people shall speak unto thee, saying, Wilt thou not shew us what thou meanest by these?

19 Say unto them, Thus saith the Lord GOD; Behold, I will take the stick of Joseph, which is in the hand of Ephraim, and the tribes of Israel his fellows, and will put them with him, even with the stick of Judah, and make them one stick, and they shall be one in mine hand.

20 And the sticks whereon thou writest shall be in thine hand before their eyes.

21 And say unto them, Thus saith the Lord GOD; Behold, I will take the children of Israel from among the heathen, whither they be gone, and will gather them on every side, and bring them into their own land:

22 And I will make them one nation in the land upon the mountains of Israel; and one king shall be king to them all: and they shall be no more two nations, neither shall they be divided into two kingdoms any more at all:

23 Neither shall they defile themselves any more with their idols, nor with their detestable things, nor with any of their transgressions: but I will save them out of all their dwellingplaces, wherein they have sinned, and will cleanse them: so shall they be my people, and I will be their God.

(Ezekiel 37:16-23).

587/3635

Ezekiel 37:26-28. The whole world will know that the African Hebrews are 'black folks' (old folks), and that they are God's chosen people.

26 Moreover I will make a covenant of peace with them; (African Hebrews) it shall be an everlasting covenant with them: and I will place them, and multiply them, and will set my sanctuary in the midst of them for evermore.

27 My tabernacle also shall be with them: yea, I will be their God, and they shall be my people.

28 And the heathen (gentiles) shall know that I the LORD do sanctify Israel, when my sanctuary shall be in the midst of them for evermore.

(Ezekiel 37:26-28).

587/3635

Ezekiel Chapter 38. What God will do to 'new folks' when they come up against Israel, when Israel becomes one nation of people again. (Gog, Magog, Meshech, Tubal, etc. = new folks of America, Persia, Ethiopia, Libya, etc. = gentile old folks or Africa.)

1 And the word of the LORD came unto me, saying,

2 Son of man, set thy face against Gog, the land of Magog, the chief prince of Meshech and Tubal, and prophesy against him,

3 And say, Thus saith the Lord GOD; Behold, I am against thee, O Gog, the chief prince of Meshech and Tubal:

4 And I will turn thee back, and put hooks into thy jaws, and I will bring thee forth, and all thine army, horses and horsemen, all of

them clothed with all sorts of armour, even a great company with bucklers and shields, all of them handling swords:

5 Persia, Ethiopia, and Libya with them; all of them with shield and helmet:

6 Gomer, and all his bands; the house of Togarmah of the north quarters, and all his bands: and many people with thee.

7 Be thou prepared, and prepare for thyself, thou, and all thy company that are assembled unto thee, and be thou a guard unto them.

8 After many days thou shalt be visited: in the latter years thou shalt come into the land that is brought back from the sword, and is gathered out of many people, against the mountains of Israel, which have been always waste: but it is brought forth out of the nations, and they shall dwell safely all of them.

9 Thou shalt ascend and come like a storm, thou shalt be like a cloud to cover the land, thou, and all thy bands, and many people with thee.

10 Thus saith the Lord GOD; It shall also come to pass, that at the same time shall things come into thy mind, and thou shalt think an evil thought:

11 And thou shalt say, I will go up to the land of unwalled villages; I will go to them that are at rest, that dwell safely, all of them dwelling without walls, and having neither bars nor gates,

12 To take a spoil, and to take a prey; to turn thine hand upon the desolate places that are now inhabited, and upon the people that are gathered out of the nations, which have gotten cattle and goods, that dwell in the midst of the land.

13 Sheba, and Dedan, and the merchants of Tarshish, with all the young lions thereof, shall say unto thee, Art thou come to take a spoil? hast thou gathered thy company to take a prey? to carry away silver and gold, to take away cattle and goods, to take a great spoil?

14 Therefore, son of man, prophesy and say unto Gog, Thus saith the Lord GOD; In that day when my people of Israel dwelleth safely, shalt thou not know it?

15 And thou shalt come from thy place out of the north parts, (North America) thou, and many people with thee, all of them riding upon horses, a great company, and a mighty army:

16 And thou shalt come up against my people of Israel, (African Hebrews) as a cloud to cover the land; it shall be in the latter days, and I will bring thee against my land, (Africa) that the heathen may know me, when I shall be sanctified in thee, O Gog, before their eyes.

17 Thus saith the Lord GOD; Art thou he of whom I have spoken in old time by my servants the prophets of Israel, which prophesied in those days many years that I would bring thee against them?

18 And it shall come to pass at the same time when Gog shall come against the land of Israel, saith the Lord GOD, that my fury shall come up in my face.

19 For in my jealousy and in the fire of my wrath have I spoken, Surely in that day there shall be a great shaking in the land of Israel; (Africa)

20 So that the fishes of the sea, and the fowls of the heaven, and the beasts of the field, and all creeping things that creep upon the earth, and all the men that are upon the face of the earth, shall shake at my presence, and the mountains shall be thrown down, and the steep places shall fall, and every wall shall fall to the ground.

21 And I will call for a sword against him throughout all my mountains, saith the Lord GOD: every man's sword shall be against his brother.

22 And I will plead against him with pestilence and with blood; and I will rain upon him, and upon his bands, and upon the many people that are with him, an overflowing rain, and great hailstones, fire, and brimstone.

23 Thus will I magnify myself, and sanctify myself; and I will be known in the eyes of many nations, and they shall know that I am the LORD.

(Ezekiel 38:1-23).

587/3635

Ezekiel 39:1-22. God will cause the 'new folks' to come upon the African Hebrews, as HE did Pharaoh back in Egypt, and destroy them before Israel's eyes. Israel will bury their bodies for seven months, and the beasts shall feast on them. God will cause the 'new folks' to come from North America and will smite them. (Gog, Magog, Meshech and Tubal = America)

1 Therefore, thou son of man, prophesy against Gog, and say, Thus saith the Lord GOD; Behold, I am against thee, O Gog, the chief prince of Meshech and Tubal:

2 And I will turn thee back, and leave but the sixth part of thee, and will cause thee to come up from the north parts, (America) and will bring thee upon the mountains of Israel: (Africa)

3 And I will smite thy bow out of thy left hand, and will cause thine arrows to fall out of thy right hand.

4 Thou shalt fall upon the mountains of Israel, (Africa) thou, and all thy bands, and the people that is with thee: I will give thee unto the ravenous birds of every sort, and to the beasts of the field to be devoured.

5 Thou shalt fall upon the open field: for I have spoken it, saith the Lord GOD.

6 And I will send a fire on Magog, (Gentiles) and among them that dwell carelessly in the isles: and they shall know that I am the LORD.

7 So will I make my holy name known in the midst of my people Israel; and I will not let them pollute my holy name any more: and the heathen shall know that I am the LORD, the Holy One in Israel.

8 Behold, it is come, and it is done, saith the Lord GOD; this is the day whereof I have spoken.

9 And they that dwell in the cities of Israel (Africa) shall go forth, and shall set on fire and burn the weapons, both the shields and the bucklers, the bows and the arrows, and the handstaves, and the spears, and they shall burn them with fire seven years: (America's weapons and war-power will cease to exist)

10 So that they shall take no wood out of the field, neither cut down any out of the forests; for they shall burn the weapons with fire: and they shall spoil those that spoiled them, and rob those that robbed them, saith the Lord GOD.

11 And it shall come to pass in that day, that I will give unto Gog (Gentiles) a place there of graves in Israel, (Africa) the valley of the passengers on the east of the sea: and it shall stop the noses of the passengers: and there shall they bury Gog and all his multitude: and they shall call it The valley of Hamongog. (The burial place for the gentiles that come up against the African Hebrews when they return to Africa)

12 And seven months shall the house of Israel (African Hebrews) be burying of them, (Gentiles) that they may cleanse the land.

13 Yea, all the people of the land shall bury them; and it shall be to them a renown the day that I shall be glorified, saith the Lord GOD.

14 And they shall sever out men of continual employment, passing through the land to bury with the passengers those that remain upon the face of the earth, to cleanse it: after the end of seven months shall they search.

15 And the passengers that pass through the land, when any seeth a man's bone, then shall he set up a sign by it, till the buriers have buried it in the valley of Hamongog.

16 And also the name of the city shall be Hamonah. Thus shall they cleanse the land.

17 And, thou son of man, thus saith the Lord GOD; Speak unto every feathered fowl, and to every beast of the field, Assemble yourselves, and come; gather yourselves on every side to my sacrifice that I do sacrifice for you, even a great sacrifice upon the mountains of Israel, that ye may eat flesh, and drink blood.

18 Ye shall eat the flesh of the mighty, and drink the blood of the princes of the earth, of rams, of lambs, and of goats, of bullocks, all of them fatlings of Bashan.

19 And ye shall eat fat till ye be full, and drink blood till ye be drunken, of my sacrifice which I have sacrificed for you.

20 Thus ye shall be filled at my table with horses and chariots, with mighty men, and with all men of war, saith the Lord GOD.

21 And I will set my glory among the heathen, (new folks) and all the heathen shall see my judgment that I have executed, and my hand that I have laid upon them.

22 So the house of Israel (African Hebrews) shall know that I am the LORD their God from that day and forward.

(Ezekiel 39:1-22).

587/3635

Ezekiel 39:23-29. The 'new folks' will know why the African Hebrews were placed in America and afflicted for 400 years.

23 And the heathen (new folks) shall know that the house of Israel (African Hebrews) went into captivity for their iniquity: because they trespassed against me, therefore hid I my face from them, and gave them into the hand of their enemies: so fell they all by the sword.

24 According to their uncleanness and according to their transgressions have I done unto them, and hid my face from them.

25 Therefore thus saith the Lord GOD; Now will I bring again the captivity of Jacob, (African Hebrews) and have mercy upon the whole house of Israel, (African Hebrews) and will be jealous for my holy name;

26 After that they have borne their shame, and all their trespasses whereby they have trespassed against me, when they dwelt safely in their land, and none made them afraid.

27 When I have brought them again from the people, and gathered them out of their enemies' lands, and am sanctified in them in the sight of many nations;

28 Then shall they know that I am the LORD their God, which caused them to be led into captivity among the heathen: but I have gathered them unto their own land, and have left none of them any more there.

29 Neither will I hide my face any more from them: for I have poured out my spirit upon the house of Israel, saith the Lord GOD.

(Ezekiel 39:23-29).

587/3635

Obadiah 1:1-16. God shewing Obadiah how HE will destroy the African Gentiles for rejoicing over the Children of Israel's destruction. (Edom = African Gentiles)

1 The vision of Obadiah. Thus saith the Lord GOD concerning Edom; (African Gentiles) We have heard a rumour from the LORD, and an ambassador is sent among the heathen, Arise ye, and let us rise up against her in battle.

2 Behold, I have made thee small among the heathen: thou art greatly despised.

3 The pride of thine heart hath deceived thee, thou that dwellest in the clefts of the rock, whose habitation is high; that saith in his heart, Who shall bring me down to the ground?

4 Though thou exalt thyself as the eagle, and though thou set thy nest among the stars, thence will I bring thee down, saith the LORD.

5 If thieves came to thee, if robbers by night, (how art thou cut off!) would they not have stolen till they had enough? if the grapegatherers came to thee, would they not leave some grapes?

6 How are the things of Esau (the land of Edom in which Esau's descendants lived) searched out! how are his hidden things sought up!

7 All the men of thy confederacy have brought thee even to the border: the men that were at peace with thee have deceived thee, and prevailed against thee; they that eat thy bread have laid a wound under thee: there is none understanding in him.

8 Shall I not in that day, saith the LORD, even destroy the wise men out of Edom, and understanding out of the mount of Esau?

9 And thy mighty men, O Teman, (one of the cities in Edom) shall be dismayed, to the end that every one of the mount of Esau may be cut off by slaughter.

10 For thy violence against thy brother Jacob shame shall cover thee, and thou shalt be cut off for ever.

11 In the day that thou stoodest on the other side, in the day that the

strangers carried away captive his forces, and foreigners entered into his gates, and cast lots upon Jerusalem, even thou wast as one of them.

12 But thou shouldest not have looked on the day of thy brother in the day that he became a stranger; neither shouldest thou have rejoiced over the children of Judah in the day of their destruction; neither shouldest thou have spoken proudly in the day of distress.

13 Thou shouldest not have entered into the gate of my people (African Hebrews) in the day of their calamity; yea, thou shouldest not have looked on their affliction in the day of their calamity, nor have laid hands on their substance in the day of their calamity;

14 Neither shouldest thou have stood in the crossway, to cut off those of his that did escape; neither shouldest thou have delivered up those of his that did remain in the day of distress.

15 For the day of the LORD is near upon all the heathen: as thou hast done, it shall be done unto thee: thy reward shall return upon thine own head.

16 For as ye have drunk upon my holy mountain, so shall all the heathen drink continually, yea, they shall drink, and they shall swallow down, and they shall be as though they had not been.

(Obadiah 1:1-16).

587/3635

Obadiah 1:17-21. God shewing Obadiah how HE will deliver Israel, and how they will possess their land in Africa again.

17 But upon mount Zion (Africa) shall be deliverance, and there shall be holiness; and the house of Jacob (African Hebrews) shall possess their possessions.

18 And the house of Jacob (African Hebrews) shall be a fire, and the house of Joseph (African Hebrews) a flame, and the house of Esau (Gentiles) for stubble, and they shall kindle in them, and devour them; and there shall not be any remaining of the house of Esau; for the LORD hath spoken it.

19 And they of the south shall possess the mount of Esau; and they of

the plain the Philistines: and they shall possess the fields of Ephraim, and the fields of Samaria: and Benjamin shall possess Gilead.

20 And the captivity of this host of the children of Israel shall possess that of the Canaanites, even unto Zarephath; and the captivity of Jerusalem, which is in Sepharad, shall possess the cities of the south.

21 And saviours shall come up on mount Zion (African Hebrews)to judge the mount of Esau; (Gentiles) and the kingdom shall be the LORD'S.

(Obadiah 1:17-21).

586/3636

The 2nd deportation to Babylon of the African Hebrews. Daniel was the next Prophet that worked 73 years for God. (607 BCE to 534 BCE). God used Daniel to shew the type of faith that the African Hebrews must have. God also told Daniel the specific year when Israel's 400 year captivity in America will be over.

534/3688

Daniel 12:1-2. The African Hebrew Messiah will deliver the Children of Israel from America. God said that everyone that will be delivered must be written in the book. (The book of 'purification'--see Jere. 31:31-37) God said when the time of trouble comes, many people will run to the Children of Israel for safety and refuge. When the day of the 'general awakening' comes, many people will wake up out of their 'deep sleep' (Slave Mentality), and realize that there is only one God and one Truth.

1 And at that time shall Michael (African Messiah) stand up, the great prince which standeth for the children of thy people: (African Hebrews) and there shall be a time of trouble, such as never was since there was a nation even to that same time: and at that time thy people (African Hebrews) shall be delivered, every one that shall be found written in the book.

2 And many of them that sleep in the dust of the earth (Even though 'Alive', without TRUTH, many people are walking around 'asleep' with their eyes wide open.) shall awake, some to everlasting life, and some to shame and everlasting contempt.

(Daniel 12:1-2).

534/3688

Daniel 12:11. God shewed Daniel the appointed time when the African Hebrews shall be delivered. This verse, along with Genesis 15:13-14 gives the specific year.

11 And from the time that the daily sacrifice shall be taken away, and the abomination that maketh desolate set up, there shall be a thousand two hundred and ninety days.

(Daniel 12:11).

520/3702

Haggai 2:3-9. The House of Israel that develops from the 'New Covenant', will experience a greater life-style than the House of Israel that dwelled in Africa in former times.

3 Who is left among you that saw this house (House of Israel-African Hebrews) in her first glory? and how do ye see it now? is it not in your eyes in comparison of it as nothing?

4 Yet now be strong, O Zerubbabel, (He was appointed governor over the African Hebrew colony by King Cyrus, who allowed the African Hebrews to return to their land in Jerusalem) saith the LORD; and be strong, O Joshua, son of Josedech, the high priest; and be strong, all ye people of the land, saith the LORD, and work: for I am with you, saith the LORD of hosts:

5 According to the word that I covenanted with you when ye came out of Egypt, so my spirit remaineth among you: fear ye not.

6 For thus saith the LORD of hosts; Yet once, it is a little while, and I will shake the heavens, and the earth, and the sea, and the dry land;

7 And I will shake all nations, and the desire of all nations shall come: and I will fill this house with glory, saith the LORD of hosts.

8 The silver is mine, and the gold is mine, saith the LORD of hosts.

9 The glory of this latter house shall be greater than of the former, saith the LORD of hosts: and in this place will I give peace, saith the LORD of hosts.

(Haggai 2:3-9).

520/3702

Zechariah 2:6-13. God will shake His hand upon North America, and free His people from false worship. Many people shall join the House of Israel, and everyone will know that there is only one true GOD.

6 Ho, ho, come forth, and flee from the land of the north, (North America) saith the LORD: for I have spread you abroad as the four winds of the heaven, saith the LORD.

7 Deliver thyself, O Zion, (African Hebrews) that dwellest with the daughter of Babylon. (America)

8 For thus saith the LORD of hosts; After the glory hath he sent me unto the nations which spoiled you: for he that toucheth you toucheth the apple of his eye.

9 For, behold, I will shake mine hand upon them, and they shall be a spoil to their servants: and ye shall know that the LORD of hosts hath sent me.

10 Sing and rejoice, O daughter of Zion: (African Hebrews) for, lo, I come, and I will dwell in the midst of thee, saith the LORD.

11 And many nations shall be joined to the LORD in that day, and shall be my people: and I will dwell in the midst of thee, and thou shalt know that the LORD of hosts hath sent me unto thee.

12 And the LORD shall inherit Judah (African Hebrews) his portion in the holy land, and shall choose Jerusalem (Africa) again.

13 Be silent, O all flesh, before the LORD: for he is raised up out of his holy habitation.

(Zechariah 2:6-13).

519/3703

Zechariah 1:14-21. God very angry with 'new folks' because they afflicted the African Hebrews more than HE intended. God will return and have mercy on the African Hebrews after they serve their 400 year captivity.

14 So the angel that communed with me said unto me, Cry thou,

saying, Thus saith the LORD of hosts; I am jealous for Jerusalem (African Hebrews) and for Zion (African Hebrews) with a great jealousy.

15 And I am very sore displeased with the heathen (new folks) that are at ease: for I was but a little displeased, and they helped forward the affliction.

16 Therefore thus saith the LORD; I am returned to Jerusalem (Africa) with mercies: my house shall be built in it, saith the LORD of hosts, and a line shall be stretched forth upon Jerusalem.

17 Cry yet, saying, Thus saith the LORD of hosts; My cities through prosperity shall yet be spread abroad; and the LORD shall yet comfort Zion, (African Hebrews) and shall yet choose Jerusalem. (Africa)

18 Then lifted I up mine eyes, and saw, and behold four horns.

19 And I said unto the angel that talked with me, What be these? And he answered me, These are the horns which have scattered Judah, Israel, and Jerusalem. (African Hebrews)

20 And the LORD shewed me four carpenters.

21 Then said I, What come these to do? And he spake, saying, These are the horns which have scattered Judah, so that no man did lift up his head: but these are come to fray them, to cast out the horns of the Gentiles, which lifted up their horn over the land of Judah to scatter it.

(Zechariah 1:14-21).

518/3704

Zechariah 7:9-14. Why God scattered and punished the Children of Israel.

9 Thus speaketh the LORD of hosts, saying, Execute true judgment, and shew mercy and compassions every man to his brother:

10 And oppress not the widow, nor the fatherless, the stranger, nor the poor; and let none of you imagine evil against his brother in your heart.

11 But they (African Hebrews) refused to hearken, and pulled away the shoulder, and stopped their ears, that they should not hear.

12 Yea, they made their hearts as an adamant stone, lest they should hear the law, and the words which the LORD of hosts hath sent in his spirit by the former prophets: therefore came a great wrath from the LORD of hosts.

13 Therefore it is come to pass, that as he cried, and they would not hear; so they cried, and I would not hear, saith the LORD of hosts:

14 But I scattered them with a whirlwind among all the nations whom they knew not. Thus the land (Africa) was desolate after them, that no man passed through nor returned: for they laid the pleasant land desolate.

(Zechariah 7:9-14).

518/3704

Zechariah Chapter 8. This whole chapter talks about the great restoration that God promises the African Hebrews when the 400 year punishment is completed. God will save His people that are scattered all over the world, and cause them to dwell in Africa again. (Zion and Jerusalem are anachronisms for the African Hebrews and Africa.)

487/3735

Zechariah 10:6-12. God will strengthen and save the African Hebrews and give Africa back to them. God will bring African people from Africa (Egypt) and from America (Assyria) and take them to a temporary resting locations (Gilead & Lebanon) until America is brought down, and until the 'new folks' that are ruling Africa depart away.

6 And I will strengthen the house of Judah, (African Hebrews) and I will save the house of Joseph, (African Hebrews) and I will bring them again to place them; for I have mercy upon them: and they shall be as though I had not cast them off: for I am the LORD their God, and will hear them.

7 And they of Ephraim (African Hebrews) shall be like a mighty man, and their heart shall rejoice as through wine: yea, their children shall see it, and be glad; their heart shall rejoice in the LORD.

8 I will hiss for them, and gather them; for I have redeemed them: and they shall increase as they have increased.

9 And I will sow them among the people: and they shall remember me in far countries; and they shall live with their children, and turn again.

10 I will bring them again also out of the land of Egypt, (Africa) and gather them out of Assyria; (America) and I will bring them into the land of Gilead and Lebanon; and place shall not be found for them.

11 And he shall pass through the sea with affliction, and shall smite the waves in the sea, and all the deeps of the river (Atlantic Ocean) shall dry up: and the pride of Assyria (America) shall be brought down, and the sceptre of Egypt (Africa) shall depart away.

12 And I will strengthen them in the LORD; and they shall walk up and down in his name, saith the LORD.

(Zechariah 10:6-12).

487/3735

Zechariah Chapter 12. God will destroy all that come up against the African Hebrews. (Jerusalem, Judah and David = the African Hebrews)

1 The burden of the word of the LORD for Israel, (African Hebrews) saith the LORD, which stretcheth forth the heavens, and layeth the foundation of the earth, and formeth the spirit of man within him.

2 Behold, I will make Jerusalem (African Hebrews) a cup of trembling unto all the people round about, when they shall be in the siege both against Judah and against Jerusalem.

3 And in that day will I make Jerusalem a burdensome stone for all people: all that burden themselves with it shall be cut in pieces, though all the people of the earth be gathered together against it.

4 In that day, saith the LORD, I will smite every horse with astonishment, and his rider with madness: and I will open mine eyes upon the house of Judah, (African Hebrews) and will smite every horse of the people with blindness.

5 And the governors of Judah shall say in their heart, The inhabitants of Jerusalem shall be my strength in the LORD of hosts their God.

6 In that day will I make the governors of Judah like an hearth of fire among the wood, and like a torch of fire in a sheaf; and they shall devour all the people round about, on the right hand and on the left: and Jerusalem (Africa) shall be inhabited again in her own place, even in Jerusalem.

7 The LORD also shall save the tents of Judah first, that the glory of the house of David and the glory of the inhabitants of Jerusalem do not magnify themselves against Judah.

8 In that day shall the LORD defend the inhabitants of Jerusalem; and he that is feeble among them at that day shall be as David; and the house of David (African Hebrews) shall be as God, as the angel of the LORD before them.

9 And it shall come to pass in that day, that I will seek to destroy all the nations that come against Jerusalem. (Africa)

10 And I will pour upon the house of David, and upon the inhabitants of Jerusalem, the spirit of grace and of supplications: and they shall look upon me whom they have pierced, and they shall mourn for him, as one mourneth for his only son, and shall be in bitterness for him, as one that is in bitterness for his firstborn.

11 In that day shall there be a great mourning in Jerusalem, (Africa) as the mourning of Hadadrimmon (a place in the valley of Megiddo where the African Hebrew King Josiah was mortally wounded--II Kings 23:39) in the valley of Megiddon.

12 And the land shall mourn, every family apart; the family of the house of David apart, and their wives apart; the family of the house of Nathan apart, and their wives apart;

13 The family of the house of Levi apart, and their wives apart; the family of Shimei apart, and their wives apart;

14 All the families that remain, every family apart, and their wives apart.

(Zechariah 12:1-14).

487/3735

Zechariah 13:2-7. The day is coming fast upon us when God will cut off all false religions, idols, false prophets and ministers. People will be able to tell the difference between 'truth' and lies, and will no longer listen to false teachings and emotional preachers that deaden the senses with their loud screaming, and provide no wisdom. False preachers will no longer dress up in robed garments that deceive the people. When the Spirit of Truth unfolds, the false prophets and ministers will acknowledge the fact that they are not teaching or preaching, the true word of God.

2 And it shall come to pass in that day, saith the LORD of hosts, that I will cut off the names of the idols out of the land, and they shall no more be remembered: and also I will cause the prophets and the unclean spirit to pass out of the land.

3 And it shall come to pass, that when any shall yet prophesy, then his father and his mother that begat him shall say unto him, Thou shalt not live; for thou speakest lies in the name of the LORD: and his father and his mother that begat him shall thrust him through when he prophesieth.

4 And it shall come to pass in that day, that the prophets shall be ashamed every one of his vision, when he hath prophesied; neither shall they wear a rough garment to deceive:

5 But he shall say, I am no prophet, I am an husbandman; for man taught me to keep cattle from my youth.

6 And one shall say unto him, What are these wounds in thine hands? Then he shall answer, Those with which I was wounded in the house of my friends.

7 Awake, O sword, against my shepherd, and against the man that is my fellow, saith the LORD of hosts: smite the shepherd, and the sheep shall be scattered: and I will turn mine hand upon the little ones.

(Zechariah 13:2-7).

487/3735

Zechariah 13:8-9. In these coming last days, 'new folks' and 'gentile Africans' will be cut off, but the African Hebrews will be purified and turn to God's Ten Commandments.

8 And it shall come to pass, that in all the land, saith the LORD, two parts therein shall be cut off and die; but the third shall be left therein. (The 1st part, or 1/3 are the Gentile old folks--The 2nd part, or 2/3 are the 'new folks', the 3rd part are the African Hebrews)

9 And I will bring the third part through the fire, and will refine them as silver is refined, and will try them as gold is tried: they shall call on my name, and I will hear them: I will say, It is my people: and they shall say, The LORD is my God.

(Zechariah 13:8-9).

487/3735

Zechariah Chapter 14. The day of the Lord is coming. God will gather all nations against the African Hebrew, but God will fight their battles as He did in the days of old. God will be king over all the earth, and everyone will know that there is only one, true GOD. After the battle, Africa will be re-established as the land of 'peace'. God will smite all the people that fight against the African Hebrews, and Israel shall possess the wealth and substance of the oppressor as recorded in Genesis 15:14. Those nations that survive the battle, will fear the Lord, turn and keep the Ten Commandments, and worship the Lord properly according to the Hebrew Holidays that God commanded. The nations and people that do not conform to the true worship, shall be punished.

1 Behold, the day of the LORD cometh, and thy spoil shall be divided in the midst of thee.

2 For I will gather all nations against Jerusalem (African Hebrews) to battle; and the city shall be taken, and the houses rifled, and the women ravished; and half of the city shall go forth into captivity, and the residue of the people shall not be cut off from the city.

3 Then shall the LORD go forth, and fight against those nations, as when he fought in the day of battle.

4 And his feet shall stand in that day upon the mount of Olives, (Africa) which is before Jerusalem on the east, and the mount of Olives shall cleave in the midst thereof toward the east and toward the west, and there shall be a very great valley; and half of the mountain shall remove toward the north, and half of it toward the south.

5 And ye shall flee to the valley of the mountains; for the valley of the mountains shall reach unto Azal: (A place near Jerusalem) yea, ye shall flee, like as ye fled from before the earthquake in the days of Uzziah king of Judah: and the LORD my God shall come, and all the saints with thee.

6 And it shall come to pass in that day, that the light shall not be clear, nor dark:

7 But it shall be one day which shall be known to the LORD, not day, nor night: but it shall come to pass, that at evening time it shall be light.

8 And it shall be in that day, that living waters shall go out from Jerusalem; (Africa) half of them toward the former sea, and half of them toward the hinder sea: in summer and in winter shall it be.

9 And the LORD shall be king over all the earth: in that day shall there be one LORD, and his name one.

10 All the land shall be turned as a plain from Geba (A town assigned to the tribe of Levi) to Rimmon south of Jerusalem:(Africa) and it shall be lifted up, and inhabited in her place, from Benjamin's (African Hebrews) gate unto the place of the first gate, unto the corner gate, and from the tower of Hananeel (A tower in the wall of Jerusalem) unto the king's winepresses.

11 And men shall dwell in it, and there shall be no more utter destruction; but Jerusalem (Africa) shall be safely inhabited.

12 And this shall be the plague wherewith the LORD will smite all the people that have fought against Jerusalem; (African Hebrews) Their flesh shall consume away while they stand upon their feet, and their eyes shall consume away in their holes, and their tongue shall consume away in their mouth.

13 And it shall come to pass in that day, that a great tumult from the LORD shall be among them; and they shall lay hold every one on the hand of his neighbour, and his hand shall rise up against the hand of his neighbour.

14 And Judah (African Hebrews)also shall fight at Jerusalem; (Africa) and the wealth of all the heathen (new folks) round about shall be gathered together, gold, and silver, and apparel, in great abundance.

15 And so shall be the plague of the horse, of the mule, of the camel, and of the ass, and of all the beasts that shall be in these tents, as this plague.

16 And it shall come to pass, that every one that is left of all the nations which came against Jerusalem (African Hebrews) shall even go up from year to year to worship the King, the LORD of hosts, and to keep the feast of tabernacles.

17 And it shall be, that whoso will not come up of all the families of the earth unto Jerusalem (Africa) to worship the King, the LORD of hosts, even upon them shall be no rain.

18 And if the family of Egypt (Gentiles) go not up, and come not, that have no rain; there shall be the plague, wherewith the LORD will smite the heathen that come not up to keep the feast of tabernacles.

19 This shall be the punishment of Egypt, (Gentiels) and the punishment of all nations that come not up to keep the feast of tabernacles.

20 In that day shall there be upon the bells of the horses, HOLINESS UNTO THE LORD; and the pots in the LORD'S house shall be like the bowls before the altar.

21 Yea, every pot in Jerusalem (Africa) and in Judah (African Hebrews) shall be holiness unto the LORD of hosts: and all they that sacrifice shall come and take of them, and seethe therein: and in that day there shall be no more the Canaanite (Gentile) in the house of the LORD of hosts.

(Zechariah 14:1-21).

397/3825

Malachi Chapter 1. God is complaining about the many sins of the African Hebrews. They were chosen to represent righteousness, and to magnify and make God's law, 'honorable'. God is still looking for His honor from the African Hebrews.

1 The burden of the word of the LORD to Israel by Malachi.

2 I have loved you, (African Hebrews) saith the LORD. Yet ye say, Wherein hast thou loved us? Was not Esau Jacob's brother? saith the LORD: yet I loved Jacob,

3 And I hated Esau, and laid his mountains and his heritage waste for the dragons of the wilderness.

4 Whereas Edom saith, We are impoverished, but we will return and build the desolate places; thus saith the LORD of hosts, They shall build, but I will throw down; and they shall call them, The border of wickedness, and, The people against whom the LORD hath indignation for ever.

5 And your eyes shall see, and ye shall say, The LORD will be magnified from the border of Israel.

6 A son honoureth his father, and a servant his master: if then I be a father, where is mine honour? and if I be a master, where is my fear? saith the LORD of hosts unto you, O priests, that despise my name. And ye say, Wherein have we despised thy name?

7 Ye offer polluted bread upon mine altar; and ye say, Wherein have we polluted thee? In that ye say, The table of the LORD is contemptible.

8 And if ye offer the blind for sacrifice, is it not evil? and if ye offer the lame and sick, is it not evil? offer it now unto thy governor;

will he be pleased with thee, or accept thy person? saith the LORD of hosts.

9 And now, I pray you, beseech God that he will be gracious unto us: this hath been by your means: will he regard your persons? saith the LORD of hosts.

10 Who is there even among you that would shut the doors for nought? neither do ye kindle fire on mine altar for nought. I have no pleasure in you, saith the LORD of hosts, neither will I accept an offering at your hand.

11 For from the rising of the sun even unto the going down of the same my name shall be great among the Gentiles; and in every place incense shall be offered unto my name, and a pure offering: for my name shall be great among the heathen, saith the LORD of hosts.

12 But ye have profaned it, in that ye say, The table of the LORD is polluted; and the fruit thereof, even his meat, is contemptible.

13 Ye said also, Behold, what a weariness is it! and ye have snuffed at it, saith the LORD of hosts; and ye brought that which was torn, and the lame, and the sick; thus ye brought an offering: should I accept this of your hand? saith the LORD.

14 But cursed be the deceiver, which hath in his flock a male, and voweth, and sacrificeth unto the Lord a corrupt thing: for I am a great King, saith the LORD of hosts, and my name is dreadful among the heathen.

(Malachi 1:1-14).

397/3825

Malachi Chapter 2. God's message to the unworthy ministers, priests and the faithless Hebrew Israelites. God's main complaint is that the priest and ministers that were over the people, did not seek the 'law', and as a result, caused the African Hebrews to 'stumble at the law'.

1 And now, O ye priests, this commandment is for you.

2 If ye will not hear, and if ye will not lay it to heart, to give glory unto my name, saith the LORD of hosts, I will even send a curse upon you, and I will curse your blessings: yea, I have cursed them already, because ye do not lay it to heart.

3 Behold, I will corrupt your seed, and spread dung upon your faces, even the dung of your solemn feasts; and one shall take you away with it.

4 And ye shall know that I have sent this commandment unto you, that my covenant might be with Levi, (African Hebrews) saith the LORD of hosts.

5 My covenant was with him of life and peace; and I gave them to him for the fear wherewith he feared me, and was afraid before my name.

6 The law of truth was in his mouth, and iniquity was not found in his lips: he walked with me in peace and equity, and did turn many away from iniquity.

7 For the priest's lips should keep knowledge, and they should seek the law at his mouth: for he is the messenger of the LORD of hosts.

8 But ye are departed out of the way; ye have caused many to stumble at the law; ye have corrupted the covenant of Levi, saith the LORD of hosts.

9 Therefore have I also made you contemptible and base before all the people, according as ye have not kept my ways, but have been partial in the law.

10 Have we not all one father? hath not one God created us? why do we deal treacherously every man against his brother, by profaning the covenant of our fathers?

11 Judah (African Hebrews) hath dealt treacherously, and an abomination is committed in Israel (African Hebrews) and in Jerusalem;(Africa) for Judah hath profaned the holiness of the LORD which he loved, and hath married the daughter of a strange god.

12 The LORD will cut off the man that doeth this, the master and the scholar, out of the tabernacles of Jacob, (African Hebrews) and him that offereth an offering unto the LORD of hosts.

13 And this have ye done again, covering the altar of the LORD with tears, with weeping, and with crying out, insomuch that he regardeth not the offering any more, or receiveth it with good will at your hand.

14 Yet ye say, Wherefore? Because the LORD hath been witness between thee and the wife of thy youth, against whom thou hast dealt treacherously: yet is she thy companion, and the wife of thy covenant.

15 And did not he make one? Yet had he the residue of the spirit. And wherefore one? That he might seek a godly seed. Therefore take heed to your spirit, and let none deal treacherously against the wife of his youth.

16 For the LORD, the God of Israel, (African Hebrews) saith that he hateth putting away: for one covereth violence with his garment, saith the LORD of hosts: therefore take heed to your spirit, that ye deal not treacherously.

17 Ye have wearied the LORD with your words. Yet ye say, Wherein have we wearied him? When ye say, Every one that doeth evil is good in the sight of the LORD, and he delighteth in them; or, Where is the God of judgment?

(Malachi 2:1-17).

397/3825

Malachi 3:1-6. There is no "true" worship to the "true" God anywhere in the world today. If it were, there would be more love and more peace. No form of worship, (especially from the African Hebrews) will be acceptable or pleasant unto God until God sends His African Hebrew 'messenger' with the 'NEW COVENANT'. (Jeremiah 31:31-37) The 'NEW COVENANT' will establish a standard of law that will be acceptable unto God.

1 Behold, I will send my messenger, and he shall prepare the way before me: and the Lord, whom ye seek, shall suddenly come to his temple, even the messenger of the covenant, whom ye delight in: behold, he shall come, saith the LORD of hosts.

2 But who may abide the day of his coming? and who shall stand when he appeareth? for he is like a refiner's fire, and like fullers' soap:

3 And he shall sit as a refiner and purifier of silver: and he shall purify the sons of Levi, (The present-day leader of the African Hebrews) and purge them as gold and silver, that they (The African Hebrew Elders and ministers) may offer unto the LORD an offering in righteousness.

4 Then shall the offering of Judah (African Hebrews) and Jerusalem (African Hebrews) be pleasant unto the LORD, as in the days of old, and as in former years.

5 And I will come near to you to judgment; and I will be a swift witness against the sorcerers, and against the adulterers, and against false swearers, and against those that oppress the hireling in his wages, the widow, and the fatherless, and that turn aside the stranger from his right, and fear not me, saith the LORD of hosts.

6 For I am the LORD, I change not; therefore ye sons of Jacob (African Hebrews) are not consumed.

(Malachi 3:1-6).

397/3825

Malachi 3:8-10. The importance of paying tithes. Economics affect 'old folks' (black folks), especially the African Hebrew in a very peculiar way. This is because they do not understand the magic of paying tithes to the true 'Storehouse' of God. God's 'NEW COVENANT' will provide a way for them to become economically solvent and sound.

8 Will a man rob God? Yet ye have robbed me. But ye say, Wherein have we robbed thee? In tithes and offerings.

9 Ye are cursed with a curse: for ye have robbed me, even this whole nation.

10 Bring ye all the tithes into the storehouse, that there may be meat in mine house, and prove me now herewith, saith the LORD of hosts, if I will not open you the windows of heaven, and pour you out a blessing, that there shall not be room enough to receive it.

(Malachi 3:8-10).

397/3825

Malachi 3:11-12. How the Children of Israel's new home in Africa will be when they receive God's 'New Covenant'

11 And I will rebuke the devourer for your sakes, and he shall not destroy the fruits of your ground; neither shall your vine cast her fruit before the time in the field, saith the LORD of hosts.

12 And all nations shall call you blessed: for ye shall be a delightsome land, saith the LORD of hosts.

(Malachi 3:11-12).

397/3825

Malachi 3:16. Many 'old folks' (black folks) reject the Bible because they feel that 'new folks' (white folks) wrote it. This is definitely true for the 'New Testament', but not for the 'Old Testament'. Even though 'new folks' were the ones who tried to interpret, revise and change the "Scriptures of Truth", (Old Testament) it seems as though God knew that this would happen. This one verse gives confirmation and comfort to the African Hebrew and all Black folks, that what exist in the Old Testament is there because God sanctioned it. Therefore once again, the 'Old Testament' is for 'Old Folks' (black folks), and the 'New Testament' is for 'New Folks' (new folks). In "TRUTH" if the African Hebrews would have kept the TEN COMMANDMENTS of GOD, there would be no New Testament, nor 'new folks'. The Old Testament was written 'before' God, for His 'chosen' people, who should 'Fear' God and keep the Ten Commandments. To prove that the Old Testament is for 'Old Folks', God said that a book **WAS** written (Old Testament), not **WILL BE** written (New Testament).

16 Then they that feared the LORD spake often one to another: and the LORD hearkened, and heard it, and a book of remembrance was written before him for them that feared the LORD, and that thought upon his name.

(Malachi 3:16).

397/3825

Malachi 3:17. God will not be sponsoring a 'membership' drive when He returns to gather the Children of Israel. God will be returning to make up the jewels of His kingdom, and the African Hebrews must get themselves together.

17 And they shall be mine, (African Hebrews) saith the LORD of hosts, in that day when I make up my jewels; and I will spare them, as a man spareth his own son that serveth him.

(Malachi 3:17).

397/3825

Malachi 3:18. The House of Israel must be cleaned out. When this is completed, some will not make it.

18 Then shall ye return, and discern between the righteous and the wicked, between him that serveth God and him that serveth him not.

(Malachi 3:18).

397/3825

Malachi 4:1-4. The last chance for the Children of Israel.

1 For, behold, the day cometh, that shall burn as an oven; and all the proud, yea, and all that do wickedly, shall be stubble: and the day that cometh shall burn them up, saith the LORD of hosts, that it shall leave them neither root nor branch.

2 But unto you that fear my name shall the Sun of righteousness arise with healing in his wings; and ye shall go forth, and grow up as calves of the stall.

3 And ye shall tread down the wicked; for they shall be ashes under the soles of your feet in the day that I shall do this, saith the LORD of hosts.

4 Remember ye the law of Moses my servant, which I commanded unto him in Horeb for all Israel, with the statutes and judgments.

(Malachi 4:1-4).

SO ENDETH A PORTION OF WHAT THE SPIRIT-GOD REVEALED TO THE WRITER CONCERNING THE 'OLD TESTAMENT.

<u>NEW TESTAMENT</u>

There are over 400 years between the Old and New Testaments. This is the time period that God used to create 'new folks' (white folks) out of the 'old folks' (black folks), and the 'beast, fowl, and creeping things'. Approximately 4222 years have gone by now, and God was ready to create and put the 'new folks' to work. Since the 'new folks' were brand new, they would require a lot of direction in order to develop to the human level.

This is why GOD prepared the Prophet Jesus and put him to work. Jesus had two primary missions: (1) To teach the 'new folks' of God. (2) To fulfill what the 16 Prophets wrote. (See St. Matthews 5:17). The first four chapters of the New Testament (Gospel) is the 'Doctrine' that the Prophet Jesus taught the 'new folks' so that they would have an idea of what the Old Testament was about before God created them. **<u>VITAL</u>**--Of all the Prophets that worked for God, why was Jesus the only one that was assassinated?. Think about it. Abraham, Moses, Isaiah and the rest of the Prophets that worked for God, passed this life in a normal manner..... the Prophet Jesus was the only one that died savagely. Why???? God sacrificed Jesus that way to shew that He was serious about destroying the Children of Israel and the Gentile 'old folks' from Africa. When GOD caused the 'new folks' to murder Jesus, it was the 'sign' that the time had come for God to fulfill what He shewed and told the 16 Prophets. Shortly after the 'new folks' killed Jesus, Africa was destroyed in thirds as God promised in Ezekiel 5:12. God prepared Jesus for death at a very early age. From the age of 12, Jesus anticipated the day when he would be sacrificed for the sins of his African forefathers, the Children of Israel, the African Hebrews. This is why Jesus said, 'Father forgive them, for they know not what they do'. **Jesus was an African/Hebrew** according to the genealogies recorded in St. Matthews Chapter 1 and St. Luke 3:23-38. The world is upside down because people are following the teachings **'about'** Jesus, instead of the teachings **'of'** Jesus. Jesus taught from the 'Holy Scriptures' which is the Old Testament, but Ministers are leading people astray by placing their emphasis on the New Testament, and calling Jesus their Saviour. We must remember that the New Testament did not exist during the time that Jesus worked for God. The New Testament was not written by the 'new folks' until many years 'after' the death of Jesus. This is why Jesus constantly referred the people to the 'Scriptures', which is the Old Testament. The New Testament is 'not' the Scriptures, and Jesus is not our Saviour. There is only one Saviour, The One, True and Living God. The God that created us and chose our bodies to be the dwelling place to express Its Spirit through. Read I Corinthians 3:16.

16 Know ye not that ye are the temple of God, and that the Spirit of God dwelleth in you?

(1Corinthians 3:16).

God is a Spirit. The Spirit is what God is. The Old Testament is the 'word of God', and the New Testament is the 'word of man'. The 'word of God' is always 'prefaced' by, **'THUS SAITH THE LORD', or 'AND THE LORD SPAKE THESE WORDS', or AND GOD SPOKE THESE WORDS SAYING, or 'THE WORD OF THE LORD CAME UNTO ME, SAYING'**. (You never see this in the Europeans New Testament) God is very angry with Ministers that are teaching false doctrine, such as 'Jesus is our Saviour', and ' the whole Bible is the 'Scripture' and the word of God.'. The whole world is cursed because of the gross misunderstanding of who our 'Saviour' is.

The following references will help us understand who our 'saviour' is, and will sensitize us to the 1st Commandment, which is **"Thou shalt have no other gods before me".**

Isaiah 43:3

God explaining who our Saviour is.

3 For I am the LORD thy God, the Holy One of Israel, thy Saviour: I gave Egypt for thy ransom, Ethiopia and Seba for thee.

(Isaiah 43:3).

Isaiah 43:11-15

Is there a saviour other than the Lord God?

11 I, even I, am the LORD; and beside me there is no saviour.

12 I have declared, and have saved, and I have shewed, when there was no strange god among you: therefore ye are my witnesses, saith the LORD, that I am God.

13 Yea, before the day was I am he; and there is none that can deliver out of my hand: I will work, and who shall let it?

14 Thus saith the LORD, your redeemer, the Holy One of Israel; (African Hebrews) For your sake I have sent to Babylon, and have brought down all their nobles, and the Chaldeans, whose cry is in the ships.

15 I am the LORD, your Holy One, the creator of Israel, (African Hebrews) your King.

(Isaiah 43:11-15).

Isaiah 44:6-8

Should we make gods out of foolish idols?

6 Thus saith the LORD the King of Israel, (African Hebrews) and his redeemer the LORD of hosts; I am the first, and I am the last; and beside me there is no God.

7 And who, as I, shall call, and shall declare it, and set it in order for me, since I appointed the ancient people? (Old Folks) and the things that are coming, and shall come, let them shew unto them.

8 Fear ye not, neither be afraid: have not I told thee from that time, and have declared it? ye are even my witnesses. Is there a God beside me? yea, there is no God; I know not any.

(Isaiah 44:6-8).

Isaiah 45:5-8

God said there is no god besides Him because God created everything.

5 I am the LORD, and there is none else, there is no God beside me: I girded thee, though thou hast not known me:

6 That they may know from the rising of the sun, and from the west, that there is none beside me. I am the LORD, and there is none else.

7 I form the light, and create darkness: I make peace, and create evil: I the LORD do all these things.

8 Drop down, ye heavens, from above, and let the skies pour down righteousness: let the earth open, and let them bring forth

salvation, and let righteousness spring up together; I the LORD have created it.

(Isaiah 45:5-8).

Isaiah 45:16-18

God will cause us to be confused when we choose 'man-made' false religions and don't serve GOD properly.

16 They shall be ashamed, and also confounded, all of them: they shall go to confusion together that are makers of idols.

17 But Israel (African Hebrews) shall be saved in the LORD with an everlasting salvation: ye shall not be ashamed nor confounded world without end.

18 For thus saith the LORD that created the heavens; God himself that formed the earth and made it; he hath established it, he created it not in vain, he formed it to be inhabited: I am the LORD; and there is none else.

(Isaiah 45:16-18).

Isaiah 46:5-9

People are so confused today, that many have made a 'man' equal to GOD, but God said that is wrong.

5 To whom will ye liken me, and make me equal, and compare me, that we may be like?

6 They lavish gold out of the bag, and weigh silver in the balance, and hire a goldsmith; and he maketh it a god: they fall down, yea, they worship.

7 They bear him upon the shoulder, they carry him, and set him in his place, and he standeth; from his place shall he not remove: yea, one shall cry unto him, yet can he not answer, nor save him out of his trouble.

8 Remember this, and shew yourselves men: bring it again to mind, O ye transgressors.

9 Remember the former things of old: for I am God, and there is none else; I am God, and there is none like me,

(Isaiah 46:5-9).

Isaiah 47:4

God is our redeemer. (Saviour)

4 As for our redeemer, the LORD of hosts is his name, the Holy One of Israel. (African Hebrews)

(Isaiah 47:4).

Isaiah 48:17

We cannot profit and know our way without the 'true' God.

17 Thus saith the LORD, thy Redeemer, the Holy One of Israel; (African Hebrews) I am the LORD thy God which teacheth thee to profit, which leadeth thee by the way that thou shouldest go.

(Isaiah 48:17).

Isaiah 49:26

Even the oppressor will know that God is our saviour.

26 And I will feed them that oppress thee with their own flesh; and they shall be drunken with their own blood, as with sweet wine: and all flesh shall know that I the LORD am thy Saviour and thy Redeemer, the mighty One of Jacob. (African Hebrews)

(Isaiah 49:26).

Isaiah 50:10

Many people are walking around in a 'deep sleep' because they are trusting in the name of 'man' and not God.

10 Who is among you that feareth the LORD, that obeyeth the voice of his servant, that walketh in darkness, and hath no light? let him trust in the name of the LORD, and stay upon his God.

(Isaiah 50:10).

Isaiah 51:15

What is the true name of our saviour?

15 But I am the LORD thy God, that divided the sea, whose waves roared: The LORD of hosts is his name.

(Isaiah 51:15).

Isaiah 52:5-6

The day is very near when people will stop blaspheming the name of God and know the proper name of our saviour.

5 Now therefore, what have I here, saith the LORD, that my people (African Hebrews) is taken away for nought? they that rule over them (new folks) make them to howl, saith the LORD; and my name continually every day is blasphemed.

6 Therefore my people shall know my name: therefore they shall know in that day that I am he that doth speak: behold, it is I.

(Isaiah 52:5-6).

Isaiah 54:5

Our saviour is the 'God of the whole earth'. We make God small when we call a 'man' our saviour.

5 For thy Maker is thine husband; the LORD of hosts is his name; and thy Redeemer the Holy One of Israel; (African Hebrews) The God of the whole earth shall he be called.

(Isaiah 54:5).

Isaiah 55:6-7

It is time for us to return and call upon the name of the true and living God.

6 Seek ye the LORD while he may be found, call ye upon him while he is near:

7 Let the wicked forsake his way, and the unrighteous man his thoughts: and let him return unto the LORD, and he will have mercy upon him; and to our God, for he will abundantly pardon.

(Isaiah 55:6-7).

Hosea 13:4

Is there a saviour other than the Lord God? There is only one TRUE GOD and Saviour, and the whole world will know it very soon. Many people are very confused calling Jesus their saviour. Jesus worked very hard trying to make people understand that God was their saviour, and not Jesus himself. Let's take a look.

4 Yet I am the LORD thy God from the land of Egypt, (Africa) and thou shalt know no god but me: for there is no saviour beside me.

(Hosea 13:4).

St. Matthew 4:10

Jesus explaining that we should worship the Lord thy God, and God 'only'. This is why there is so much confusion, sickness, death, curses, sorrow, grief and disappointment in the earth. It is because people are worshipping a 'man' (Jesus), that God chose to teach people about God.

10 Then saith Jesus unto him, Get thee hence, Satan: for it is written, Thou shalt worship the Lord thy God, and him only shalt thou serve.

(Matthew 4:10).

St. Matthew 5:45

Jesus giving honor to the 'true' God, and teaching people what to do so that they may be the children of God. (Not himself)

45 That ye may be the children of your Father which is in heaven: for he maketh his sun to rise on the evil and on the good, and sendeth rain on the just and on the unjust.

(Matthew 5:45).

St. Matthew 5:48

Jesus teaching us to be perfect as God is. Notice how Jesus gives no reference unto himself as being our 'saviour'. Jesus constantly referred people to; "Your Father which is in heaven". (God)

48 Be ye therefore perfect, even as your Father which is in heaven is perfect.

(Matthew 5:48).

St. Matthew 6:1

Jesus teaching that our reward comes from God, not man, as Jesus was.

1 Take heed that ye do not your alms before men, to be seen of them: otherwise ye have no reward of your Father which is in heaven.

(Matthew 6:1).

St. Matthew 6:4

Jesus teaching that God is the 'spirit' that dwells in darkness, or in secret. God is a 'spirit', Jesus was a 'man'.

4 That thine alms may be in secret: and thy Father which seeth in secret himself shall reward thee openly.

(Matthew 6:4).

St. Matthew 6:6

Jesus teaching the people to pray unto 'God', not Jesus.

6 But thou, when thou prayest, enter into thy closet, and when thou hast shut thy door, pray to thy Father which is in secret; and thy Father which seeth in secret shall reward thee openly.

(Matthew 6:6).

St. Matthew 6:9-13

Jesus teaching the people what to say unto God when they pray. Jesus taught them to pray to God, not Jesus. God said many folks call this the 'Lord's prayer'. God said it is not the 'Lord's prayer'.

God said this is the prayer that Jesus taught his disciples and should be called 'the disciples prayer', not the 'Lord's prayer', because God does not need a prayer.

9 After this manner therefore pray ye: Our Father which art in heaven, Hallowed be thy name.

10 Thy kingdom come. Thy will be done in earth, as it is in heaven.

11 Give us this day our daily bread.

12 And forgive us our debts, as we forgive our debtors.

13 And lead us not into temptation, but deliver us from evil: For thine is the kingdom, and the power, and the glory, for ever. Amen.

(Matthew 6:9-13).

St. Matthew 6:14-15

Jesus teaching that all power and might is in the hands of God, and again we find Jesus referring us to our heavenly Father, (GOD) not himself.

14 For if ye forgive men their trespasses, your heavenly Father will also forgive you:

15 But if ye forgive not men their trespasses, neither will your Father forgive your trespasses.

(Matthew 6:14-15).

St. Matthew 6:18

Jesus teaching the importance of rendering unto God, and not unto man, as Jesus was.

18 That thou appear not unto men to fast, but unto thy Father which is in secret: and thy Father, which seeth in secret, shall reward thee openly.

(Matthew 6:18).

St. Matthew 6:26

Jesus teaching that it is God, that provides everything, and it is God that is our saviour.

26 Behold the fowls of the air: for they sow not, neither do they reap, nor gather into barns; yet your heavenly Father feedeth them. Are ye not much better than they?

(Matthew 6:26).

St. Matthew 6:30

Jesus teaching that it is God, that we should have faith in, because God is our saviour.

30 Wherefore, if God so clothe the grass of the field, which to day is, and to morrow is cast into the oven, shall he not much more clothe you, O ye of little faith?

(Matthew 6:30).

St. Matthew 6:32

Jesus teaching that, only God knows our needs, and only God can do something about our needs; not Jesus. God said if Jesus was our saviour, where in the New Testament does Jesus say that he is our saviour?

32 (For after all these things do the Gentiles seek) for your heavenly Father knoweth that ye have need of all these things.

(Matthew 6:32).

St. Matthew 6:33

Jesus teaching us to seek the kingdom of God, which is God's law, or the Ten Commandments.

33 But seek ye first the kingdom of God, and his righteousness; and all these things shall be added unto you.

(Matthew 6:33).

St. Matthew 7:21

Jesus teaching that God's Ten Commandments is the only way.

21 Not every one that saith unto me, Lord, Lord, shall enter into the kingdom of heaven; but he that doeth the will of my Father which is in heaven.

(Matthew 7:21).

St. Matthew 10:20

Jesus referring the disciples to the Lord God, who is our saviour. Jesus also is teaching that, God is the 'spirit' within us.

20 For it is not ye that speak, but the Spirit of your Father which speaketh in you.

(Matthew 10:20).

St. Matthew 11:25-27

Jesus thanking and acknowledging the Lord God. People today thank, praise and acknowledge Jesus-- a man.

25 At that time Jesus answered and said, I thank thee, O Father, Lord of heaven and earth, because thou hast hid these things from the wise and prudent, and hast revealed them unto babes.

26 Even so, Father: for so it seemed good in thy sight.

27 All things are delivered unto me of my Father: and no man knoweth the Son, but the Father; neither knoweth any man the Father, save the Son, and he to whomsoever the Son will reveal him.

(Matthew 11:25-27).

St. Matthew 12:50

The Prophet Jesus did not tell us to praise and serve him. Jesus taught that he was human like everyone else.

50 For whosoever shall do the will of my Father which is in heaven, the same is my brother, and sister, and mother.

(Matthew 12:50).

St. Matthew 15:13-14

Jesus teaching that when we do not plant the seeds that the Lord God told us to plant, we wander in darkness. (Even with our eyes wide open.)

13 But he answered and said, Every plant, which my heavenly Father hath not planted, shall be rooted up.

14 Let them alone: they be blind leaders of the blind. And if the blind lead the blind, both shall fall into the ditch.

(Matthew 15:13-14).

St. Matthew 19:16-17

Jesus taught that God's Ten Commandments is the only way that we can be saved.

16 And, behold, one came and said unto him, Good Master, what good thing shall I do, that I may have eternal life?

17 And he said unto him, Why callest thou me good? there is none good but one, that is, God: but if thou wilt enter into life, keep the commandments.

(Matthew 19:16-17).

St. Matthew 19:25-26

Jesus confirming the fact that 'God' is our saviour.

25 When his disciples heard it, they were exceedingly amazed, saying, Who then can be saved?

26 But Jesus beheld them, and said unto them, With men this is impossible; but with God all things are possible.

(Matthew 19:25-26).

St. Matthew 21:11

Jesus is not our saviour; God is. Jesus was a prophet of God, and we must learn to rightly divide.

11 And the multitude said, This is Jesus the prophet of Nazareth of Galilee.

(Matthew 21:11).

Jesus was a man; a prophet. Jesus came and did his work for God just like all of the prophets, and passed on. God, our true and living saviour, is a 'spirit', and those that worship God, must worship in SPIRIT and in TRUTH. GOD IS OUR SAVIOUR..

If people say that Jesus is their saviour, why don't they follow the teachings of Jesus, which would be, to keep the Ten Commandments? Many people are following the teachings of the apostle Paul, who wrote 14 of the 27 books in the New testament. People with common sense would read those 14 books carefully and check Paul out with real curiosity. Paul could be considered a good politician. He would say and do anything to save his own neck. Paul spoke Greek and lived in a city noted for its Greek culture; Paul considered himself a Roman citizen (Read Acts 22:25-29 and 21:39); Paul called himself a Jew; Paul called himself a Christian. One can clearly see why Paul told Timothy (11 Timothy 2:15) to 'study' so that he could rightly divide the 'truth'. Paul wrote two letters to the church at Thessalonica, two to the Corinthians, one to the Galatians, and one to the Romans. (All 'new folks') These writings took place while Paul was in prison for thirteen years. After Paul's imprisonment in Rome, he wrote the letters (or books) known as Philemon, Colossians, Ephesians, and Phillippians. When Paul was free, he wrote two letters known as 1 Timothy and Titus. He was imprisoned again in Rome. Just before his death at the hands of Nero, Paul wrote 2 Timothy. **There is more in the New Testament from Paul than it is from Jesus. Many people say that Jesus is there saviour, but when you read the New Testament, it appears that Paul has more influence on their 'spiritual' lives. Many people profess to being a 'Christian' without understanding the 'history' of Christianity. Christianity is Euro-Centric in total, and was established by 'new folks' after the death of Jesus. Many believe that Jesus died for the sins of the world. That's true as long as we understand that the only world that existed before Jesus, was the world of Africa. Africa was where the sins were committed. The sins that Jesus died for were committed by his ancestors , the African Hebrew Israelites, the Children of Israel. (Read St. Matthew 5:17) After Jesus fulfilled the 'law' and the 'prophets', he was crucified, Africa was destroyed, and the African Hebrew Israelites and Gentile 'old folks' were taken to many 'new folk' countries where they were reduced to the level of a 'slave'. All because they broke the Ten Commandments of God.**

ABOUT THE AUTHOR

The writer is a seasoned musician, counselor and author who has developed a "Human Betterment" program that has helped scores of people improve their lives. He believes that the development of the individual life is a natural process, and will unfold perfectly once natural order has been restored. After graduating high school, the writer served six years in the United States Air Force. During his 35 years working in Corporate America, he studied Psychology at Penn State; Theology at Shaw Univ; Business Management at Pace and Lincoln Colleges, and music at SUNY, Binghamton...He was also a minister for eight years.

The writer was born in Penna, brought up in a foster home with his siblings and helped raised 78 children. Little did he know that he was being raised by a Hebrew woman who kept the 7th day Sabbath, the Passover, and all other Hebrew holidays, and the writer was subjected to strict adherence to these laws. As a child and even as a young adult, the writer regarded this way of life as a stumbling block due to 'no fun', 'no sports', and 'no games' from sundown Friday to sundown Saturday , not to mention the ridicule he received from his peers.

Little did the writer know that this life style was ordained by a high power who was preparing him for a greater work..Very early in life the writer was stricken with the discomfort of 'injustice' that he observed among the peoples of the earth, especially the African America people who were receiving the greatest affliction of all peoples.

The writer began his investigation of this dilemma by studying most religions and delved into many aspects of world histories searching for the truth.

The writer was not satisfied with the report that a band of bad people went to Africa, stole a whole people, drained Africa of it's natural civilization, brought the African people to a strange land and sold them for slaves

Well after years of this intense search and investigation with no satisfactory true results, the writer turned this travail over to the high power through prayer and meditation. In 1971 he received the unfoldment of a revelation and 'Truth at Last' was born. The writers first attempt to document this revelation was in 1973 with a 100 page first edition. Since that time the writer has expanded Truth at Last almost three-fold. The writers other works include: another book titled 'Why Me'—Why things happen to you and you don't know why"...He has written over 200 poems and composed over 150 songs...

Printed in the United States
60325LVS00003B/94-96

9 781420 852417